Scottish Natural Heritage
An Insider's View

Roger Crofts

TIPPERMUIR
BOOKS LIMITED

This first edition published and copyright 2026 by Tippermuir Books Ltd, Perth, Scotland.

mail@tippermuirbooks.co.uk – tippermuirbooks.co.uk.

ISBN 978-1-913836-55-9 (paperback).

A CIP catalogue record for this book is available from the British Library.

Project coordination and editorial by Dr Paul S Philippou.

Editorial support by Steve Zajda and Jean Hands.

Cover design by Matthew Mackie.

Co-founders and publishers of Tippermuir Books: Rob Hands, Matthew Mackie and Paul S Philippou.

Typeset by Palimpsest Book Production Ltd, Falkirk, Stirlingshire

Text set in Adobe Garamond Pro Regular 10.5/14pt.

Printed and bound by Ashford Colour Ltd

This book has been printed in the UK to reduce transportation miles and their impact upon the environment. It has been printed to comply with the Forest Stewardship Council (FSC) Chain of Custody requirements and paper sourcing from responsibly managed sources.

Dedicated to all colleagues and friends who have worked on natural heritage, nature conservation and countryside in Scotland.

'I had the privilege of working with Roger Crofts at SNH between 1999 and his retirement in 2002. I can think of no better person to compile this authoritative history of the organisation and to have the energy, enthusiasm, and tenacity to see it through to publication.'

Dr John Markland, CBE
Chairman SNH (1999–2006)

'The establishment of Scottish Natural Heritage (SNH) in 1992 was momentous for the conservation and enhancement of nature in Scotland. I was part of the organisation from inception, seeing it evolve in response to political and environmental challenges and opportunities. This book provides a vividly insightful commentary on the journey made by SNH. It is instructive and essential reading for politicians, public servants, environmentalists and students, each of whom should be uniquely better informed about how an 'independent' public body operates. Professor Crofts is unstinting and unsparing in his excellent narrative.'

Professor Des Thompson, MBE, FRSE, FCIEEMFormer Principal Adviser on Science and Biodiversity with SNH and successor NatureScot. Currently Leverhulme Emeritus Fellow with the University of the Highlands and Islands, and adviser to the United Nations on climate change.

'This book is an invaluable record of the creation of SNH (now NatureScot) and of the people and institutions involved in the birth of a new approach to nature conservation in Scotland. Very few people 'who were there' have the combined insight and overview of the stresses and tensions involved. Indeed, Roger is perhaps the only person who could write this book, and I am delighted that after some considerable persuasion from Des Thompson and I, that he has done so.

It is a fascinating read and is historically important in the context of modern nature conservation. It is, however, much more than that. It shows how governments work, how important people and their personalities are in shaping organisations and how taking a long-term view is important in tackling the key issues and pressures nature now faces across Scotland.

I am acutely aware in my role as Chair of NatureScot that we are able to help nature now so effectively thanks to the efforts of Roger and the others involved in the creation of, and in the early years, of the organisation.

Professor Colin Galbraith, FRSE, Chair of NatureScot

PREFACE

I HAVE known Roger Crofts since the early 1990s, and worked very closely with him from 1991 to 1999 when he was Chief Executive of Scottish Natural Heritage, of which I was chairman. I was constantly impressed by his prodigious capacity for hard work, his meticulous attention to detail, his administrative skills, his shrewd judgement, and his drive for excellence throughout the organisation.

His expert knowledge of the geography and geology of Scotland, and his love of the outdoors, were an inspiration to us all. He always prepared himself (and me!) very carefully ahead of meetings, where his observations were always helpful, constructive and very much to the point.

As a person, Roger is an affectionate and steadfast friend, and an enjoyable and energetic companion. He does not always suffer fools gladly, but usually manages to disguise the fact. He has dedicated his life to public service in one form or another. He also has an enviable talent for summing up long discussions neatly, lucidly and succinctly – and impromptu.

Magnus Magnusson, KBE
2002

FOREWORD

I CAN still vividly remember the first time I met Roger Crofts. Sometime in the autumn of 1991, I represented Plantlife, the plant conservation charity, at a meeting of non-governmental environmental bodies (NGOs) that Roger hosted in the boardroom of the Chester Street office where the nascent new body to be called Scottish Natural Heritage (SNH) was based. By then, the Nature Conservancy Council (NCC) had been split up by government decree. An interim organisation called the Nature Conservancy Council for Scotland was in operation, but Roger had been appointed as Chief Executive of SNH, the new, broader-based organisation tasked with bringing together the nature conservation agenda and the countryside protection priorities of the Countryside Commission for Scotland, which had been operating in Scotland since 1968.

Roger and a small team were developing the priorities and principles of the new organisation, before inheriting the staff of the two existing bodies and beginning work in April 1992. I remember realising at that meeting that Roger was a very different civil servant. He was clearly motivated by a vision and determined to create an organisation that would realise that vision, based around the simple but eloquent motto for the new body: 'working with Scotland's people for our natural heritage'. With his background as a geographer and research geomorphologist, Roger had a clear view that large landscapes had to be seen in totality and to be managed and protected as whole systems. As a keen hillwalker, he knew that accessibility for people was an important aspect of the conservation contract with the public. It was also clear that he recognised that, for his vision to be realised, it had to appeal to the mass of the predominantly urban population of Scotland. To do that, he knew that he needed the various countryside and wildlife organisations to be on his side, and he was keen to listen to our views, to debate them, to challenge them, but also to learn from them.

Once SNH was formally launched, I increasingly found myself working alongside Roger and his staff (several of whom were longstanding friends). In 1996, I became chair of Scottish Wildlife & Countryside Link (the NGO network body, now known as Scottish Environment LINK). Roger had instigated regular informal working meetings with the heads of the largest environmental NGOs in Scotland, including LINK, to discuss current issues of the day. Roger used these to sound out his future aspirations and plans, and to test how the NGOs might respond. We did the same in reverse for NGO campaigns. The meetings ensured that there were rarely unpleasant surprises and often meant that we could agree to work together from our own perspectives for the common good of the Scottish environment.

I owe Roger a huge personal debt for encouraging me and supporting me in getting more involved in this work. In April 1997, having lived for seven years in Wester Ross, Roger facilitated my appointment onto the North Areas Board of SNH. The board was chaired by Simon Fraser, a distinguished solicitor and land reform advocate from the Isle of Lewis, and we worked with Jeff Watson, as Director of Operations (North Scotland), a friend since my days at Aberdeen University, who I respected greatly as, amongst other things, the leading expert on Golden Eagles. The Board had a very diverse membership so meetings were often challenging, but I enjoyed working with them for what we all saw as the common good.

At Roger's instigation, SNH had pioneered open Board meetings. I remember North Areas Board meetings in Thurso, Barra, Fair Isle and elsewhere that were a huge learning curve for me. I began to appreciate that there was a lot of support for the broad vision that we had for Scotland, but that SNH had to get much smarter in how we lived up to our motto of 'working with Scotland's people' if we were going to achieve that vision.

After one of Roger's NGO head meetings in early 1999, I remember walking up Dundas Street in Edinburgh with Roger when he suggested, out of the blue, that I should apply for the post of SNH Chair to replace Magnus Magnusson who was due to retire. He generously thought I might have the communication skills and the conservation credentials to take on the post. To become chairman, I would also first have to apply for Board membership, which I duly did. To my eternal relief, John Markland was appointed as Chair, but I was invited onto the Main Board. When Roger Wheater resigned as Deputy Chair in November 1999 to become Chair of the National Trust for Scotland, Roger and John invited me to take up that post. I served as Deputy Chair through to March 2005 with Roger and his successor Ian Jardine as Chief Executives. It was a role that I hugely enjoyed. John had exactly the right skills and network of contacts to navigate the evolving relationship with the Parliament as it became established, and, together with Roger, they made a formidable leadership team. I was much better suited to taking a lead on some of the scientific issues that we were addressing, like the burgeoning interest in species reintroductions and the growing recognition of the impact of climate change. I am amused, and a little embarrassed, to reflect on how my views matured over that time from the quotes that Roger selects from me in this book.

It was a pleasure working with Roger on the Board. He was always happy to listen to the advice of Board members, but also prepared to argue his ground if he felt that was justified. As often as not, it was the Board who changed our views, on the basis of the careful research and analysis that Roger had undertaken on any issue. It was teamwork at its best, and Roger clearly relished the challenges this presented. He was always supportive of staff, and keen to ensure that they gave of their very best in taking forward their work. I was impressed by how he seemed to know everyone in the organisation, not just in their roles with SNH but in their lives beyond work as well.

There is one lesson that I particularly remember from Roger. Each year the Board agreed management targets for the year ahead, with specific actions that had to be monitorable and measurable. The first time I attended the year-end review process, I remember being pleased that we had met most of the targets, but was worried that there were several where we had only achieved perhaps 80 per cent or 90 per cent of the target. I worried that this would be seen as failure, but Roger was sanguine. He argued that there was no point having targets that you could easily achieve. Good targets needed to be genuinely challenging and, if they were, then you could not expect to fully achieve them all – a slight shortfall was just a powerful incentive to do even better the next year.

I am hugely proud of what we achieved in my time with SNH. Roger reflects on some of the outcomes in his final chapter, and I would add others from my period working with Ian Jardine. However, this book is not a celebration of SNH's achievements; someone else will have to write that. It is about Roger's insights into setting up a management system that made these achievements possible. It is about being laser-focussed on the ultimate vision and ensuring that the system is fit for achieving that purpose. It is about encouraging individuals and bringing them together as a team to take forward the objectives of the organisation. I'm sure senior executives of other government – and indeed non-governmental – bodies, maybe even some corporate bosses, could learn much from the ideas that Roger discusses. With an eye to the news as I write this, I might tactfully suggest that a few Government Ministers might also benefit from Roger's insights as they struggle to bring together dysfunctional departments! I hope it might also encourage current Scottish Ministers to reinvigorate their support for the rebranded NatureScot that now takes forward the work of SNH.

Michael Scott, OBE
Deputy Chairman, Scottish Natural Heritage (1999-2005)
Lochcarron, November 2025

Foreword

ORGANISATIONAL AND OTHER ABBREVIATIONS

ADMG – Association of Deer Management Groups
CCS – Countryside Commission for Scotland
CCW – Countryside Council for Wales
COSLA – Convention of Scottish Local Authorities
DCS – Deer Commission for Scotland
eNGOs – environmental Non-Government Organisations
EN – English Nature
EU – European Union
HIDB – Highlands and Islands Development Board
HIE – Highlands and Islands Enterprise
HLF – Heritage Lottery Fund
IUCN – International Union for the Conservation of Nature
JNCC – Joint Nature Conservation Committee
MAB – Man and the Biosphere programme of UNESCO
MBA – Master of Business Administration degree
MCS – Mountaineering Council of Scotland
NC – Nature Conservancy Great Britian until 1973
NCC – Nature Conservancy Council until 1991
NCCS – Nature Conservancy Council for Scotland 1991-92
NDPB – Non-Departmental Public Body
NE – Natural England successor to English Nature
NERC – Natural Environment Research Council
NFUS – National Farmers Union Scotland
NGO – Non-Government Organisation
NHA – Natural Heritage Area
NHMF – National Heritage Memorial Fund
NNR – National Nature Reserve
NP – National Park
NSA – National Scenic Area
NTS – National Trust for Scotland
QUANGO – Quasi Autonomous Non-Government Organisation
RBGE – Royal Botanic Garden Edinburgh
RSPB – Royal Society for the Protection of Birds
SAC – Scottish Agricultural College
SAC – Special Area of Conservation for habitats and species
ScotLINK or SEL – Scottish Environmental LINK a consortium of environmental NGOs (formerly SWCL - Scottish Wild and Countryside LINK)
SE – Scottish Enterprise
SEPA – Scottish Environmental Protection Agency
SH – Scottish Homes
SLF – Scottish Landowners Federation
SSSI – Site of Special Scientific Interest
SNH – Scottish Natural Heritage
SPA – Special Protection Area for birds
SWT – Scottish Wildlife Trust
UNESCO – United Nations Educational, Scientific and Cultural Organisation
WCPA – World Commission on Protected Areas a component of IUCN
WWF – World Wide Fund for Nature

Scottish Natural Heritage

CONTENTS

INTRODUCTION

THIS BOOK is for anyone interested in how government works, the role of a public agency in the real politic and what a public sector Chief Executive does in practice. I hope also that anyone engaged in, or concerned about, the management of Scotland's natural heritage will learn from this very personal assessment of the opportunities and challenges faced by Scottish Natural Heritage (hereinafter SNH).

This is one person's account of SNH, its life and times over its first decade. It is written by the person who had the lead in varying roles over thirteen years. I add a short time frame to help the reader.

July 1984 to October 1988: Head of Highland and Tourism Division, Industry Department for Scotland, Scottish Office - responsible for policy and the oversight of the Highlands and Islands Development Board and the Scottish Tourist Board. This included the battles between development and conservation, especially in the Flow Country of Caithness and Sutherland and ski development.

November 1988 to August 1991 Head of Rural Affairs Division, Scottish Office Environment Department – responsible for policy on nature conservation, countryside, rural affairs coordination, oversight of the Countryside Commission for Scotland, and developing proposals and legislation for establishment of Scottish Natural Heritage.

September 1991 to March 1992 Head of Scottish Natural Heritage Implementation Team.

April 1992 to March 2002 Chief Executive Scottish Natural Heritage.

Prior to SNH, I was responsible in the Scottish Office for advising Ministers on the need for organisational and cultural change on nature conservation and countryside, advising on new policy and direction, and leading the team of officials as the Natural Heritage (Scotland) Bill (1990-1991) was taken through the UK Parliament. I was appointed to the leadership role for the first decade of SNH as its Chief Executive, through three contracts – five, three and two years, as was the norm at the time. It was a wonderful opportunity to be allowed to establish, develop and lead a new organisation with strong political and public support. I was a very fortunate person to be appointed to this role.

This book is definitely an insider's perspective and unique at that. I tell how one individual seeks to use their own personal strengths in leadership, creativity and dynamism to deal with internal and externally imposed issues, and to develop styles of working that make a real difference. I am the first to admit that my approach to leadership and management is not a blueprint. Nevertheless, I hope that my insights into working relations between government and an agency, and between an agency and its diverse clientele, will resound with others who have followed this path. I also hope that it will help those who aspire to take on leadership roles in the public sector and with the public whose resources are being used.

Not everyone will agree with me. At least, I feel that I should put down some markers from my perspective for others to comment on, to judge and to hopefully learn lessons from the experience. I hope that my version of events, both positive and less so, will help and inspire others, whether for improving the care and understanding of Scotland's priceless natural heritage, or in taking on leadership roles.

Readers might well ask, surely this is history and times have changed. Yes, times have changed, but there is too rarely the opportunity to look back and to describe what was happening at the time. That might be useful in itself, especially as corporate memories these days are very short. Moreover, we also fail to reflect on whether lessons can be learned from the past. Proponents against this view argue that the pace of change is so great and the scene ever changing that looking back and reflecting cannot really be relevant. How many people have shaken their heads when someone with long experience offers a comment from the past? Surely it is irrelevant for today's situation, one hears them say as context, focus, culture and many other attributes have changed fundamentally. I disagree. Persuaded by former colleagues, I have set down my story of what happened, and why and what were the many and various influences prevailing to do things in a certain way or to respond to the strictures that we were placed under.

There has been no thorough account or appraisal published of SNH. However, a number of works, referred to later in the text, have made passing reference. See, for examples, Donald Mackay, *Scotland's Rural Land Use Agencies*, Peter Marren, *Nature Conservation*, and J Morton Boyd, *The Song of the Sandpiper*.

This book is relatively unusual as not many public sector leaders in the

UK have published such accounts. The literature by government insiders in the UK appears to be limited, whereas in the USA it is voluminous. Sir Martin Holdgate's *Penguins and Mandarins - the memories of natural and unnatural history* by a world leader on nature conservation is a fine example. Alistair Campbell's account of *The Blair Years* is another. Notable others are Charles Rossotti's *Many Unhappy Returns* about the Internal Revenue Service of the USA, and James Wilson's *Bureaucracy*. More widely, corporate leaders in business and politics, such as Phil Knight's memoir of the creation of Nike, and Jacinda Ardern's *A New Kind of Leader* are insightful. Hopefully, this book will be a valuable addition both to the literature on leadership and to the work of government.

Readers might also ask why I have waited for over two decades before writing this account. The answer is simple. I have been busy on other things and, more importantly, distance from the events can hopefully give me a more rounded perspective. Now is the time to reflect as the 35th anniversary of the legislation is celebrated in 2026, and it will be a third of a century since the establishment of SNH in 2027. I hope that readers will feel better able to plan the way forward stimulated by lessons from the past.

There was a sea change in thinking about the natural environment and society from the publication of *The World Conservation Strategy* in 1980 and the World Commission on Environment and Development's report *Our Common Future* in 1987. Both espoused the cause of Sustainable Development. It was obvious, therefore, that when proposals for changing both the organisational structures for nature conservation and countryside in England, Scotland and Wales that this new perspective should be at the heart. This was certainly the case in Scotland as the then Secretary of State, Malcolm Rifkind, made clear in a series of public statements towards the end of the decade.

The basic political decision was to bring together the Nature Conservancy Council in Scotland and the Countryside Commission for Scotland and to add wider powers to meet the challenges of the time and bring a more integrated Scottish approach. It was not 'out with the old' as the many professional and experienced people in the existing bodies, the Nature Conservancy Council (NCC) and the Countryside Commission for Scotland (CCS), were needed for the new approaches. The challenge was to create a bigger canvas, to remove the barriers built up over many decades, ossified in legislation and organisational arrangements. In tune with this emerging environment was the need for fresh approaches, and giving statutory recognition to the role of people as individuals, communities and society more widely as players.

This is the essential background to the story I tell in this book. By necessity, it starts with what has happened since the mid-1930s and how our understanding and attitudes on ecologically-based conservation and on countryside access and management have changed. This evolution was fraught with inhibitions and traditional approaches, setting up silos of operation and areas of dispute between separate bodies. These structures and mindsets were never going to be able to address the agenda emerging in the 1980s and formulated internationally and adopted nationally at the Earth Summit in Rio in 1992.

I set out in Chapter 1 the case for change as an historical perspective of the separate strands of policy and activity on nature conservation and countryside. Chapter 2 tells the story of the progress of the legislation from the policy papers to the approved statute. Chapter 3 discusses the establishment of SNH as an organisation: people, structures, activities and more. In Chapter 4, the development and delivery of SNH policies and activities are examined. Chapter 5 focusses on the all-important relationship between the government in Scotland and SNH, its ups and downs and outcomes. Chapter 6 describes the fundamental changes to SNH ways of operating and the establishment of its trailblazing *Natural Heritage Futures* programme. There were many controversial issues to be dealt with and these are assessed in Chapter 7. Chapter 8 portrays the many elements of working with others in the public, private and charitable sectors and the approaches which we tried and tested to better or lesser effect. In Chapter 9, I reflect on the journey, what worked and what did not, what were the obstacles and how we overcame those that we could. Finally, in Chapter 10, I reflect on what has changed over the last quarter of a century on the key issues for the natural heritage, in government and partner relationships and my reflections on leadership and management.

To avoid confusion about the various labels to describe the government in Scotland, I have used the term Scottish Office for the pre-devolution period and Scottish Government for the period thereafter.

Roger Crofts
Musselburgh, February 2026

CHAPTER 1

Arguing the Case for Change

> 'The thesis of this book is that planning for the preservation of rural beauty must be directed to the deliberate conservation of much of our native vegetation, since this is an essential element of natural beauty, and that such planning must be balanced and harmonised with land utilisation for agriculture and forestry.'
> **A G Tansley,** ***Our Heritage of Wild Nature***

AT THE time of writing, SNH, now informally named NatureScot (until the name is formally changed in primary legislation), has become an established part of government machinery for the protection and enhancement of nature and landscape and public access to and enjoyment of the outdoors. To understand the reasons for the decisions made in the late 1980s and the establishment of SNH under the Natural Heritage (Scotland) Act 1991, we need to go back a little in history.

The journey to its establishment goes back to the separation of nature and countryside functions in the interwar years, ossified in early postwar legislation and in Scottish politics. What ultimately led to the merger of two distinctive streams of public leadership and administration for nature and the countryside? Why was a change justified in the later 1980s? How did it come about? What was the result? And what were the issues that it had to wrestle with? These are the questions addressed in this chapter.

Why Was a New Organisation Needed?

There are many reasons why political leaders across the spectrum of opinion in Scotland and also in Westminster and Whitehall, and closely followed by Wales, thought that the arrangements for looking after nature needed radical change. In Scotland, there were also concerns about the effectiveness of the arrangements for looking after the countryside and public access to it and enjoyment of it. The story in England differed from that in Scotland in terms of the reasoning and the outcomes. The initial view of consultants hired by the UK Department of the Environment to review the early experience of SNH was negative, perhaps because the commissioning bureaucrats in Whitehall did not wish to emulate our approach. Ironically, the arrangements in England a decade or so after the Scottish changes demonstrated that the Scottish model was a reasonable one to follow as an organisation with similar roles and responsibilities to SNH was established.

It is not my purpose to provide a history of natural conservation or countryside in Britain. There are many accounts, some more reliable than others, dependent on the author's perspective, by Sheaill, Stamp, Marren and others. Rather I spell out my views on why change was necessary.

Nature Conservation – An Uneasy Compromise

Nature conservation was undertaken by the statutory body, the NCC. One of its primary roles was the identification and notification of Sites of Special Scientific Interest to provide a representative selection of the best sites and areas for the protection of flora, fauna, geological and physiographic features in the counties of England, Scotland and Wales. This system had many critics throughout the 1980s following the seminal Wildlife and Countryside Act of 1981. The provisions in the Act necessitated the re-designation of all existing Sites of Special Scientific Interest (SSSIs) plus the addition of others. It led to SSSIs being regarded as the *bête noire* of owners and occupiers of land despite the fact they were based on the *Voluntary Principle*. In practice, this meant that what NCC decreed could be ignored by owners of land and water or they could be paid compensation for not doing what they claimed they wanted to. How about that for a contorted system! In other words, the Act represented a kind of truce between conservation interests and landowning interests. Once the statutory body had identified an area justifying designation as an SSSI, it was not protected against damage until all of the arrangements between the owners of the site and the NCC were complete. This led to many examples of damage to the putative site through deliberate action by owners, or at least on their behalf. Notable cases occurred in the Somerset Levels. As a result, the UK Parliament passed amendments in 1985, to the effect that once a site had been identified as an SSSI it should be treated as if it were fully protected, and any damage would result in action against the owner in the courts.

These disagreements were the result of the inevitable clashes between owners and managers of land, farmers and foresters. Their interests were well articulated through the representative bodies, such as the Country Landowners Association in England and the Scottish Landowners Federation in Scotland, and by members of the House of Lords, as well as by the National Farmers Unions.

The best, or worst, manifestations were the forestry planting proposals in Scotland. I well remember being at the denouement meeting between the then Secretary of State and his political adviser with a Forestry Commissioner. The latter sought to justify the existing arrangements of allowing government money to be paid to those who claimed that their forestry planting proposals were being thwarted by the nature conservation body, even though the proposers had no intention of carrying out the tree planting. As the person responsible for the policy on nature conservation, I just listened to the unravelling of the arguments. It may surprise those who know me that I said nothing during the formal part of the meeting, as the case by the Forestry Commission was regarded as so ludicrous by the Secretary of State. At one point, he turned to his political adviser and speculated whether they should obtain some land, wait until NCC proposed the area as an SSSI at which point they would say that this would stop them from planting trees and apply for compensation. The sheer ludicrousness of the argument were not recognised by the Forestry Commissioner, despite the obvious forensic point from the Secretary of State. As a result, the real revolution from a compensatory approach to a more progressive relationship of positive management arrangements providing public benefit between the nature conservation agency and the owner was born.

Adding fuel to the flame was the publication by the NCC of its report *Birds, Bogs and Forestry* making the scientific case for protection of the whole of the Flow Country. The launch of the report in London rather than in the area or even in Inverness was very insensitive and added strength to the arguments by the Chair of the HIDB for a new Scottish nature body. Having to use the SSSI mechanisms, as it was the only one available for such a large area, made the situation worse.

In effect, the nub of the political rationale for changing the arrangements for statutory nature conservation came out of this argument about compensation, or as it was termed the 'loss of future income foregone' argument. It was an indefensible system. It favoured unscrupulous owners to claim that they were being stopped from making land use changes by the NCC and demanding compensation for the putative income foregone from the operations they claimed they were going to undertake.

There were many cases in Scotland, particularly in the Flow Country of Caithness and Sutherland, where compensation arrangements were agreed, and the costs were paid by the Secretary of State for the Environment for the UK. Not unreasonably, he challenged the notion that he should be paying the bill for such arrangements in Scotland. Not only did this trigger his Scottish colleague's reaction, as described above, it led the Secretary of State for Scotland to argue the case for having control on what happened in Scotland. There was an easy meeting of the minds of the two Secretaries of State on this point. Hence, the devolution of nature conservation was determined politically.

There were other arguments which led to agreement on the new arrangements. There was an emerging argument about the loss of rights by local communities and farmers. This was in part the result of the implementation of the SSSI provisions in the 1981 Act (as amended) that required all of the existing SSSIs to be redesignated, and new agreements reached with owners and tenants. Disputes flared up around Scotland, the ones perhaps most remembered were in Islay and Orkney. David Bellamy visited these islands at the invitation of the RSPB and immediately found himself in opposition to farmers resulting in the burning of his effigy and his rapid retreat from the islands.

There were also some much deeper, and more fundamental, issues regarding the role of science, and who pulled the strings in the NCC. In what follows, I should emphasise that this is my ringside view of affairs. Others have wholly different interpretations as set out, for example, by Thompson, Birks and Birks in their monumental assessment of the life and legacy of Derek Ratcliffe *Nature's Conscience.*

Despite some fundamental work by the NCC in Scotland on the relationship between nature conservation and forestry, and nature conservation and agriculture in Scotland, led by some first class policy analysts and creative thinkers like Alan Mowle, there appeared to be a loss of ecological thinking as the science of ecology became muddled with the pursuit of nature conservation purism within the Chief Scientist's Directorate of NCC. It felt to me and others working on the structural changes, as if the conservation movement, led by NCC and its acolytes in the RSPB, were acting as what I called 'Conservation Imperialists' - they knew best and apparently had the scientific credentials to back them. The close personal links of staff NCC and the RSPB raised questions as to who was running statutory nature conservation. Ironically, the RSPB President at the time was Magnus Magnusson, and Scottish Ministers considered it a coup to appoint him successively as the Chair of the interim NCC Scotland and then SNH.

Lest the reader feels that I am too biased, I should record what a former Chief Scientist of English Nature told me about his old organisation - the NCC. Put bluntly, he said, 'It was too fragmented, too scientific, too authoritarian, too reactive' and he 'doubted its effectiveness'.

NCC was not helped by the appointment of a senior civil servant from the Department of the Environment as its Director in 1988. The individual seemed determined to become the ultimate 'gamekeeper turned poacher' much to the annoyance of his original employers administratively and politically. It did seem that the organisation was out of control, running its own (and clearly others') agendas and was a thorn in the flesh of the many protagonists, particularly in the land fraternity.

Of course, the lobby movement against the proposals came to the fore, including from the NCC Chief Scientist. Writing in *New Scientist*, 9 September 1989, Derek Radcliffe, days after his retirement, said:

> The British government has strange ways of demonstrating its commitment to conserving the environment. While we wait for some meaningful deeds to follow Margaret Thatcher's words on the subject, Britain's environment ministers have announced their intention to carve up the Nature Conservancy Council between England, Scotland and Wales...By an impenetrable logic, the different bits will be amalgamated with the Countryside Commissions in Scotland and Wales, but not in England. This is a job engineered by Malcolm Rifkind, the Secretary of State for Scotland, with the Scottish landowning, farming, forestry development and local political establishment standing behind him.

That view remains widely held as the primary reason for change. Interestingly, Derek Ratcliffe wrote to me at the end of 2000 saying:

> I understand the difficulties that nature observation faces in Scotland and the sensitivities that have to be observed in the context of the socio-economic situation.

A Weak Countryside Body

There is another angle to the arguments leading to the establishment of a new body in Scotland which is rarely if ever articulated. These revolve around the status, standing, location, culture and effectiveness of the CCS. It was established under the Countryside (Scotland) Act 1967 and its premises were at Battleby, a small country house and grounds north of Perth. It had many able staff, who fortunately stayed on to become very effective colleagues in SNH and who played a formative role in, for example, the creation of new access laws and the creation of footpaths, the development of the countryside ranger service and the fundamental role of environmental education. However, the politically appointed leadership of CCS was rather askew from the political reality, all the more surprising given the political links which some Commissioners had in the past and at the time.

CCS had a long-standing mission to 'right the wrong' of there being no national parks in Scotland. There was an oft asked question. Why should a country that had been the birthplace of the Father of National Parks, John Muir, be thwarted from having them and being the only other country in Europe without them, along with Albania? The answer had been clear for many decades, since the attempts in the late nineteenth century to secure legislation, led by the MP James Bryce. More recent arguments came from the UK Government appointed Commission on National Parks for Scotland led by Sir Douglas Ramsay and reporting in 1949, and later in CCS's own publications setting out the case - in *A Parks System for Scotland*, for example. There had been long-standing objections from local authorities not wishing to lose powers and authority, and from landowners not wishing to have a new regime imposed upon them over which they had little control. We were clear in the Scottish Office in the late 1980s that Ministers would not support the establishment of national parks. However, we gained ministerial agreement for CCS to examine arrangements for what we called *popular mountain areas.* The CCS did not read the political runes clearly and still felt, despite being given private briefings to the contrary, that this would prepare the way for national parks.

CCS's report *The Mountain Areas of Scotland: conservation and management* was published in 1990. It usefully identified key problems, such as fish farms, forestry, housing and tourism development, land use conflict, recreation as a land use and the lack of management incentives. Many of these issues we grappled with later in SNH and, sad to say, some still exist 35 years after the CCS report, as I shall spell out in Chapter 10. Interestingly, CCS argued for the establishment of local land use forums; a far-sighted suggestion which still has not quite come to fruition despite experiments in regional forums arising from the requirements placed on the Scottish Government in the Climate Change (Scotland) Act 2009 for the establishment of a land use strategy. CCS also recommended the establishment of four national parks: Loch Lomond and The Trossachs, Cairngorms, Ben Nevis/Glencoe/Blackmount, and Wester Ross, misreading the political runes. Nevertheless, in what many in the pro national parks lobby regarded as a spoiling tactic, Scottish Ministers agreed to the establishment of two working parties to examine the possibilities for better recreation and access provision and management and improved landscape protection for Loch Lomond and the Trossachs, and for the Cairngorms. The inability of the appointed leaders of CCS to read the politics of the time was a major issue. Only when there was a change of government following the 1997 election, was the time right politically for the establishment of national parks, as well as clarifying the rights and responsibilities of public access to the countryside.

Lest the reader thinks that it is only the national parks issue that resulted in CCS being merged with the NCC to form SNH, there were other issues. On the policy front, there was concern that the earlier work on assessing the diversity and quality of Scotland's landscape and its ability to withstand changes in land use and in economic activity had not been taken to fruition, beyond the responsibilities of local planning authorities for National Scenic Areas. Furthermore, design guidelines for properties in the countryside were never brought to a strategic level despite earlier work.

Perhaps the most telling point was that CCS was a small organisation based on a small estate north of Perth, what might be called 'out of sight out of mind' of the mainstream of political and policy thought and action. This was certainly a view told to me in no uncertain terms by my colleagues in the Scottish Office who had previously had responsibility for CCS, when I was appointed to the conservation and countryside portfolio role in the Scottish Office Environment Department. CCS had also suffered from ineffective leadership. At executive level, this was most apparent after the retirement of its outstanding first Director, John Foster Also, too many of its senior Commissioners, albeit appointed by the Secretary of State for Scotland as non-executive Board members, seemed to lack the necessary political nous. 'Get them out of Battleby' was the clear advice from my Scottish Office colleagues. It was, therefore, curious that the appointed leadership of CCS, once the merger into SNH was announced, spent much time and even more political capital on arguing for Battleby to be the SNH Headquarters. Again, a lack of political nous was evident.

Ministers' frustrations came to the fore when the time came to appoint new Commissioners. Scottish Office officials were tasked with seeking candidates who were not wedded to the current culture and would bring new thinking. Three appointments were particularly significant: Mark Turnbull, Ian Cunningham, and Adam Watson.

Mark Turnbull was a well-known and highly-respected landscape architect and planner. Ian Cunningham was the leading figure in agricultural education as Principal of the West of Scotland College of Agriculture and later Chair of the Macaulay Institute. Adam Watson was, without doubt, Britain's leading scientist on the ecology of the uplands and the living fountain of knowledge on the Cairngorms. Given the strong personalities and their complementary expertise and experience, we had hopes for changes. But sad to say, their influence was largely nullified by the conservative single-track thinking in CCS about national parks and defending Battleby as the centre of operations.

Two Separate Intellectual Traditions No Longer Appropriate

There were other matters which were influential in the arguments for a new Scottish body. Philosophy, natural science or social science, linkages in landscapes or disconnections were some. Let me elaborate.

The intellectual origins for countryside conservation and nature conservation are quite different and, some might argue, provided the rationale for keeping their execution separate. However, strongly influenced by my training and research career as a geographer and geomorphologist, I felt that nature and landscape are so inextricably linked and that public interest in, access to and enjoyment of the whole countryside should be integrated. That is not how matters had evolved through the earlier twentieth century.

Landscape was really an aesthetic issue to be seen, perceived, admired and enjoyed for its intrinsic qualities. It was less regarded for its genetic underpinnings from a wide range of abiotic earth processes; what we can reasonably classify as 'nature'. The 'love of nature' was in many respects born out of this non-scientific personal appreciation, which I first became aware of from reading the writings of noted US Geological Survey staff in the nineteenth century, such as G K Gilbert and J W Powell, and the writings of Sir Walter Scott, John Ruskin and George Perkins Marsh. This appreciation was later developed, for example, in Aldo Leopold's seminal work *Sand County Almanac* and in W H Murray's inspiring and thoughtful analysis of Scotland's mountain landscapes, *Highland Landscape*, commissioned by the National Trust for Scotland (NTS). The latter became the blueprint for the definition of National Scenic Areas a decade or so later.

From the 1930s, more scientifically-based approaches came to the fore led by the new generation of ecologists, particularly Sir Arthur Tansley and Professor W H Pearsall. In effect, they established the new science of ecology, focussing on the mapping of vegetation complexes and the descriptions of habitats. That was not regarded as sufficient and Tansley led the argument on the need for nature conservation in his 1945 monograph *Our Heritage of Wild Nature: A Plea for Organized Nature Conservation.* He was clearly influenced by his observations in both lowland and upland Britain, commenting that most of the land surface is man-made. His argument for nature conservation partly stemmed from the scientific value of the land and its economic implications, and interestingly also its natural beauty and the sentiment attaching to wild country for people to escape to from the strains of modern life, and partly from its educational value. Tansley placed great stress on the links between nature and beauty. In similar vein, in his 1947 report on national parks for England and Wales he argued that public access and enjoyment of nature went side by side. He was joined by others, including the geographer Sir Dudley Stamp who had masterminded the land use survey which gave Tansley an insight into land use change and its causes and effects. Tansley and ecologically-based thinking was influential in the nature conservation components of the trailblazing National Parks and Access to the Countryside Act 1949, in particular the provisions for the establishment of National Nature Reserves. It is interesting to note that one of the first of these was at Beinn Eighe in Wester Ross, where an area of wetland was subsequently named as the Tansley Bog. It is also interesting to note that, although the label 'nature conservation' was the critical one, the arguments were as much about wildness and naturalness, and the beauty and aesthetics of landscape; yet these were not translated into the roles and responsibilities of government nature conservation bodies. How far sighted Tansley was.

The separate stream of development of landscape conservation through national parks and access to the countryside emerged particularly in the post-World War Two reconstruction period with Government commissions led by John Dower for the UK as a whole and by Sir Douglas Ramsay in Scotland.

The 1949 National Parks and Access to the Countryside Act, therefore, set a course of three separations. England and Wales emerged with a national park system; Scotland did not for the reasons stated above. The rights of access differed between England and Wales on the one hand and Scotland on the other with more permissive and legally-binding approaches in England and Wales. Arrangements for nature conservation were separated from those for care of scenery and wild places.

Two traditions therefore emerged from the 1949 Act: nature conservation, and landscape protection and its enjoyment. This separation was legalised and became institutionally ossified over the coming decades.

New statutory bodies in England and Wales and in Scotland for the countryside were borne out of a series of informed debates, with the Duke of Edinburgh playing a key role. *The Countryside in 1970* conferences held in the later 1960s arose from concerns about changes to the countryside, especially from the intensification of agriculture and the extension of commercial forestry. The CCS was established through the Countryside (Scotland) Act 1967.

A parallel development was the increasing demand for public access to the countryside. The renowned public march on Kinder Scout in the southern Pennines by urban folk from Manchester, Sheffield and other cities in the 1920s, demonstrated the irritation with the lack of rights to access and the need for connection to the hills and mountains. In Scotland, this irritation was reflected in the continuing failure of legislative attempts, begun by James Bryce in the 1890s, to gain a formal right of access to the open countryside.

The scientific underpinning of nature conservation from its origin in 1949 proved to be an ongoing debate, or maybe a running sore, as each time changes were made, they led to more confusion of roles and responsibilities between government bodies. The sense, or, as I strongly believe, the nonsense, of separating science from advice, policy and management of nature is the point at issue. The point of departure was the split of the Nature Conservancy (NC) in the 1970s when the scientific branch was subsumed within the Natural Environmental Research Council (NERC) as a separate entity – the Institute of Terrestrial Ecology and the NCC formed the remainder under NERC. Thereafter, the demand for nature conservation to remain science based in its work was never resolved. The customer/contractor principle of the 1970s, whereby the NCC should obtain its research from external sources, principally the research institutes of NERC, was the operating approach determined by the government. This was devised by Lord Rothschild, commissioned by the Conservative administration of the day, to recognise that the customer should have a clear view of their requirements and negotiate their delivery through a contractor. NCC fought back by establishing a Chief Scientist Team (later Directorate) headed by the redoubtable Derek Radcliffe, a role he played until retiring in 1989; he had previously been Deputy Director (Science) of the NC. It is not my intention to assess his significance in nature conservation, except to say that he was a seminal figure; readers should refer to the monumental appreciation of his role and influence in *Nature's Conscience* written by those who knew him, worked with him and understood his power and influence. The issue at stake throughout his tenure as Chief Scientist and which ran on into the formation and early years of SNH, was the status and positioning of science and its role in determining, or otherwise, the credos of the organisation and its approach to its nature conservation work on policy and action.

Following a visit to Peterborough to meet Ratcliffe and a few of his staff to discuss the Flow Country, the Under Secretary and myself from the Scottish Office could readily understand the importance of the scientific basis for nature conservation. Equally, we could see that in NCC the scientists wanted to drive the agenda rather than accepting the new norm of science being the servant of the strategy and policy for nature conservation. This manifested itself most pointedly in the Flow Country debate - the highly contentious issue about the deep ploughing of carbon, habitat and species rich peats and small lochs to plant non-native species of trees for commercial reasons and economic development. The scientific basis for conservation was clearly set out in the report *The Flow Country*, but science was somewhat set aside in the earlier polemical report *Birds, Bogs and Forestry* because of the NCC's determination to win an argument for the protection of the area from afforestation. Maybe this was a result of NCC feeling it had to take on both scientific and policy advocacy roles as the UK Environment Ministry were not doing the latter. Nevertheless, we came away convinced that the role separation between scientific knowledge and policy advice had become at best blurred. Was it really science or some mystique between science and propaganda that was at work? It led me to coin the phrase 'Conservation Imperialism' in that conservation staff of the government agency saw their role as a fight and that dictating the terms of engagement from an apparently scientific perspective would win the day. Clearly, it was a grave error of judgement as it did not win the day with decision makers. This episode influenced my own thinking when establishing the culture of SNH and its approach to policy and influencing, and establishing the role of science and scientists, as I shall describe in a later chapter.

An Emerging Scottish Agenda

Added to these issues were the emerging debates about devolution to Scotland. Whilst the Conservative government was not in favour of a Scottish Parliament, it wished to have greater control over matters in Scotland which had been traditionally run on a UK or Great Britain wide basis. This definitely included nature conservation as indicated earlier. The agenda was manifested in the establishment of new statutory bodies in Scotland to deal with issues at arm's length from government, such as Scottish Homes and the two Enterprise agencies.

A New Global Agenda

The final driving force for organisational change was the emerging global agenda of sustainable development. Debates about new international agreements began to firm up resolution internationally at the UN Conference on the Human Environment in 1972 and especially with the establishment of The World Commission on Environment and Development in the mid-1980s chaired by the Prime Minister of Norway, Gro Harlem Brundtland. Its report, *Our Common Future,* published in 1987, was particularly influential, and led ultimately to the Earth Summit in Rio in 1992 and the agreement to the sustainable development agenda and the three specific Conventions on Biodiversity, Climate Change, and Combating Desertification.

Scottish Office officials suggested to the Secretary of State that he might focus on sustainable development in his speech at the annual forum of the Scottish Council (Development and Industry) held in Aviemore. He duly agreed and, in September 1989, took his audience by surprise in spelling out the sustainable development agenda and the Scottish Office's commitment to taking it forward. As a result, a small but highly significantly element in the Scottish Office's proposals for the natural heritage was on sustainable development, leading to a Section of the Natural Heritage (Scotland) Act 1991 having wording to this effect.

Overview of Reasons For Change

This detailed review I hope will have given readers an understanding of the multifaceted reasons for change in policy and organisational arrangements. In summary, the arguments for establishing a new agency integrating and extending the functions of nature conservation and countryside in Scotland were as follows:

First was the need for accountability in policy and finance on Scottish matters to be the sole responsibility of the Secretary of State for Scotland.

Second was the increasingly weak arguments of retaining separation of the two sets of functions, especially in the light of the driving forces of the sustainable development agenda.

Third both of the existing organisations had poor public images in Scotland, partly as a result of the unresolved questions of who called the shots.

Fourth and related, both organisations seemed to have lost their way by failing to deliver effectively on their key responsibilities.

These were, therefore, the arguments that drove the decision to establish a Scottish-based body accountable directly to Scottish Ministers and the UK Parliament. The next steps were to set the policy framework, to develop the legislative proposals and to develop the culture of the new organisation, and appoint the key people, specifically the Chair and the Chief Executive. I will consider each of these elements in turn, once I have reflected on the backlash to the UK Government's proposals and the compromises which were made by the government to get their main proposals of devolution of nature conservation administered by separate bodies for England, Scotland and Wales through the UK Parliament

Recognising the Seminal Figures From the Past as Our Inheritance

Before leaving this analysis, I want to recognise the leadership of the past and the inheritance the new body would have as a result of the work of some key individuals in nature conservation and countryside. I have been selective in terms of the stature and esteem in which the individuals were held by colleagues at the time as was indicated to me when I became the SNH CEO. I have reproduced summaries of the appreciations written by those who knew them.

> ***Dr John Berry, CBE, FRSE***
> ***Director Scotland the Nature Conservancy (1948-1968)***
>
> John Berry was a naturalist who made a difference...Following a degree in Zoology at Cambridge, his career began to prosper as a researcher into fish biology. In 1936 he was elected to a Fellowship of the Royal Society of Edinburgh at the age of 29. He was a Fellow for 66 years: elected the youngest and he died the oldest... From this period, too, comes his only book. In collaboration with Misses Baxter and Rintoul, he amassed data for the *Wild Geese and Wild Duck of Scotland* (1939), which for the first time of any regions in the world, described the distribution of wildfowl and gave a scientifically based estimate of their numbers. It was an account on which all further work of the group in Scotland came to be based.
>
> There were exciting initiatives in nature conservation in the late

1940s. In 1948 John was sent to Fontainebleau for the founding meeting of IUCN...At much the same time, he was approached to become Director of the new Nature Conservancy in Scotland, a post he held for 18 years, in which the character of the organisation was formed, and its operations became part of the fabric of Scottish Government and life.

His greatest achievement was to establish the great series of National Nature Reserves, beginning with Beinn Eighe in 1951, when he was sent to buy a pine wood for £4000 and returned with the whole mountain. He added to Beinn Eighe a whole stream of other nature reserves, including Tentsmuir and Morton Lochs, Loch Leven, the Cairngorms (by agreement) and Rùm, purchased from a wealthy lady owner over the horses at Newmarket. He achieved wonders, and the award of a CBE was some recognition of this. 'I am not a Scottish Nationalist', he was wont to say, 'I am a Scottish Naturalist'. We owe him a debt for his stewardship of Scottish nature that is hard to calculate.

Abbreviated from T C Smout Obituary (Dr John Berry) in Scottish Birds (1994)

Dr W Joe Eggling, CBE, FRSE
Conservation Officer and Latterly Director (1955-1970)

Joe Eggling was one of the outstanding figures in Scottish conservation and ornithology. Following studying forestry at Edinburgh and Oxford Universities, he worked in East Africa, becoming the Chief Conservator for Tanganyika, focussing on the survey and management of the natural resources. Returning to Scotland, he speculatively wrote to Dr John Berry, then Director Scotland of the Nature Conservancy, inquiring about a job. As he was a forester he could not be appointed as a scientist according to the rule book. However, both Berry and Sir Athur Duncan, the Chair of the Nature Conservancy in Scotland, recognised his qualities and invented the post of Conservation Officer for him. Although NC was a small organisation, in a pioneering way it grappled with major issues like designating the first SSSIs and generally bringing a more orderly approach to the welfare of wildlife. Joe Eggling relished the challenge which this presented, both in terms of directing practical conservation work on the ground and also the humdrum and long drawn-out bureaucratic processes which lay behind it.

He played a formative role in the Scottish Ornithologists' Club as a Councillor and as Vice President and then President. He spent much time on the Isle of May which was close to his heart. He was Honorary Secretary to the Bird Observatory and kept the most meticulous records and led the designation of the May as a National Nature Reserve through negotiations with the Northern Lighthouse Board. On his last visit to the May before he died, he had the pleasure of seeing the ownership being formally handed over to the NCC.

He will be remembered for achieving state ownership for the Isle of May. He will be also remembered with affection for his generosity of spirit, his thoughtfulness towards others and for his good company. He was not just a big man; he was a towering presence.

Abbreviated from John Arnott Obituary of Dr Joe Eggling in Scottish Birds (1994)

J Morton Boyd, CBE, FRSE
Regional Officer and latterly Director Scotland the Nature Conservancy/NCC (1956-1985)

Morton Boyd was one of Scotland's leading nature conservationists. His multiplicity of skills as an author, lecturer, raconteur, photographer, artist, educator and evangelist were focussed to great effect on the conservation of nature in his beloved Scotland. His crusade was to achieve a better understanding of nature through scientific endeavour and to instil into friends, colleagues and the wider public an enthusiasm for nature. His writings and lectures bear testimony to his skills.-

...Meeting Morton Boyd for the first time, I was struck by his sense of history and his vision: he was truly someone who could relate to past, present and future. I was also struck by his enthusiasm and motivation which remained undiminished right to the end of his life. We all remember the twinkle in the eye and the passion of delivery combining head and heart, which certainly brought a tear to Morton's eye and often to those of his listeners as well. Many of us have benefited from talking with him about environmental issues of the day – which were the issues of his day. He helped me and many others to appreciate the continuity of ideas, the wisdom and challenge of bold visions, the importance of relating global with local perspectives, and the dynamics of the natural world.

...His philosophy, partly born from his deep religious belief and long term association with the Kirk, was to humanity and environment as an inextricable whole. To him the cultural landscapes were no less important than the more natural areas. Equally, he was clear in his own mind, no doubt influenced by Fraser Darling, of the degree of degradation of our natural heritage due to human activity. His vision was to redress this wherever possible. Indeed the work which he and his colleagues began on the revival of habitats and species at keystone sites, such as Rùm and Beinn Eighe, were all part of his vision. Morton provided enthusiastic leadership when these and other sites were purchased for the nation and looked after by the Nature Conservancy and latterly the Natural Conservancy Council.

Abbreviated from Roger Crofts in SNH Occasional Paper No 8, A Celebration of the life of John Morton Boyd (2015)

John Foster, CBE
Director CCS (1968-1985)

John Foster was one of Scotland's pre-eminent national parks and countryside leaders. As the first Director of the Countryside Commission for Scotland, and in retirement, he was dedicated to protecting the scenery and natural beauty of the countryside and to improving people's access to and enjoyment of it. His innovative leadership provides a legacy which lives on in the work of the statutory and charitable sectors in Britain and further afield.

...Given his Scottish ancestry, and his innovative and highly successful leadership at the Peak District National Park, it was not surprising that he was appointed the first Director of the Countryside Commission for Scotland in 1968. He established the Commission's base at Battleby, north of Perth. This provided an excellent location for the demonstration of countryside interpretation and visitor management, the training of rangers and the development of environmental education, with a unique innovative education facility and conference centre that is still in use today. He had a *tabula rasa* to develop many innovative approaches to the countryside. He instituted the Scottish Countryside Ranger Service and developed the training of rangers. He pioneered countryside interpretation in Scotland with Don Aldridge as his lead, and he espoused environmental education as a key to the future wellbeing of the Scottish countryside. But it was for the protection of the countryside from unplanned and unwarranted development that he is perhaps best remembered. Living through the early days of many bids for the development of onshore oil and gas facilities in scenic locations, he ensured that there was a sound basis for characterising Scotland's landscapes and for identifying the areas of highest scenic value and natural attraction, notably through the report, *Scotland's Scenic Heritage*, which led ultimately to the statutory establishment of National Scenic Areas. He was less successful in persuading the many interests arrayed against national parks to change their minds. But he was shrewd enough to prepare the ground through a thoughtful and carefully crafted report, *A Parks System for Scotland*, which established the basis for Regional Parks and Country Parks, and set out the arguments for the eventual establishment of national parks in Scotland.

...Roger Crofts, one of his successors, says, 'John's innovative work was an inspiration to me in protecting the beauty of the landscape, developing high quality ranger services, arguing the case for national parks in Scotland, and recognising the great value of international collaboration.'

John believed strongly in the value of international cooperation in the field of landscape protection and nature conservation.

...His work was widely recognised with the award of a CBE in 1985 and other honours. International recognition came with the Fred Packard International Parks Merit Award in 1992.

Abbreviated from Obituary John Foster, The Scotsman (August 2002)

CHAPTER 2

Securing the Statutory Basis

'The proposals are designed to improve the way we handle conservation of wild fauna and flora and the countryside...the circumstances and needs of England, Scotland and Wales are very different, and the present system of nature conservation is inadequate...The conservation and countryside functions should be the responsibility of a single body in each country.'
Nicolas Ridley, UK Secretary of State for Environment 1989

'Conservation is about local action in a global context. Scotland can and must contribute to the changes in attitude that are required worldwide...The government believe that this organisational change will encourage new attitudes to landscape and nature conservation in Scotland.'
Malcom Rifkind, Secretary of State for Scotland 1989

THIS CHAPTER sets out the evolution of the political decision and the establishment of the new body. In particular, it traces some of the political pitfalls that had to be negotiated by Ministers due to lobbying from vested interests.

Responding to the Backlash

'The death of nature conservation' as it was seen by some with the establishment of three separate bodies for England, Scotland and Wales respectively resulted in many challenges. Nature NGOs, like the RSPB and WWF, as well as the NCC Council and its senior staff, led the charge. This backlash was ferocious, and took Ministers in Whitehall and Edinburgh by surprise. Ministers, however, retained their resolve, but realised that some compromises which did not undermine their key objectives needed to be given.

The major compromise, spearheaded in the House of Lords by the Lord Carver, representing the major nature NGOs, led to the establishment of the Joint Nature Conservation Committee (JNCC). At a meeting of three Secretaries of State – Environment, Scotland and Wales and their Permanent Secretaries, which I attended, it was clear that a statutory body was needed which the new devolved nature agencies should have joint responsibility for and fund. It was to have a Chair and three other members independent of the three devolved agencies, as well as two members appointed by each of the agencies. Staff were assigned from each of the devolved agencies to undertake the agreed programme. This mechanism worked politically and meant that the formal establishment of the JNCC and the reorganisation of the NCC into three devolved bodies received Parliamentary assent at the same time as the three agencies were established under the Environmental Protection Act 1990. Its main responsibilities were to ensure consistency in site designation standards; maintain comparable standards and protocols for survey, monitoring and analysis; provide advice at a national and international level; and manage services collectively where it could deliver conservation or value for money benefits. Its effectiveness has been a source of constant debate ever since, partly due to tensions between the devolved agencies and the independent members, but that is not an issue for this book.

In Scotland, in order to give time for the preparation of the new devolved and integrated agency and to find space in the programme of the Scottish Standing Committee of the UK Parliament, an interim one year body, the Nature Conservancy Council for Scotland (NCCS), was established. Certain Fellows of the Royal Society of Edinburgh who had close links with either the CCS or the NCC or both, and environmental NGOs, made their views known to Ministers and publicly about the deconstruction of the NCC and the establishment of the new integrated body. Again, Ministers were not prepared to change their main aspiration, but they recognised the need for a refreshed and more robust scientific approach to Sites of Special Scientific Interest. In deciding to establish an Advisory Committee on SSSIs, Ministers made it clear that they meant business. The Committee's role was to rigorously review the approaches taken to SSSI notification and the rationale for site selection. Eminent conservation scientists were appointed who were independent of the Board of NCC Scotland or the soon to be established SNH.

Consulting on the Proposals

A short consultation paper written by colleagues and me in the Scottish Office Environment Department was released in July 1989 entitled *Scotland's Natural Heritage: a consultation paper*. The centrepiece of the front cover was a red deer stag with Scots pine and commercial forestry in the background of a moorland setting with a raptor overhead to emphasise the importance of interaction with land management interests. Noting the distinctiveness of Scotland's natural heritage within Britain, the paper stated the government's aim as 'to continue to protect and manage Scotland's natural heritage, while ensuring that people can enjoy it and continue to live and work in it'. The purpose of the consultation was to solicit views on the merger proposals which the government claimed reflected a growing groundswell of support for changes in the organisational structure. The outcome of the consultation was broad support for the merger, albeit anxieties were expressed about nature conservation being lessened and also about the countryside responsibilities being swamped by those for nature.

The Scottish Office's new approach in philosophy and culture, again written by colleagues and me, was spelt out in more detail in *Scotland's Natural Heritage: the Way Ahead*. It was released in summer 1990 for consultation and input to drafting of the legislation. The Secretary of State for Scotland made clear the government's intentions by stating, 'We must improve our understanding, increase awareness, promote cooperation and find ways of allowing our rural communities to grow and prosper by managing natural resources wisely and well'. He went on to say 'Conservation is about local action in a global context. Scotland can and must contribute to changes in attitude that are required. The government believe that this organisational change will encourage new attitudes to landscape and nature conservation in Scotland'. Magnus Magnusson, who had been appointed the Chair of SNH, said, 'We are at the start of something hugely exhilarating and constructive'.

What's in a Name?

When Ministers were asked to decide on the name of the new organisation they were given a number of options by civil servants. We recognised that use of any of the words in the titles of the two predecessor organisations would be a mistake, either because it might signal one of the functions being regarded as more important that the other, or that it would fail to signal that the new body was not as different from its predecessors as Ministers were claiming. The word Scottish had to be in the title to signify that the responsibility lay with the Secretary of State for Scotland and that the body was to be separate from its nature conservation predecessor. Heritage was seen as a reflection of the sustainability ethic, meaning that it embraced inheritance from the past, caring at the present and passing on responsibly to future generations. Adding the word natural to heritage made a clear distinction from the cultural heritage, which was the responsibility at the time of Historic Scotland (HS) and the Royal Commission on Ancient and Historic Monuments of Scotland (RCAHMS). Alternative names did not have the resonance of what the government wished to signal with the establishment of its new body. Two examples suffice to make the point. Nature Police may have been favoured by the Conservation Imperialists but would send entirely the wrong signals. The Nature and Countryside Agency for Scotland would signal a bolting together of two existing bodies rather than a new start.

In retrospect, the word 'heritage' did give confusion as the media, in particular, seemed incapable of understanding that heritage related to nature as well as to culture. Clearly, they had not read or were even aware of, Tansley's excellent monograph referred to earlier, *Our Heritage of Wild Nature.* It is somewhat ironic that the name of the organisation resulting from the merger of HS and RCAHMS is Historic Environment Scotland, as if in the pre-human period there was not an environment; a total misnomer, if ever there was one, compared with SNH.

But names do reflect the thinking of the time. Hence it is no surprise that after almost 30 years of the name SNH, the leadership persuaded Ministers to change the name to NatureScot. Formalisation will have to await a change in the primary legislation. Given the many references to SNH in extant legislation this is likely to prove too cumbersome a task, and presumably why it has not been included in the Natural Environment (Scotland) Bill currently before the Scottish Parliament. As I have written elsewhere, this name would not have been possible in 1990:

> It is somewhat ironic that those developing nature conservation in the middle of the 20th century took 'nature' onto a narrow path

> focusing almost entirely on plants and animals and the ecological systems in which they existed. In the by-going, geodiversity played second fiddle at best, and people were too often regarded as a nuisance factor, forgetting the close association between people and nature.

It has led me to conclude 'nature is the solution if we have the political and public recognition of its vital importance to the wellbeing of current and future generations'.

A Clear Statutory Basis

Drafting legislation is an interesting experience for a civil servant. As the head of the policy division and head of the Bill team it was an exciting time. You were personally in the lead working directly with the relevant Ministers. Or so you thought. Perhaps surprisingly to readers, the system works as follows.

The policy civil servant agrees the way forward with Ministers. In the case of the Natural Heritage (Scotland) Bill this was the relatively easy element. Trying to persuade the Scottish Office Solicitors that Ministers had a clear view of what they wanted was protracted, especially as we wished to break new ground by amalgamating the most positive elements of the legislation from the two predecessor bodies and adding a clear aim and purpose that were distinctively different. The reference to sustainable development proved to be the most difficult for the Solicitors to understand as it had never before been proposed in a UK Bill; maybe no more should be said on that point! Once past the solicitors' hurdle, the next step is to ask the Parliamentary Draftsman to draft the Bill. Their role is to ensure that protocol is not breached and that the meaning of Clauses is clear in the context of historical drafting. One interesting instance of this was the definition of natural heritage where the term 'physiographical features' was the common statutory parlance. This was old-fashioned in terminology focussed on what existed, that is a feature, not on the more important issue of the processes by which it was formed and potentially was currently being altered; this latter reflected the shift in the approach arising from the most recent research. As a former geomorphologist, I wanted this changed to use the now more common term - geomorphological features and processes. Needless to say, I was defeated by the Parliamentary Draftsman. Anyway, all was eventually done and the draft Bill published.

The rubric used in setting out the contents of the Bill was 'taking the best of the past in the legislation and adding new approaches to meet the government's ambitions for the new body'. The major unique feature was the reference to sustainable development, giving the new organisation the first ever duty of paying attention to sustainability. In addition, natural heritage was defined so that it 'includes the flora and fauna of Scotland, its geological and physiographical features, its natural beauty and amenity'. Balancing duties to take account of other interests were included from the earlier legislation. The powers which CCS had for undertaking with partners 'development projects and schemes' were provided for the new body. This was a breakthrough from the original nature conservation legislation and enabled SNH to develop positive measures, such as the groundbreaking habitat management schemes. The advisory role of SNH not only amalgamated the roles of the predecessor bodies, but substantially extended them and identified the importance of an integrated approach in providing advice. The proposals for a new designation to protect nature and countryside, termed *Natural Heritage Areas*, was included. Organisationally, we wanted to ensure that SNH had the powers to set up committees to suit its operational requirements, hence a permissive Schedule was written into the Bill. This was important as both of the former bodies had seemed remote, and much of the angst around Scotland about nature and landscape was due to lack of effective contact and working with local organisations and local communities, especially at the senior levels within both organisations. The ability to establish companies and set up partnerships was added, following powers given to the newly-established Scottish Enterprise and Highlands and Islands Enterprise bodies. An important repeal was the removal of the statutory concept of the countryside as this meant that the detailed maps defining the boundary between countryside and non-countryside (ie urban, sub urban and peri urban) was no longer necessary.

Parliamentary Debates and Legislative Approval

Scottish Ministers decided to introduce the Bill in the House of Lords, not unprecedented but relatively unusual. The vagaries of the Parliamentary timetable largely dictated this, particularly the capacity of the Scottish MPs working in committee, which would be the main vehicle for Parliamentary scrutiny of the Bill. As a result, the Bill once it had completed its scrutiny in the

Commons had to revert to the Lords for its Third Reading and completion of the statutory process.

Lord Strathclyde, as Minister of State in the House of Lords, had responsibility for piloting the Bill through the upper house. His only query about the provisions in the Bill, as I recall, was what the sustainability duty meant. As I knew he came from an Ayrshire farming family, I asked what the most important natural capital asset on the farm was. He quickly understood the question and answered, 'The soil'. I was, therefore, able to explain to his satisfaction that the sustainability duty meant caring or stewarding natural assets, of which the soil is one of the most fundamental, for the benefit of current and future generations of farmers and the public.

The passage through the House of Lords was not without its difficulties, given the protective attitude of some Members to the old NCC and by those seeking to ensure that there would be no dilution of the nature conservation. On the other hand, there were those landowners in the Scottish uplands who were concerned that the management of Highland Estates would be interfered with by nature bureaucrats. Hence a clause was added that would have meant that any owner or occupier of land notified as an SSSI or where SNH had notified its intention to do so would have the right to appeal to the Secretary of State. This would have resulted in wholesale challenges to the existing notified sites and skewed the work of SNH in its early years. It was regarded by many as 'a wrecking amendment' to the whole government approach. Foremost amongst these opponents was Lord Pearson of Rannoch.. His continued lobbying did not gain much traction with Ministers. Other landowners with interests in sports shooting, including Earl Peel, who had extensive landholdings in the northern Pennines, remained concerned. Underlying these concerns were the effect of protecting raptor species from persecution and undermining the successful breeding of grouse. This Bill, nor the debates on it in the Lords, could resolve this problem. In introducing the Bill to the Commons at its Second Reading, the government categorically stated that these specific provisions were unworkable and technically flawed. In effect, it remained a standoff for many years, until scientific studies based on Langholm Moor in the Scottish Borders and ultimately the passing of the Wildlife Management and Muirburn (Scotland) Act in 2024 changed the approach. As always, under a Conservative administration, there were concerns expressed from the government benches about the establishment of another

Non-Departmental Public Body (NDPB) to give it its formal nomenclature, otherwise known colloquially as a QUANGO (a Quasi Autonomous Non-Government Organisation - which is neither politically, nor administratively, nor legislatively correct phraseology).

The Bill passed to the House of Commons. It was introduced on 11 February 1991 by the Secretary of State for Scotland, Ian Lang, who had recently replaced Malcolm Rifkind on the latter's promotion to Secretary of State for Defence. It lasted for six hours (Hansard, 11 February 1991 Orders of the Day Natural Heritage (Scotland) Bill [Lords] Order for Second Reading). The Bill was then committed to the First Scottish Standing Committee for detailed scrutiny. The cross-party committee membership deliberated through eight sittings concluding on 14 March 1991.

There was strong cross-party support for the proposals and for the Clauses in the Bill, with only one fundamental challenge to the proposals. Nevertheless, the Bill was in committee for nineteen hours with Will Scott and me in the officials' box throughout providing the Minister responsible, Lord James Douglas Hamilton, with speaking notes and briefing. One hoped the package for the Minister was sufficient, but inevitably an issue would be raised that came out of left field so to speak. This meant that the officials in the box had to provide a speaking note, hand written but hopefully legible, to the Minister in short order. The provisions on water management and abstraction, led by a colleague, took less than an hour to conclude in the final session. On completion, the two Ministers took Will and me for a drink in the House of Commons Bar to celebrate the successful outcome.

The major issue arising from an amendment in the House of Lords was the Clause stating that SNH must review an SSSI if the owner or occupier requested it. This amendment reflected the strength of landowning opinion in the House of Lords who took a negative view of this designation. It was not until the final session in the House of Commons committee deliberations that a revised Clause was found acceptable to all parties. It placed responsibility on the Secretary of State to establish an Advisory Committee on SSSIs (Section 12). Its members were to be independent of SNH and have scientific qualifications and expertise. Its role was 'to have the function of giving advice to SNH on such matters concerning areas of special scientific interest as are specified in this section'.

Sam Galbraith and Brian Wilson, who led for the official Opposition, were supportive and only ever gently tested Lord James, who led for the government throughout the House of Commons stages. They did demand greater clarity of the intention to establish Natural Heritage Areas and to revoke the clause of owners and occupiers being able to challenge SSSI notification. There was pressure from some interests for the government to accept a clause for the establishment of national parks in Scotland. The government, in effect, made some administrative concessions with the establishment of working parties to consider future possibilities for the Cairngorms chaired by Magnus Magnusson and for Loch Lomond and the Trossachs chaired by Sir Peter Hutchison.

The debate on the reintroduction of extinct native species was perhaps the most fascinating. It was not serious about amending the Bill, but to be able to debate whether, and under what circumstances, animals such as the auroch (a large version of modern domesticated cattle which became extinct in the post-glacial period) might be reintroduced, which of course is not feasible but merely added spice to the debate. Nicholas Fairbairn, the MP for Perth & Kinross and a former Solicitor General for Scotland, led these debates. More fundamentally, the role of the new body in relation to local communities and to local government was questioned; initiated by the MP for the Western Isles, Callum MacDonald. This led to a modest rewording of the purposes of the new body to include what are termed 'balancing duties', to take into account in the work of the body the needs of others, particularly local communities, owners and occupiers of land, and archaeological and historical interests. I think the most lasting phrase stated by MPs was by Ray Michie, the MP for Argyll and Bute, who said that 'to meet the legitimate intention (of the organisation dealing with the Scottish countryside) it would have to have the wisdom of Solomon and the patience of Job' (Hansard, 11 February 1991, col 660).

CHAPTER 3

Establishing the Organisation

'SNH has a tremendous task. Sustainability and working with people are our watchwords. We take up the torch from NCCS and CCS to whom Scotland owes a great debt...We have a great challenge. We are going to accept with happiness and determination, with a good history behind us and the exciting future in front.'

Chris Smout, SNH Deputy Chair at the Official Inauguration, 11 May 1992

'This is a new beginning for those who support conservation in Scotland. The tide is on the turn. It will be for SNH to ride the crest of this wave and to ensure that we have both high visibility and a high energy in relation to the range of possibilities that will lie in our path.'

Magnus Magnusson, Speech to Royal Society of Edinburgh Conference, January 1991

TO HELP the transition to the new body, we decided collectively that there should be a joint implementation committee comprising appointed members of both organisations. Inevitably, a great deal of politicking went on with each party staking out its territory on approaches and the balance within the remit. One particularly divisive issue was the location of the headquarters. CCS Commissioners were insistent it had to be at Battleby, whereas those from the NCC felt that Hope Terrace, in the Grange area of Edinburgh, was more suitable.

Nevertheless, we issued joint newsletters to members of staff of both bodies under the heading *Natural Partners.* We even had some sweatshirts made for staff; I still have mine.

The important issue for me, as the lead civil servant, was to recognise, and have others recognise, the positive bequests from CCS and NCC and the implications for our programmes. The table below sets out my perspective.

CCS Inheritance	**Status**	**Issues Requiring SNH Attention**
National Scenic Areas	*Established*	*Stronger Protection*
Regional Parks	*Established*	*Local Authority Commitment & Funding*
Country Parks	*Established*	*Local Authority Commitment & Funding*
Countryside Ranger Services	*Established*	*SNH Commitment & Funding*
Long Distance Footpaths	*Established*	*SNH Funding and Bids for New Ones*
Environmental Education	*Enviable Reputation*	*Scottish Government Policy & Funding*
Countryside Interpretation	*Enviable Reputation*	*Adopting new approaches*
Countryside Access	*Effective Review in Progress*	*Develop Policies & Promote Path Networks*
Planning Advice	*Highly effective*	*Build on Competence Achieved*

National Parks	*Proposals Politically Unacceptable*	*Support Cairngorms & Loch Lomond & The Trossachs Working Parties*
Countryside in and Around Towns	*Many Initiatives Running*	*Continue the Work and Assess What More is Possible*

NCC Inheritance	**Status**	**Issues Requiring SNH Attention**
Nature Conservation Review	*Published*	*Review Gaps, Develop Ecological Networks and Linkages on the Ground*
Geological Conservation Review	*Underway*	*Complete & Publish Through JNCC. Notify as SSSIs Those Sites Needing Protection*
Renotification of SSSIs	*Completed*	*Promotion of Benefits, Joint Responsibilities, and Positive Management Agreements*
Land Use & Nature Conservation	*Policy Papers*	*Develop Further Under Wider Remit & Lobby Within Government*
Science Base	*Central Role*	*Build on Expertise & Readjust Basis as Foundation for Internal & External Advice*
Regional Structure	*Limited Discretion*	*Evolve & Develop Partner Interaction*
Area Teams	*Part Established*	*Increase Scale & Discretion Over Time*

The most important inheritance was the staff. Their knowledge and expertise was essential to deal with the many issues needing to be addressed in the shorter and longer terms. The staff views of the new arrangements and, therefore, the extent of their commitment to the past or to the future were vitally important. This is always the case with fundamental changes in organisations' functions, approaches and structures that are driven externally, including changes in political authority and responsibility.

Building the Organisation

A great deal of advice was sought by the Scottish Office from external consultants. This was the norm for new bodies established by and paid for by them. For example, the accountancy firm, Ernst & Young were commissioned to undertake an Analysis of Operational Options. This approach can be helpful as it provides an independent perspective and brings in additional hands to share the work.

Appointment of the Chair

Ministers were keen to appoint a Chair of the new organisation at an early stage and to give the same person the responsibility for chairing the one-year body, the NCCS. What was in their mind was to appoint someone with experience of chairing a public body in Scotland, who was a well-known figure on the Scottish scene and had empathy with the role which they wished the new body to play. Magnus Magnusson fitted all of these informal criteria. He had the added advantage, presentationally, that he was the President of the RSPB, a body whose Council and staff were largely against the UK Government's reforms of nature conservation bodies. Ministers regarded his appointment as a coup. And so it turned out to be. He was also a consummate scholar, more particularly on the history of Scotland and the links with the Norse cultures. He remained a major figure as an Icelandic citizen all of his life since being brought to Scotland as a nine month old when his parents moved to Leith, his father as a shipping agent. Hence his knighthood for services to Scotland was Honorary and he used with great pride the KBE after his name. Among his more recent writing assignments, he had edited a book with Graham White, *The Nature of Scotland*, providing a comprehensive overview of all aspects of Scotland's nature and its interaction with its people written by well-known experts.

Magnus was very much his own man in dealing with Ministers. He had ready access to the media which he could use, or at least threaten to use, to turn an argument in favour of the new body. A clear recognition of his role and status within the government was that on his retirement on 31 March 1999, after seven years as SNH Chair, he was given a private dinner at Bute House by two former Ministers, Sir Hector Monro and The Earl of Lindsay, and the current Minister, Lord Sewel, (two Conservative and one Labour) with Government officials plus Chris Smout, the Deputy Chair, and me present.

Magnus proved to be the most diligent and enlightened person I have ever had the pleasure of working with in his preparation for meetings within and outwith the organisation and in preparing and delivering speeches. I was fortunate in meeting Magnus soon after he was appointed and we clearly struck a chord about what was needed and how it should be done, long before I was appointed as Chief Executive. Very quickly, after my own appointment, we built a working relationship of trust and common goals to the extent that sometime later one of the Board members said to me in all seriousness that I was too close to the Chair. I admit having smiled at this observation and responded by saying that this was so much better than in another Scottish Office body, Scottish Enterprise, where the media had publicised that the Chair and Chief Executive were at loggerheads. Such an approach was anathema to both of us, and we were privately dubbed 'the old master' and 'the young master'. What a privilege it was to work alongside such a consummate person dedicated to the public interest and with such exacting standards. I learned so much; not least the better use of English grammar such as the use and misuse of the split infinitive which became a standard source of fun between us.

We only differed in one way in how we did things - delivering speeches. Magnus would always ask for a briefing from staff leading on the subject at issue alongside myself. He would record the conversation, then draft a speech and let me review and comment on it. He then revised it. His delivery was perfect. Most people did not know that he read the speeches word for word such was his outstanding declamatory style. I differed. I had been brought up in the 'preaching tradition' of the Baptist Church. As a teenager in Hinckley Baptist Church and later at the Baptist Student Societies in Liverpool, Leicester and Aberdeen, I was frequently asked to preach sermons. These were delivered from notes, usually based on three points, something I had learned from a notable Welsh Baptist preacher in Hinckley, the Reverend T Tudor Rees. I have done this ever since. Yes, I know that I cannot always predict precisely what I am going to say. Magnus said he could not use that approach. He agreed that I could and should. And so that has proved ever since. One occasion when we were in Iceland together in 1996, I gave a public speech on our work in SNH with the guiding phrases being positive action, always using the 'ing' suffix to my key points. He was full of praise.

Magnus gave the most uplifting speeches on our visits to the North Isles, one in Kirkwall and the other in Lerwick, where, with his Nordic culture, he was well-known and a kindred soul of these islanders. On both occasions, he captured the audience from the outset and his words stimulated in-depth discussions for hours afterwards. He did sometimes stray from his brief to make a point. Speaking at the annual conference of the National Farmers Union of Scotland, that well-known bastion of conservatism, he challenged their view that farmers were the real stewards of the environment. That did not go down well, but as time passes this was clearly accurate and reflects a lack of acceptance that food production, whatever the environmental consequences, is not the only social responsibility of the farmer, as many of the younger generation of farmers are proving. He also challenged the golfing community when we agreed that he should warn his audience of the likely effect of sea level rise and increased storminess at the coast potentially causing the loss of the links golf courses. This went down very badly, but has nevertheless proved to be the case as part of the treasured links golf courses at St Andrews, Montrose and Royal Aberdeen have been endangered by coastal erosion despite the attempts to forestall the sea.

The point about the many speeches we both gave was that they were setting out SNH's stall not only to an external audience, but also internally. We made sure that the full text of our speeches was available to staff and Board members throughout the organisation so that they were aware of our thinking and the nuances of our arguments and could use them in their interactions with their colleagues and with those they worked with in other organisations.

My Credentials to be Chief Executive

Some people have a career plan and pathway to follow. That was certainly not mine. Following my decision that I was not cut out to be a classroom teacher of geography as the subject rather than the students were more interesting and important to me, I embarked on an academic research career at Aberdeen University and then University College London. What is relevant to my future roles in government and SNH is that I began work as a research scientist, but increasingly became interested in how the scientific knowledge and growing experience could be used to inform and maybe influence decision-making process in local and national government and in government agencies.

My major project at Aberdeen University was the creation of a geomorphological map of upper Deeside in the context of a wider study of tourism potential there. *Royal Grampian Country* was funded by the Scottish Tourist Board. My challenge was how to use the mapping data to inform decisions on development ideas for roads linking Deeside and Speyside and skiing on Mar Lodge Estate and to identify both the potentials and the obstacles from a natural environmental viewpoint. My interest in assessment of natural resources and their management was kindled.

My own personal research at the Sands of St Cyrus at the mouth of the River North Esk was to work out a time sequence of events for the evolution of the area below the cliffs. This later proved to be helpful in determining the management of the NCC Reserve. I advised that trying to turn the clock back was not naturally possible and the management of the Reserve needed to be adjusted accordingly. My work also enabled the abiotic natural evolution of the site to be better understood both by visitors and by the site managers.

Most significant in scale was the work with colleagues Bill Ritchie and Sandy Mather, on contract from the CCS, to undertake resource inventories and assess the use and management of sandy beach systems in Wester Ross, North Argyll and West Inverness-shire, mainland Argyll, and Islay, Jura and Colonsay. We were able to objectively assess what was happening and to make recommendations for management changes, for example by Argyll County Council at Calgary Bay on Mull, and at Tralee Bay in Benderloch, north of Oban. A CCS senior staff member, however, felt that we were over-reaching our remit, but the fact that the local council responded positively proved our point.

My scientific work continued with studies of the evolution of sand dunes on the Mullet peninsula in County Mayo, Eire, and of raised beaches and coastal processes in the Arctic environment of Vest Spitsbergen. My mapping work continued with two years spent compiling the Geomorphological Map of Great Britain for the British Geomorphological Research Group, based at University College London.

Having realised that a career in the academic world was never going to materialise as I was most interested in applied research and its use in everyday situations, I was fortunate to be appointed to the Scottish Office. I joined a group of social researchers in the Central Research Unit. For most of my decade there, I was on the pragmatic side working in the North Sea Oil Support Group helping my colleagues and Ministers understand the demands of the industry for onshore facilities and being able to use my geographical knowledge to identify sites for developing facilities, such as petrochemical works and sites where oil and gas pipelines from the central and northern North Sea could be brought ashore. Inevitably, this brought challenges from local communities and from the countryside and conservation agencies. After spells reviewing sea fisheries law enforcement and local government structure and financing, I was appointed into the Senior Civil Service. I had only two jobs there prior to SNH. Both proved to be of great value as they meant being the sponsor of Non-Departmental Public Bodies: the Highlands and Islands Development Board, the Scottish Tourist Board, and later the CCS and the Scottish arm of the NCC. The latter job also involved environmental input into land use issues, especially agriculture, fisheries and forestry which were to become major areas of activity in SNH.

One of the many things I learned was how to use my research and analytical skills to review both sides of an argument in the hope that the decisions which Ministers took were on a well-informed basis. After all, this is an essential purpose of a civil servant's role.

As a lifelong geographer, I have certain personal characteristics. I enjoy fieldwork - gathering data and information to increase understanding of situations, people and places. I have had the good fortune to be able to visit all parts of Scotland during my working career and to develop an understanding of Scotland as the most naturally and culturally diverse small country in the world. I am also a pragmatist who loves to see issues resolved and progress made. Part of that attribute is recognising that 'the perfect is the enemy of the good' and that it is better to make decisions than to obfuscate. I am also a 'strategic opportunist' meaning that I prepare for potential opportunities in the hope I can use them for good causes when they arise. And I am a 'completer/finisher' which is an essential driver for me rather than leaving tasks undone because they are in the too difficult category, even when your end point may not have been the most appropriate one.

I have worked in Scotland all of my career and in my own time over the last two decades. I celebrated half of my life in Scotland on 17 December 1992 and, as I write, the total is over 58 years. I wear the kilt on appropriate occasions, such as leading the National Trust for Cruises for eleven years, wearing the Clan Davidson tartan as my mother's maiden name was Dawson which is a sept of the Clan Davidson. I have only a modicum of Scottish genetic heritage, 8 per cent, being predominately an English East Midlander, with a touch of Nordic/Scandinavian genes (14 per cent).

It has been a privilege and pleasure to visit so many parts of our country and to meet and work with so many people. The networks developed have been of great value at every stage of my life as I always seem to know somebody or to know the place in question. Indeed, my daughter often teases me by saying, 'Dad can we go somewhere where no one knows you?' This is the essence of what we call *Village Scotland*. The fact there are so many dimensions to one's activities also helps a great deal.

The one dimension missing from my experience was leading and managing a large cadre of staff. My small Division in the Scottish Office had 24 staff.

Appointment of the Chief Executive

To return to the story. The Chief Executive was appointed following public advertisement for the post in spring 1991. It was decided that the appointment process should be run by the Civil Service Commission responsible for senior appointments in government. The appointment board was chaired by the First Civil Service Commissioner with the Principal of Edinburgh University, the head of the Scottish Office Environment Department, a CCS Commissioner and the Chair designate of SNH. I understand that there were 90 applicants. I was unsure about applying as I saw a potential career path in the Senior Civil Service, but Magnus was keen that I did. The appointment had to be approved by the Secretary of State in terms of the 1991 Act. I was both totally surprised and also elated when I was telephoned by Gavin McCrone, my head of department, one evening in April 1991, to be told that Ian Lang had approved my appointment as Chief Executive. Not only did I have the privilege of leading the development of the government's policy and statute for the new body, but was tasked to lead this body, implement the new approach and nurture the staff of the two predecessor bodies to deliver our message and way of working. *The Scotsman* headline of my appointment was 'Insider at the helm' and I liked the *Sunday Post* headline, 'Nature boss is no April fool'. In the many letters I received congratulating me on my appointment, colleagues and friends made it clear that the challenge of the task was enormous. One colleague whom I greatly admired and worked with when he was the Chief Planner at the Scottish Development Department, Derek Lyddon wrote, 'you are clearly the right person in the right place at the right time'.

Mr Lang stated in the press release:

> I am sure Roger Crofts will approach his task as Chief Executive with commitment and enthusiasm and with Magnus Magnusson as Chair, the staff and the board will develop a formidable team."

Having had no experience of leading and managing a large organisation, what would my approach be? I have always had a strong view of what leadership is all about. Whilst management is important, the leader is precisely that: to demonstrate creativity, to be a good listener, to know one's colleagues and what makes them tick and what they don't like. Along with my aforementioned attitude to work it was, so to speak, second nature to me to take and develop initiatives and to ensure that all of the rhetoric of Minsters and officials about SNH was delivered. At times, it meant I did fly a kite to see what reaction I might get. The essential element in that approach is to listen and assess the reactions and talk to those who reacted and make a judgement to either continue or to change one's mind. As my Management Team colleagues asked on a number of occasions at the end of these exercises in sounding out possibilities, 'Have you changed your mind then and is that a decision?' It was easy to answer 'Yes' and move forward. Another important aspect was to judge what was needed and essential now and what could wait, what potential there was for change now and what needed more mature reflection, particularly in our case at a stage when the organisation had become more mature and confident in itself. Another question was how to remember what I needed to do. I am blessed with a good memory. I added a simple way of remembering by having lists of tasks and activities in small notebooks. Unlike other Chief Executives I knew, I did not have A4 size notebooks which they brought to meetings and recorded relevant material, as I never knew how they would find certain information when they needed it. I preferred to use separate sheets of paper for each topic and to place those in my relevant working folder. These simple working practices intrigued colleagues, including Alan Mowle, our first class head of corporate planning and review, who adopted this approach.

There were two roles I gave high priority to throughout my tenure. First, was to know and understand staff and the issues they were dealing with. Hence, I had a continuous programme of visits around the organisation to the offices and to be taken into the field as that was one of the two coal faces of SNH. When I was asked, 'How do you have the time to visit us, Roger?' my answer was easy but surprising to some staff: 'Because it is one of my highest priorities to meet you and spend time with you.' The other priority was networking within Scotland. Although I only came to live and work in Scotland at the age of 22, after school and university, I had quickly built up networks of people and knowledge of the country from my previous academic roles and government jobs. I understood the actuality of *Village Scotland.* It is one of the country's most important attributes for those who work within the public realm. Maintaining connections and networks throughout my tenure was an important role. Meeting, in all sorts of formats and places, senior officials in the government and CEOs in its agencies, in the business and commercial sectors and in the NGOs was a key role to make sure that SNH was 'at the table'. It was essential to understand the perspectives of others and to ensure that our perspective was fully understood from the horse's mouth rather than by hearsay. It was a role which some staff did not understand. When asked by staff why I met so many organisations and attended so many functions, Lindsay Manson, my Personal Assistant at the time, said that if I did not do this it would be interpreted that SNH was not interested and was aloof rather than a player.

My good friend and hill walking companion, Bob Aitken, wrote this ditty to me on my appointment to point out some of the difficulties we would undoubtedly face:

Frae the pines o' Rothiemurchus tae the dunes o' Sandwood Bay
The word gaes oot this mornin': 'SNH starts work the day!'
Ilk crofter chiel an' fermer loon foresees a muckle grant
For daein' what he ocht tae dae, bit somehoo' finds he can't.
Wi' management Agreement n' NHAs in hand,
Oor Roger leads his stalwarts oan toward the Promised Land.
Whaur gleam thon high objectives, Conservation a' Enjoyment.
Their only hope – it proves to be sustainable employment.

Personal Assistants

One crucial appointment to help me as Chief Executive was a Personal Assistant. I am sure in management speak it has a different title. This role was shared with the Chair. It was needed to filter the volume of business coming onto my desk, to judge the priorities for action, and to serve as the Secretary to the Board and the Management Team - developing agendas, chasing papers, writing the minutes, and pursuing the follow-up action. It was also crucial to 'keep our door open' to colleagues and visitors and to be 'the eyes and ears' of what was happening around the organisation and to say what the Chair and/or Chief Executive was thinking on an issue.

I was very fortunate to have four excellent colleagues in that role during my tenure. All were different personalities and played the role slightly differently, but that was a strength. Lindsay Manson understood the role, having been a Private Secretary to the Head of the Scottish Office Development Department. She had very sound judgement and acute insights, a level-headed and calm demeanour, was hard working and a good interlocutor (she was Personal Assistant from September 1991 to October 1993). Clive Hurley also came from a government administrative background and joined me on the closure of our Riccarton Office. He was the classically sound, reliable, get on with the job Personal Assistant. He was a keen birdwatcher and that gave him credibility with like-minded staff (October 1993 to February 1997). Roddy Fairley, an ex CCS staff member, joined me from the Policy Directive. He was an intelligent and creative spirit with wide networks in the organisation, ready to take initiatives and to inspire confidence (February 1997 to October 1998). Iain Rennick was also with CCS where amongst other roles he chaired the Trade Union Side very effectively. He was calm, highly reliable, straight talking when necessary, and was well known, well liked and highly trusted throughout SNH (November 1998 to March 2002, albeit with a brief interlude when Andy Dorin ably stood in).

This role and the careful choice of person in it is an essential one in any organisation, whatever title it is given.

Appointment of the Board

As the Secretary of State was responsible for the appointment of the Board members, as per the enabling legislation, we were soon told the names of those appointed. Chris Smout, the well-known and highly-regarded historian and Historiographer Royal for Scotland was appointed Deputy Chair. He had made his views known about the weaknesses of the existing situation and the opportunities which the government's proposals offered in an article in *The Scotsman*. More particularly, he was a leading and active scholar in the nascent field of Environmental History initiating many seminars on this subject and producing many books, most notably his outstanding series of lectures given at Oxford University in 1999 and published as *Nature Contested*. A self-taught field naturalist of the highest order from his childhood in Kent, as I discovered on many occasions then and forever since from excursions into the field with him and his wife Anne-Marie. He was the perfect complement to Magnus, with a measured, thoughtful and insightful approach to calm the more questionable ideas of the Chair and Chief Executive when needed.

To reflect the importance of science to the organisation, Professor George Dunnett, the Regius Professor of Zoology at Aberdeen University, and himself a leading ornithological scientist, was appointed to the Board. He had taught many of the staff of SNH, including those like Jeff Watson and Colin Galbraith, who later became key figures in the top management of the organisation. To complement this expertise, Dr Bill Mutch, a forest and land use scientist at Edinburgh University, was appointed and led the South East Regional Board of SNH, having previously been a CCS Commissioner, giving continuity to the merger. The farming community was well represented with the appointment of Bruce Cowe, a leading farmer in the Tweed Merse and a leading figure in the Farming and Wildlife Advisory Groups which he chaired in Scotland. Duncan McPherson farmed near Cromarty on the Black Isle and was also a leading figure in local government as Convenor of Highland Regional Council and involvement in COSLA. David Laird owned a mixed farm in the Mearns north of Forfar and was also a land agent and solicitor. He brought all of the wisdom of land management to our considerations, as well as his close connection with the Royal Household through his working relations with the Lord Privy Seal, the Earl of Airlie. He chaired the North East Regional Board where he worked closely and effectively with Ian Jardine. Nan Burnet, who with her husband farmed in the Borders south of Broughton, also brought knowledge of local government and other bodies and took over as Chair of the South East Regional Board when Bill Mutch's term ended.

The Earl of Dalkeith brought a wealth of knowledge of land use and organisational management from the sizeable estates and business interests of the Buccleuch family. He chaired the South West Regional Board bringing his close connections to the area and through estate ownership to great effect. He demitted office on his appointment as a Millennium Commissioner because he did not wish there to be any conflict of interest in his roles, such was his thoughtfulness on these matters. Sir John Lister-Kaye was an environmental educator, having established the highly-successful Aigas Field Centre near Beauly, training future rangers and educating all ages about the natural world, as well as being a burgeoning nature writer. He chaired the North West Regional Board and worked closely with its outstanding and highly-respected Regional Director, Peter Tilbrook, and the rising star, Jeff Watson. Alan Blackshaw represented access and outdoor recreation interests having authored the classic guide on mountaineering and skied the length of Scandinavia and, following early retirement from the civil service, was a leading figure in the access reform movement. Last, but by no means least, was Roy Dennis, the well-known leading figure in bird reintroduction in Scotland from his work on the return of the Osprey, initially to Loch Garten on Speyside when he worked for RSPB and, later, working with NCC colleagues on the return of the Sea Eagle. He brought an entirely different dimension in arguing the case for the redistribution of government money from defence spending to environment improvement, as well as playing a key role in bird reintroductions in Scotland and England.

Refreshing the Board

Over the following years, Board members changed as their terms were extended or ended, and new members were appointed. The appointments, as far as I could read the thinking in government, sought to cover the range of interests which SNH's remit demanded and to encourage links with the many partners. Gender balance did not seem to be an issue over this period, although more women were appointed at later stages. It was a sign of the times in government.

Magnus completed his term in March 1999 having led the organisation with distinction and aplomb for eight years.

Writing in 1999 Magnus said:

> I shall always think of my time with SNH as one of the highlights of my life – nothing else can quite compare with the challenges we have faced and dealt with over the years.

The new Chair appointed by the Secretary of State, Donald Dewar, on the recommendation of the Minister of State, Lord Sewel, was Dr John Markland. John came from an entirely different background. As a geography undergraduate and research graduate from Dundee University, we had a common academic heritage albeit one on the social side and the other on the Earth science side. He had been the Chief Executive of Fife Council before retirement. He quickly made connections with the relevant Ministers in the government and was invited onto various working parties, specifically those related to sustainable development and agriculture. This meant that SNH had an inside track on these important subjects, although not necessarily the one which Ministers adhered to when there were more prominent voices, such as those presenting the farming interests. He oversaw the transition of the political scene when the Scottish Parliament was established, adhering to my advice that we needed a new strategy in the light of the new political dynamic of more Ministers and more national politicians who were likely to want to know what we were doing and why, especially when given contrary messages by their constituents and others who were not necessarily on our side. It is often difficult for a former Chief Executive in a chairing role to work alongside a current one, but we worked effectively together, with John respecting my approach and giving me the support to continue.

Roger Wheater was appointed Deputy Chair at the end of Chris Smout's tenure. He was a leading figure internationally in conservation of animals in the wild having led the Uganda National Parks Service, and also in *ex situ* animal conservation having been Director of the Royal Scottish Zoological Society for many years. He was also a key figure in the NTS (of which he became Chair after completing his term on the SNH Board) and deftly chaired and steered the Access Forum.

The environmental NGO movement was well represented by Seaton Baxter who at the time was President of Scottish Wildlife and Countryside LINK as well as an academic of a most interesting philosophical bent at Robert Gordon University. Later on, Kevin Dunion, the former Chief Executive of Friends of the Earth Scotland and one of the leading thinkers in the environmental movement, brought a wider perspective to the organisation founded on sustainable development principles. Dr Patricia MacDonald was a leading environmental interpreter, commentator and photographer who, with her husband as the aircraft pilot, produced stunning images of the Scottish landscape which we used in many publications. Michael Scott, who became the third Deputy Chair, was an outstanding nature writer, conservationist and specialist on upland flora and Scottish flowers as evidenced by his books on these subjects. He was a leading figure in the formation and development of Plantlife as its first Scottish Officer and in ScotLINK (as it became known). Jeremy Rowan-Robinson was a lawyer and planner working at Aberdeen University. He brought wise counsel to our deliberations on many legal and planning issues, especially when we were tasked by government to bring forward proposals on access legislation and were being challenged by environmental NGOs on the Cairngorms mountain railway proposal.

The farming and rural community were always well represented on the SNH Board. Barbara Kelly, a partner in a dairy farm in Dumfriesshire and the doyen of rural representation in Scotland, made sure we understood the rural community dimensions of our work; she was also an experienced board member of NDPBs. She became the Chair of the South West Regional Board on the Earl of Dalkeith's resignation. Bill Ritchie, an Assynt crofter and secretary of the community buyout group in the area, brought hard-headed pragmatism and challenging thinking on the role of communities. He chaired the North West Regional Board. Simon Fraser succeeded him and chaired the reformatted North Areas Board. A solicitor in Stornoway and with a strong base on the land and deep knowledge and experience of community land purchases, he too challenged our thinking and approaches on rural communities and landownership. Peter Chapman, a partner in a Buchan mixed farming enterprise with his brother, brought a down-to-earth pragmatism on what was possible about the use of farmed land he sought to exemplify on his farms. He later had a short spell as an MSP. Sir Peter Hutchison, who had chaired the Loch Lomond and Trossachs Working Party for the government and was to become the Chair of the Forestry Commission, was briefly a Board member bringing calm advice.

Local government experience was presented by Peter Peacock, who succeeded Duncan McPherson as Convenor of Highland Council. He was alert to our need for making alliances with rural communities in the Highlands and Islands and understood the need for economic development. He later became an MSP and a Minister for Education in the coalition government. Keith Geddes, who had been the Convenor of Lothian Regional Council and subsequently of Edinburgh City Council, brought a wealth of local government and community engagement experience, as well as a deep interest in the countryside, including his role on the Board of Greenspace Scotland.

The scientific community were represented throughout. Professor Janet Sprent, a senior biologist at Dundee University, brought her academic cadre and straightforward thinking and talking to the table. Professor Fred Last, who had been an early critic of SNH with other Fellows of the Royal Society of Edinburgh, quickly became a valued ally in debates on the use and value of science. Professor David Ingram, who had recently retired as Regius Keeper of the Royal Botanic Garden Edinburgh, brought a deep scientific ethic to our Board and enabled the close working of our two organisations on plant conservation and plant reintroductions. Sue Walker had moved to Scotland from a middle ranking management role in the Environment Agency. As a water management specialist, she brought a new dimension.

Business interests were represented in various ways over the years. Alice Lambert, a co-owner of a mussel farm on Mull, brought a knowledge of island communities and the interface between natural resource use and its care to our deliberations. Lady Isabel Glasgow had a land-owning background with broad interests in the environment. She not only became Chair of the West Areas Board, but also chaired with distinction the Moorland Forum. Sadly, both Alice and Isabel died at all too young an age. Ivor Lewis worked for Diageo, the French-owned drinks conglomerate who had interests in whisky distilling in Islay, where we had continuing debates with farmers about goose management.

Peter Mackay, formerly Head of the Industry Department of the Scottish Office, was the only retired civil servant appointed to the Board. He brought his characteristic passion for outdoors activity as well as his keen political nous to our deliberations.

Appointing the Management Team

I moved to head the SNH Implementation team in September 1991, based on an upper floor in Chester Steet in Edinburgh's West End. It was owned and occupied by the Scottish Council (Development and Industry). One of the first of many tasks was to identify the top management structure and to recruit colleagues to fill those roles. Already, there were staff at senior levels in NCCS, some appointed to the one year body, and the Director of the CCS, all of whom had been guaranteed jobs in the new organisation by the government. The other ruling factor was the need in the early years of SNH to build on the existing organisational structure of NCC Regions, given the importance of working at regional and local levels with the whole range of partner bodies and seeking to change the dynamic in the relationships to a more positive one.

It was clear at the outset that SNH had two major roles which needed to be reflected in its staffing and organisational structure - national policy advice and local delivery. In addition, we needed to have staff responsible for the infrastructure of the organisation and for providing the scientific and other knowledge base for our national and local operations. So the structure was rapidly formed around the four existing NCCS regions: North West, South West, North East and South East. Dr Peter Tilbrook was appointed as Regional Director for North West still based in Inverness. He was a biologist by training having worked in the Antarctic and was just the measured, knowledgeable and conscientious individual needed in that role where there were so many hot issues to contend with. Dr Ian Jardine, who had been in the Scottish Office working among other matters on housing and social deprivation, had opted to join the NCCS, and given his biological background and his interests, wished to work in SNH. He was to become the long-standing member of the team throughout my tenure, later moving to a policy lead role. His incisive mind and the respect which colleagues had for him was invaluable. His ability to work productively with Scottish Office officials stood us in good stead on the reviews which I shall deal with later. I was delighted when he was appointed as the second Chief Executive. I had been given a final year performance target by the Chair of having one internal candidate. The Chair thought there was not one, I knew differently. John Markland clearly changed his mind when he saw the quality of Ian compared with other external candidates. In the southwest, we appointed Chris Fox who had been the Senior Land Agent in NCC responsible for negotiating management contracts with owners and who was tasked with also supporting our new approach to positive management contracts in key areas of the country. Jane Dalgleish had joined NCCS from the Scottish Office Solicitors Office having shown a strong interest in working on the environment. She proved to be a caring and thoughtful leader of her staff. For the Director of Policy, I was fortunate in being able to recruit John Thomson. A historian by degree, he had worked in the Countryside Commission for England and Wales, and in the Department of the Environment and more recently in the Planning administration in the Scottish Office. He was ideal for taking on the lead on policy development deploying his intellect with rigour. The scientific and knowledge based services were led by Professor Michael B Usher. A highly regarded biological scientist, he had been recruited to a similar role in NCCS and took on the role of bringing together the large and knowledgeable specialist staff on all aspects of our work. As Director of Resources, we recruited Lindsay Montgomery. He was primarily a finance person, but proved adept at covering all of the other infrastructure roles. A tough negotiator, he proved his worth by playing significant roles post SNH as Chief Executive of the Legal Aid Board for Scotland and on the Audit Commission. The need for good external relations and communications meant it was essential to appoint a Director of Communications. Duncan Campbell, who had been the Director of CCS, took on this role with great energy, integrity and enthusiasm.

Giving Staff Jobs to Fit Their Expertise and the Organisation's Needs

Before I was appointed Chief Executive, the Head of the Scottish Office Environment Department, Gavin McCrone, determined that I needed additional staff to establish an SNH Implementation Unit. He suggested one of his former Private Secretaries, Lindsay Manson, for this role. We knew little of each other and decided, as we were both working in the Scottish Office's office at Dover House in London, we should meet to discuss the role. Unfortunately and unintentionally, I was sitting at a desk with the light behind me, not a good start. Anyway, Lindsay liked the idea of helping to set up this new body and the once-in-a-lifetime chance of working with Magnus Magnusson. She already had experience in setting up government agencies having worked on the establishment of Scottish Homes. So the deed was done. Unbeknown to either Lindsay or me at the time, this was to become a deep romance, and she eventually left SNH to return to the Scottish Office in December 1993 so that we could begin our real lives together. Both Magnus and Gavin were delighted when they found out, as both being old sentimentalists they thought that this was a necessary and most desirable outcome for us both. And so it was!

The other staff member who came with me to join the Implementation Team was Betty Peacock. Those were the days when members of the Senior Civil Service used Dictaphones to produce text which was then transcribed by one's Personal Secretary. Betty played that role wonderfully from when I first joined the Division responsible for nature conservation, countryside and rural affairs in November 1988. And she had been our stalwart typist during the passage of the Bill, spending hours typing briefings and speaking notes for Ministers. She was level-headed and a delight to work with.

Given the focus on staff placement into jobs, it was also essential at the outset to recruit someone with personnel experience and expertise. Cathy Marshall was duly appointed and worked with Lindsay and me on the slotting of staff into the emerging structure.

I regarded meeting staff to gain understanding of what they thought of the merger proposals as vitally important. Before I was appointed Chief Executive, I had visited Battleby and met all of the staff. Trying to secure the same access to staff in NCC Scotland proved to be more difficult, but it was unlocked by the Chair of the NCC trade union side, Alan Mowle, who became one of the leading corporate strategists and analysts in SNH. Once appointed, I decided to meet all of the staff in the two organisations, around 460, individually and as far as possible in person. In preparation, I invited them to set down their aspirations for the organisation, their role in it, where ideally they would like to work and what their personal ambition was. Magnus accompanied me on some of these discussions. Over a three month period from mid-September to mid-December 1991, I talked to everyone and developed a workable organisational structure for the early years and began to allocate staff to jobs. A huge chart was set up behind a locked door in the temporary office with only Cathy Marshall, Lindsay Manson and me having access until the point when staff had been given a job offer, had replied and been sent a formal job offer of job title and office location. I made decisions that affected not just their roles, but also their office location and who they were working alongside. One aspect which gave me great pleasure was to find out where partners were based, and where it was in opposite locations to get a better solution for them both. It was so easy to ask these colleagues what their preferred location was together, and to seal the deal to their benefit and to the organisation as a whole. Signing the 460 letters individually to indicate to every member of staff their job, title, location and grade was a most rewarding task for me. It was all done in time for every member of staff to have their job secured before Christmas 1991.

The two organisations had different grading structures, promotion regimes, performance measurements and pay regimes. Worst of all was that there were 39 'occupational groups' which populated the structures. This could not continue if we were to have any chance of building an organisation where there was opportunity for everyone to move roles for their own and the organisation's betterment and for a positive culture to be imbued. The solution to me was simple: scrap the whole lot and have one single occupational structure. At a joint Trades Union meeting of the two organisations in the old CCS boardroom at Battleby, I announced to the astonished attendees that I had just made that decision. They looked askance and asked how this could be. I responded that we were our own masters and, provided that the unions were all supportive, the decision was taken. Without any hesitation, all of the union representatives agreed immediately. A major log jam had been broken and a new basis for the organisation achieved by an administrative fiat.

One very important issue was the determination of the staff disposition within the four regions. We decided that we should establish Area teams led by an Area Manager. Thirteen Areas were established. These new roles required those who knew the business of natural heritage and who were natural leaders and managers. It had struck me in my meetings with my new colleagues that there were a cadre of people who had been Wardens in NCC and who had these characteristics. However, in the old structure they were held back from any promotion higher than the equivalent of the Senior Scientific Officer in the NCC, apparently on the grounds that they did not have a university degree. What arrant nonsense! It reflected the narrow-mindedness of the nature conservation hierarchy in those days. The decision reported in the previous paragraph opened the door to appointing Senior Wardens to management posts and, where this was right and proper for SNH and the individual, this was done. The result was a mixture of staff of varying backgrounds and expertise leading our newly-established Area Teams. It was a seminal change to the culture of the NCC by appointing four former Wardens as Area Managers: Dick Balharry, Chris Eatough, Laughton Johnston and Carmen Placido. Some traditional NCC Assistant Regional Officers were disconcerted as they saw these appointments as reducing their traditional route to promotion, but the appointments won widespread support and, furthermore, proved successful.

Where Should the Headquarters Be?

We did not change the office locations at the beginning of SNH as there was no reason to do so. It was an issue to be dealt with sequentially if and when circumstances changed in terms of our organisational requirements and changes in the type and cost of offices needed. SNH therefore operated from 38 locations around Scotland.

There remained, however, the outstanding issue of the location of the SNH headquarters. CCS Commissioners had lobbied long and hard for Battleby to be the location. Their argument was based on its central location in Scotland and fairness to the smaller organisation in the merger. As I reported earlier, Battleby was never regarded as a suitable location by colleagues in the Scottish Office. A location in the Edinburgh area where most business was transacted with all parts of government and with many partner bodies in the land, business and environmental sectors made most sense to the SNH Board. Nevertheless, there was a reasonable argument for considering an alternative to the NCC HQ at Hope Terrace in the Grange district of the city. Consultants were hired to advise us. Sites were considered in the Central Belt, including Stirling (ironically near where SEPA's HQ was eventually located). Old hospitals, such as Beechmount House on the Glasgow Road in Edinburgh, were found to be unsuitable. In the end, too much time and energy could have been spent on finding a different answer to sticking with Hope Terrace and that was decided. Chair and Chief Executive and support staff were based there on the ground floor for accessibility to staff and to visitors (compared with the locked door situation in the NCCS days on the first floor), along with the majority of the Policy Directorate Staff, and many of the infrastructure support functions, specifically finance, personnel, cartography and information systems. This position remained throughout my tenure.

The issue of what to use Battleby for needed to be addressed in the early period of SNH. Continuing to use the office for staff dealing with the countryside elements of our remit was reasonable, but we needed to bring other staff there to help with the merging of functions and to ensure that the facility was fully utilised. At the same time, the accommodation for the South East Regional Office at Riccarton on the Heriot Watt University campus was inadequate for our emerging requirements and there was a high likelihood of a substantial rent rise. The Board decided at its meeting in June 1992 that the functions based at Riccarton should be transferred to Battleby and that staff should transfer with them provided that was in keeping with their terms of employment. All seemed well but behind the scenes a considerable backlash was building, and the Board took the decision to have a deeper look at the issues by setting up a Task Force led by Sir John Lister-Kaye, who ran a successful environmental education centre near Beauly. They enlisted consultants to assess the relative cost of options, especially as the Scottish Office made it clear that they would have a role in the decision-making if the option chosen was not the best value for public money. Staff and unions were consulted. The Board received its conclusion in a closed session with me in February 1993 and took its final decision the following month that the South East Regional Headquarters should be relocated to Battleby, staff would be given the option of moving there or reassigned to our Edinburgh offices. The Board also took into account the opportunity for building up the environmental education function as the Secretary of State's Working Party on Environmental Education was about to report and Scottish Office officials had made it clear that the government wanted to make progress in implementing the proposals with SNH given a formative role. Needless to say, as is often the case with such decisions, it required some careful management to bring it into operation and to make it work.

One point was made to me about Battleby by our very savvy property adviser, Ian Darling. He said that the conference facilities, which we and others used, were unique and if we sold that site, we would not be able to replicate those facilities elsewhere as the costs would be too great. We took his advice. Later on, we also converted the old countryside workshops into more office space and filled it with staff who opted to move there from Edinburgh; some no doubt to avoid the possibility of being relocated to Inverness when the HQ was moved after my retirement.

I cannot let this consideration of HQ end without some comments on the relocation of the HQ to Inverness. The new building is not even in the city centre but on a hillside site overlooking the city. This all came about because of the power of the Highland lobbyists, including former Board member and later government Minister Peter Peacock. There is a long history of dispersal of government bodies and even departments from capital cities. I was told, quite rightly, that this was an issue for my successor and his team along with the SNH Board. Clearly, Ministers had made their minds up, despite the advice from the SNH Board that Inverness was much the costliest of the options they had considered and was far from the centre of power and influence. The Board, therefore, had no choice but to tell the Minister that they did not support the government's decision. SNH were formally Directed by the Scottish Government to adopt the move to Inverness; that was a formal instruction, and the Board had no choice! So a geographically eccentric location, where additional public sector jobs were not needed economically, was chosen. For the one and only time since we had retired from SNH Magnus and I felt compelled to publically express our concerns about the government's processes and decision publicly in a letter to *The Scotsman* newspaper. I reproduce here for readers to make their own mind up about the veracity of the decision, and the cost to the public purse.

> RELOCATION: POLICY OR POLITICS?
>
> The proposed relocation of the Headquarters of Scottish Natural Heritage raises important issues about the use of public money and the disruption to the delivery of activity for Scotland's natural heritage. The public deserves open and unambiguous answers on these issues.

It is perfectly legitimate for the Scottish Government to have a policy to relocate government jobs out of Edinburgh as a result of the overheating of its economy and other factors. But why are the reasons for the choice of receiving locations so obscure? It is in the public interest that explicit criteria are articulated, and this has not yet been done. The policy appears to have been silently changed from reviewing options in terms of efficiency gains to automatic decisions on relocation. In the case of SNH, it is far from obvious to anyone who knows the economic and employment status of Inverness why that City needs a pulse of new high-quality jobs. There needs to be a clear statement of the compelling reasons for moving SNH HQ there. It is also in the public interest to be clear of the costs of relocation of government business. Not only will there be the direct costs of new office space, support to staff who decide to relocate, compensation for those who do not, and recruitment and training of new staff, there will also be a loss of delivery of government activity on the natural heritage. By any reasonable assessment from those of us familiar with such changes, there will be a loss of momentum for probably about 5 years on crucial areas such as biodiversity conservation and improving public access. Have all of these factors been considered in the Scottish Government's decision? If so, when will the total direct and indirect costs be made publicly available? If not, why have these costs not been anticipated? When public expenditure decisions are supposed to be based on 'best value', why was the independent analysis by a highly respected firm ignored and the worst financial case chosen? Clearly the Auditor General and the Audit Committee of the Parliament will wish to review these issues and report publicly on their conclusions. Also there appears to have been no consultation before the decision was taken. This is not in accord with the now normal process of decision making in Scotland. These are legitimate questions on which the public and the staff of SNH deserve answers before Ministers issue any Direction to SNH to undertake the relocation.

Both the SNH Trade Unions and the SNH Board should be

pressing these points through every legitimate means available. We hope that they are doing so.

Magnus Magnusson, Founder Chair and Roger Crofts, Founder Chief Executive, Scottish Natural Heritage

Regional Boards

The establishment of the four Regional Boards to sit alongside the four Regions was a very logical step. The prototype had been established in the one year body NCCS. SNH needed to demonstrate to partners around Scotland that we were serious about working more closely with them. The Boards comprised members recruited to represent different networks, different areas of expertise and to improve our interface with partners. They were given clear roles and responsibilities approved by the SNH Board to reflect the common sense management style, which we former civil servants in the Secretariat operated, of making sure that everyone was clear on their roles and responsibilities. In the event, they each operated differently, partly dependent on the personality of the Regional Board Chair - some more hands on and interventionist and others taking a more measured and nuanced approach.

Overall, they were successful in helping us to achieve our objectives. They were a success in sending the signal to partners and having those who were critics of us inside our tent so to speak. They were a success in giving additional pairs of hands in meeting with partners and with adversaries who were too often dismissive of staff trying to do their job. And they brought added dimensions to the debates about what we were doing and how we were doing it. Like main Board members, they were paid for their contribution as a fee. This ensured that those appointed, who had to take leave from other paid work, were included as Board members.

It was not always comfortable to the organisation, as inevitably some appointees saw their role as protecting the interests which they represented. Some felt that they had been given an executive role which made life difficult at times for staff, so that the Chair and I had to intervene to settle matters. Personally, I made it my business to meet all of the Regional Boards collectively and their members individually so that I understood their perspective and contribution, and they were clear about their role and responsibilities to

SNH. The most difficult individuals were those who were officials of other organisations in the government realm too often wishing to protect their organisation, rather than help us. To be frank, they should never have been appointed but, after all, the Chief Executive does not have control of every decision when it comes to internal Board appointments!

The Advisory Committee on SSSI

This committee (ACSSSI) was a statutory requirement placed on the Secretary of State for Scotland by Section 12 of the Natural Heritage (Scotland) Act 1991. It was established during the Implementation Phase with the terms of reference and appointment of members approved by Ministers. Most important was the identification and appointment of members who had scientific expertise in relation to nature conservation as deployed through the SSSI mechanism and were not involved in any SNH Committees or Boards. Surprisingly, it was an easy task to identify, gain their agreement to be nominated and to obtain Ministerial approval for the appointments. Eminence and scientific rigour in the conservation field was clear to all when the appointments were announced.

After the public announcement, I recall being telephoned by Charles Clover, at the time the Environment Correspondent of *The Telegraph*, to tell me he was both surprised and delighted at the speed of action and the calibre of the appointees. He said he would report his assessment in the paper whose readership included many who wanted tougher approaches on SSSIs or no change to the conservation body arrangements in Britain. Hence, another step in winning the argument about the changes to nature conservation bodies was made.

In practice, the Committee was effective in doing its job, and its work led to a considerable improvement by SNH in the preparation of cases for designation and in response to objections from owners of existing sites. Around a dozen cases were dealt with by the committee over the decade. There was no case where the Committee disagreed entirely with SNH's case for new notification or for retaining an existing notification when an objection had been raised. The Committee helpfully commented where it considered the SNH case was weak or inadequately prepared. Generally, it commended SNH on the high standards of submission of cases. After each case, the Committee

Chair and I discussed what lessons could be learned so that I could feed them back to colleagues leading on SSSIs practices and on particular cases. Any disagreement between the Committee and SNH was about the details. Three examples suffice to illustrate this point. The precise drawing of the boundaries for the Muirkirk SSSI in Ayrshire were adjusted. The extent of the buffer zone around the Lake of Menteith SSSI was modified. Where the site contributed to a wider conservation objective, such as the Sandness Coast SSSI on west mainland Shetland, the details were amended to reflect its contribution to the Papa Stour SAC.

Ultimately, the political deal in the UK Parliament which led to the establishment of the ACSSSI was a practical success in creating an independent avenue for objectors, in defusing opposition to SSSIs and to improving our presentation of cases - wins all round.

Establishing and Developing the Culture

Much is written by social scientists about developing the culture of an organisation. I have never read any of this. Whether that was obvious at the time or in retrospect is for others to judge. But I did read John Harvey-Jones' book *Making it Happen: Reflections on Leadership,* Roger E Allen's book, *Winnie-the-Pooh on Management,* and C S Forester's insightful novels on the development of leadership in the form of Horatio Hornblower. At the time, I did not realise that Forester's portrayal of the role of leadership was often used in training in Management Science departments of universities. My own personal essay on Hornblower written in about 1986 is very revealing of the characteristics that he had that I hoped also applied to me: self-critical, quick-witted, contemplative, daring, challenging, unremitting, committed, knowledgeable, prepared and with a sense of duty. I did not recognise his other characteristics in myself, such as disciplinarian, restrained, aloof, studious, and restive. The message is to know yourself and what makes you tick. I had been through a self-perception process, with the help of close friends in the mid-eighties, which I believe helped me to know myself better and, more important, how I would react in this new and challenging role.

The rubric, which was emerging from government, in other words from Ministers briefed and advised by me as the lead civil servant on the establishment of SNH, was for a more people focussed approach, without necessarily having a firm view on the role and positioning of science. A more human friendly approach was sought after the battle between nature conservation and forestry in particular and about the case for national parks.

It should have been no surprise to anyone, therefore, that the slogan of SNH was, '*Working with Scotland's people to care for our natural heritage*'. There are three key words in this slogan:

'Heritage' was born out of the sustainability ethic of intergenerational equity of receiving, caring for and handing on hopefully in a better state than at the point of inheritance.

'Care' meant that looking after the heritage was a critical issue, especially given the indicators of damage to landscape, scenery and habitats. More significantly, it was a commonplace word to represent stewardship in the traditional meaning of the term.

'Our' reflected the role of the people of Scotland, in the broadest sense of that term, to be involved and to be partners in providing a better outcome for the natural heritage.

A longer wording was agreed by the Board:

> Our task is to secure the conservation and enhancement of Scotland's unique and precious natural heritage. We shall advise on policies and promote projects that aim to improve it and support its sustainable utilisation. Our aim is to help people to enjoy Scotland's natural heritage responsibly, understand it more fully and use it wisely so that it can be sustained for future generations.

So the basis of our philosophy was simple: *We must sustain the natural heritage if we want it to sustain us.*

This thinking was also reflected in the logo. Yes, it was different from other new government agencies established at the time, but we were determined to demonstrate a difference. We gave three small contracts of £1,000 each to design firms to come up with a logo. We got from them what was best described by my teenage children at the time as symbols more akin to banks and building societies. The easy solution was to invite a small group of staff representing both of the original organisations and not involving any of the senior management to come up with ideas. Their proposal shocked the Management Team at first, but it is one we adopted and was in use for

30 years until the recent rebranding to NatureScot. The formal design was delivered by Ron Burnett of the Edinburgh company Graphic Partners.

The framework was based on a pictogram, as used in the Celtic period of Scottish history, in other words a reference to Scotland's cultural history. The components of the pictogram were the thistle as the plant emblem of Scotland representing the Scottish flora, the sea, land and mountains representing the major biogeographical parts of Scotland, the bird of prey representing the iconic raptors, most especially the Golden Eagle, and a domesticated animal, deliberately not readily identifiable, representing the human use of the ground to produce food for human consumption. Because of its difference it received reasonably positive response with one exception. The chair of the Red Deer Commission, Partick Gordon-Duff-Pennington, throughout his tenure felt that we wished to take over the work of his Commission and interpreted the domesticated animal as a red deer and a signal of our intent. The last thing we wished to do was to take on that role, although ironically that is what eventually happened years later by government diktat: an enduring mistake I fear, which I shall discuss later.

What I also had to take on board in developing the culture was the inheritance from the two predecessor bodies. I discussed this with staff representatives on numerous occasions during the seven-month implementation period. Their leaders, Andrew Bachell and John Theaker for NCC and Iain Rennick for CCS, well recognised the issues. When I termed the NCC, 'the most rigidly organised and unmanaged organisation I had ever seen', NCC representatives asked if I could say that again so they could write it down. Their reaction was to nod their heads in agreement. Just as they well knew that certain *causes célèbres,* such as the commercial afforestation in the Flow Country, the refusal to agree to the Glen Lochy proposals by John Cameron for planting trees to shelter sheep hefts, were crosses that they wished to discard. Likewise, CCS representatives recognised the closet culture of this small organisation, although they and their colleagues were nervous about the so-called merger being a takeover by the much larger NCC with its markedly different culture and approach. They were reassured partly as I was an incomer and partly because I was familiar with both bodies, having been one of a team of consultants from Aberdeen University on the beach studies mentioned earlier and being annoyed in my oil development days at the lack of nature conservation knowledge about Nigg Bay in the Cromarty Firth when plans were mooted for its reclamation to build an oil refinery.

There were always cultural clashes between the different interests. The trick was to manage these positively. One example emphasises this point. I decided to bring the two sides of the debate about the future of the uplands together to argue their case in front of their colleagues. The critical issues included the dispute between open heather moorland or naturally tree covered areas, the role of deer culling to reduce pressure on the habitat, the effect of grouse moor management on raptor persecution, and whether or not to fence off areas to allow natural regeneration. I well recall Des Thompson, coming from a scientific background, and Dick Balharry, coming from a practical management perspective, pitting their arguments against the other's views, surely a healthy activity in any organisation. The fact that I could invite two very knowledgeable and charismatic Board members into the argument, Roy Dennis and Sir John Lister-Kaye, demonstrated both an openness to debate and the need to come to a corporate resolution rather than letting an argument simmer for years and so confuse staff working locally.

In seeking to build the culture and bring together staff from different ideologies and with different expertise, I tried two approaches in the early period of SNH. I will freely admit, in retrospect, that they were both mistakes, but it is important to spell out briefly what they were and why I came to that conclusion.

In the first year, the nine members of the Management Team agreed that we should spend a few days on an external course at a venue in the Lake District in Cumbria to develop our working relationships. A company called Impact was commissioned. They focussed on how to operate leadership and management under extreme pressure; they also used physical training exercises to get us to work collectively. I admit to being wrecked by the experience, but in a curious way that helped us to come together as we realised that we could be better at team building ourselves.

The second programme was more prolonged and involved middle and senior staff. It was organised and run by members of the Strathclyde University Business School led by Professor Colin Eden and his assistant Dr Fran Ackerman. It used confidential computer based tools to elicit the views and opinions of participants about the organisation, its formative players and the direction it was going. Not everyone felt that it was a useful exercise, and that included me. It was premature and we were not in control of the process. It is interesting to note that the course directors produced a book *Making*

Strategy in which I contributed a short case study on our experience. As I will recount later on, in the future we relied on our own resources of expert trainers to produce and run courses tailor-made to our requirements in terms of both content and style.

More support came from the then Prince of Wales. He invited a group of us to spend time with him at Sandringham in April 1992. He selected the attendees in addition to Magnus and me and Bruce Cowe, one of our Board members. They were Bob Aitken, the recreation expert, Andrew Bradford, owner of a small estate on Deeside, Robin Callander, a consultant on land management living in Feughside, Johnnie Grant of Rothiemurchus, Alwyne Farquharson of Invercauld, Simon Pepper, head of WWF Scotland, David Minns, RSPB Scotland, Patrick Gordon-Duff-Pennington, Geoffrey Lean, the journalist, plus Kenneth MacKenzie and Harold Mills from the Scottish Office. We discussed anything and everything, focussing on the Prince's view of the need for change, but knowing that there was reluctance from some parties, especially in relation to the reduction in deer numbers, and a shift in financial support for agricultural to a more environmentally sensitive system. Hence, the conclusion of our gathering was the need for solutions on deer and agriculture and the need for closer working. It did mean that right at the outset we had spent time with key figures in the land and environment business in Scotland which stood us in good stead for future discussions on moving the agenda forward. For example, we received a visit from Alwyne Farquharson at his request to begin discussions with the deer management interests on resolving some of the access issues and beginning talks about reduction in deer numbers. That was a very welcome start particularly as our relationships, as I shall describe later, with the Chair of the Deer Commission, Patrick Gordon-Duff-Pennington, were not the easiest.

We held induction briefings for all new members of staff. I gave presentations to all of these on our origins, the meaning of the three words in our title and the type of culture and mind set we aimed for. Both Magnus and later John supported me in many of these briefings. At appropriate moments, we held a series of staff conferences to include over 90 per cent of staff at different locations. I deliberately ensured that there was a mix of staff from different offices and undertaking different functions to help in developing a corporate spirit. From the outset, we also produced our own internal magazine so that all staff and Board members knew what was going on and were briefed on any significant changes. As time passed, we gave staff much more scope to provide content for the newsletters. Also, we used more simple measures in response to staff requests and suggestions. For example, many staff wished to be able to wear something signifying they were working for SNH. As a result, all staff were issued with a metal badge of the logo and name, neckties were available for men and, after lobbying, scarves were available for women staff.

The Role of Science and Scientific Advice

Was SNH to be a science-based organisation and resolve the tensions apparent through the previous 30 years of the role of science in nature conservation policy and practice? It was clear to me from my academic research years that science was an essential component in the creation of policy, and of action on the ground, but it should not be the sole determinant. In other words, the science and the scientific specialists should be advisory, but when the analysis demonstrated the need for changes in policy and/or action these should be rigorously considered and acted on.

This proved to be a 'red rag' to the scientists appointed to the Scientific Advisory Committee of the interim body NCCS and in the early days of SNH. One member, whom I greatly respect as a scientist and know as a friend and colleague in geography, David Sugden (one of the leading figures in glacial geomorphology internationally) resigned, and the Chair of the Committee, George Dunnet, soldiered on until throwing in the towel after two years of SNH. This disagreement was diverting us from the main tasks of determining the focus of our work and the balance between advice and action. One can 'never satisfy all of the people all of the time' on such matters. Indeed, Morton Boyd, whom I much admired as a scientist and leader, and gained so much from in our conversations, in his autobiography, *The Song of the Sandpiper*, headed a chapter 'The Breaking of the Nature Conservancy Council' with the subheading 'Scottish Natural Heritage and the Fall of Science'. He still took the view that 'The Scientific Advisory Committee contained some of the best scientists in Scotland, but its role was limited to providing advice and it was not long before its standing was reduced to that of a committee, and Michael Usher, its Chief Scientific Adviser and gifted naturalist was excluded from the Management Team'. Well that is a point of view backed up by Morton's statement that although he admired the personal and professional qualities of the Chair, Deputy Chair and Chief Executive, '...I was disappointed. None of the triumvirate was, as I hoped one would have been, a laureate in natural science'. Interestingly, he took a different line in writing to me on my appointment:

> I am sure that wisdom as a geographer will serve you well in finding the blend of scientific interest and natural beauty, which may escape the ecologist on the one hand and the landscape designer on the other.

Matters proved nasty at times with a triumvirate of Fellows seeking to use the Royal Society of Edinburgh to undertake an independent review of our work, and in particular our scientific status and standing. This threat at such an early stage was diverting to say the least. Magnus proved to be the saviour by ensuring that the President of the RSE did not support such a review. A more positive relationship was born through an annual joint lecture by an eminent conservation scientist on our invitation and the text published in the SNH Occasional Paper series between 1992 and 1999. Martin Holdgate (former Chief Scientist in NC and later Director General of IUCN), John Selbourne (Member of the House of Lords and senior conservation scientist) and Jeff McNeely (Chief Scientist at IUCN) were among those who participated.

A telling critique of the scientific approach to nature conservation was published by Paul Evans, at the time the Conservation Director of Plantlife, headed 'When science should stop hiding behind science's clock'. He argued in *The Guardian* of 6 December 1991 that:

> Professional conservationists must begin to communicate a broader sense of values to find new directions...Professional nature conservationists tend to steer clear of political argument ...but nature conservation is also about values and societies changing attitude to nature creates conflicting views...This means we cannot hide behind the science to say what we think is right or wrong. Doing deals, making the most of opportunities means we have to be more sure of ourselves.

Within SNH, the Board agreed with the advice of the Chief Executive that science should play the role of adviser to staff working on policy and on action on the ground. Rather than establishing a Chief Scientists Office and role, we established the Research and Advisory Services Directorate led by Professor Michael B Usher, a leading biological scientist whose knowledge of nature conservation science and nature itself was second to none. Even then, there were tensions, with staff elsewhere in the organisation giving the nickname of the scientific and advisory staff based in a separate building in the Bonnington area of Edinburgh, as 'The University of Bonnington'. It is interesting to note, in passing, that NCCS had debated the possibility of out posting its research staff to Scottish research institutes, but decided to retain the expertise inhouse. That was a very helpful decision for SNH not to have to go over the same ground again.

The fact that SNH has retained, throughout its existence and to the present day, a Scientific Advisory Committee of eminent scientists and other academics across the relevant disciplines is testament to the importance of this type of check and balance built into the organisational structure and the personalities who engage in it. That they have been able to check on the veracity of SNH's scientific work and be a touchstone of the direction of scientific thinking, demonstrates that science has not been emasculated, as some have claimed.

This point is further emphasised by the output from SNH's commissioned research programme. The plethora of excellent SNH research and advisory reports, summarising externally-commissioned research, and the research briefing notes, provided a more client-focussed approach to inputting knowledge into our national and local decision-making .

I tell this story of science because it reflects the hangover from the separation of science from policy in NCC in the 1970s and the continuing tension between scientific advice and policy development. Furthermore, it is highly relevant to many other organisations who seek to utilise scientific knowledge and information to better inform their strategies and actions.

Trade Union Relationships

An important partnership was the relationship between senior management and staff representatives through their trade unions. We met prior to the formal establishment, as I recorded earlier, and began to build a relationship based on openness and cooperation, leading to greater trust for the benefit of the organisation and its staff. These were my first dealings with trade unions. I recall my father, a non-union semi-skilled employee in a nationalised industry, saying he did not think I should have dealings with them. For once, I disagreed with his down-to-earth view.

We were fortunate in SNH in having staff who were genuinely supportive trade union leaders inherited from the NCC and CCS. Over the years, I was able to have regular one-to-one meetings with the head of the trade union side (I hate the terminology of 'sides'). The leader for a long time was John Theaker, a former Nature Warden in NCC, who was keen to develop his role as staff representative. This proved to be an excellent arrangement as he was trusted by colleagues and by myself and senior managers, hence the notion of 'sides' was not really applicable as many issues which might have gone awry due to misunderstandings were readily resolved before they became a problem. I was also happy to support the career move by Malcolm Currie, formerly an Area Officer on Speyside, to develop as the trade union lead. This was beneficial to both parties and certainly for Malcolm who later enjoyed a successful career as a mediator.

Where we had a problem was with the national full-time paid staff of some of the unions who had their own agendas. SNH union members could not follow or understand what these agendas were and how they could possibly help their specific circumstances in the organisation. These were the unfortunate days when the adversarial approach was the normal behaviour of the permanent trade union staff. We knew that having meetings in the morning, rather than after lunch, was essential to progress the business that SNH staff and management wished. I recall only one occasion when one SNH trade union representative decided to be heavy-handed; this made his colleagues uncomfortable, especially when he would not back down. To the consternation of my management colleagues, I abruptly terminated the meeting to allow a cooling-off period. This seemed to work and the point at issue was readily resolved as both 'sides' could see a way forward and the individual in point realised that they had overplayed their hand.

Developing the Policy Framework

Like all government bodies, we had to produce corporate plans setting our aims and objectives, and our policies and activities. Increasingly, these became more driven by the need to identify and deliver our work against targets, either directly set by the government or by inference to achieve outcomes which the government wanted or those of our own volition. From the outset, we published a Corporate Plan and an Operational Plan detailing the work and activities and expected outcomes for the year ahead. We produced detailed Annual Reports, including many facts and figures about our work. As the latter became more voluminous and we had better information systems and a dedicated team, led ably by Ed Mackey, we later produced that material as a separate volume annually, *SNH Facts and Figures*. Importantly, we included from the outset the list of all recipients of money in grant and management agreements, a first among Scottish public bodies. Our approach was never followed up by others, least of all the Department of Agriculture in providing information on grants to farmers. We developed how we represented all of this material to improve its accessibility to our partners and to the public. From 1995, we issued each year *Plans and Progress* documents detailing what we had done and achieved in the previous year and our work plan for the coming year in the context of our evolving Corporate Plan. All of this material should still be available online for readers to access.

Board members never found these strategic planning exercises easy, but this was not something that could be left to staff, even though staff were the workhorses in producing the goods. Our way forward was, therefore, to establish joint Board member/staff working groups and task forces with specific remits and timelines to develop our policies on a wide range of topics including our approach to deer management, agriculture, access, forestry, designations including NNRs and SSSIs, and species management. We also used joint Board member/staff working to make progress on critical internal matters. One example was a Citizens Charter (our approach to working with others, termed Customer Care) which was developed into *Natural Standards* through a joint Board/staff working group chaired by Chris Smout and completed in late 1993. We also used this approach to review our external grants programme and the future role and functions of Battleby. This may seem an unusual approach, but Magnus and I were convinced that the joint working of Board members and staff, calling on the wide expertise and experience that staff had, would help to develop the new ethos of SNH and aid the process of integration of functions. I believe that this was certainly achieved, alongside producing valuable and considered proposals for our policies and activities across many aspects of our wide remit. This in turn gave the Board a set of clear proposals to debate and agree and for staff to know exactly how to progress them internally and with external partners.

The critical points we decided to address affected elements of our remit where there might be clashes and where the policies and activities of other parts of the government machine were likely to have a deleterious effect on the natural heritage. These were responsibilities clearly given to SNH in its founding legislation, so we had to address them.

One was the relationship, or otherwise, between conservation and access. Alan Blackshaw quite accurately called this 'the double duty' and he helpfully set out his own thoughts on this for debate by the Board and senior staff. This work, together with other analysis, led to a consultation paper on access (see below for more details).

Another topic was to tease out the meaning of the sustainability duty given to us. The 1991 Act states at Section 1 (1):

> *SNH shall have regard to the desirability of securing that anything done whether by SNH or any other person in relation to the natural heritage of Scotland is undertaken in a manner which is sustainable.*

The following is quoted from an internal Scottish Office briefing, which my Bill team and I produced for the Third Reading of the Bill in the House of Lords by way of clarifying the thinking at the time:

> Sustainable is intended to be interpreted in a common sense way which encompasses uses and activities that would not cause irreparable damage to the natural heritage. Influencing the type, rate and extent of land and water use rather than necessarily seeking to halt such uses is the key role. It is not intended, for example, that SNH should try to prevent extractive industries *per se* but to ensure that they operate in an environmentally sensitive manner. Similarly for the production of food and timber the aim is to ensure that the processes of production are sensitive to the natural resource base and ensure its productive capacity in the longer term.
>
> (Unpublished Notes on Clauses for Third Reading of the Natural Heritage (Scotland) Bill in the House of Lords)

We produced a guidance paper, *Sustainable Development and the Natural Heritage: The SNH Approach* in late 1993. Our guiding principles were:

1. *Wise Use*: non-renewable resources should be used wisely and sparingly at a rate which does not restrict the options of future generations.
2. *Carrying Capacity*: renewable resources should be used within the limits of their capacity for regeneration.
3. *Environmental Quality*: the quality of the natural heritage as a whole should be maintained and improved.
4. *Precautionary Principle*: in situations of great complexity or uncertainty we should act in a precautionary manner.
5. *Shared Benefits*: there should be an equitable distribution of the costs and benefits (material and non-material) of any development.

We produced posters for each one which I purposely displayed on the walls of my office for all visitors to see. In addition, we produced Teachers' Notes and widely distributed these to schools. Interestingly, SNH produced a new statement in 2003 retaining, but elaborating on its work in relation to the five principles.

We needed to tease out the import of the six 'balancing duties' in Section 3 of the Act relating to 'actual or possible ecological and other environmental changes; the needs of agriculture, fisheries and forestry; the need for social and economic development; the need to conserve sites and landscapes of archaeological or historical interest; the interests of owners and occupiers of land; and the interests of communities'. These stated that SNH should 'take appropriate account of'. Of particular import was what these duties meant legally and what they meant in practice.

We had inherited a grants programme from CCS. To our surprise, and to my irritation as Accountable Officer (the formal role for financial management and accountability held jointly with the Head of the Scottish Office Environment Department and ultimately responsible to Parliament), we rapidly discovered that there was an over-commitment of £1.13 million in the grants budget. Fortunately, some forensic work by the finance team under Lindsay Montgomery's critical eye planned a path out of the dilemma which the Board accepted, and recipients were carefully informed about. The Board approved the grants policy early in 1993. Thereafter, with the lessons learned about improving the process of decision-making and allocations, we set up a process of delegations to the Regions and to other expenditure programmes accompanied by detailed guidance for staff.

We needed to consider and resolve how to balance activities across our broad remit. We were putting approximately 90 per cent of our resources into the protected sites and areas. I did question publicly in speeches and in *The Environment - Who Cares?* (SNH Occasional Paper No 2) whether this was the appropriate distribution. We recognised that more resources needed to be applied to the rest of the country, what many called the wider countryside, but in our case, it also meant the urban environments where semi-natural areas and access were important issues for residents.

Overall, we were forced back to the protected sites and areas as a result of the UK Government, albeit reluctantly, signing the EU Species and Habitats Directive having previously signed the EU Birds Directive. These combined together to form the Natura 2000 programme with a clear target of completing the work by the beginning of the new millennium. Failure to achieve this target was likely to bring criticism from the European Commission at least or, at worst, Infraction Proceedings against the UK Government. The pressure was cascading down the system. In our case, via the Scottish Government to SNH and specifically to our Area Teams and the habitats and species specialists in support of the identification and definition of these areas. The environmental NGOs, particularly WWF International and Birdlife International, and their national chapters, were hawkish in monitoring our progress and some difficult confrontations occurred. Our problem was the lack of enthusiasm for implementing this programme at UK levels. This was also emphasised at the Scottish level when we were told quite emphatically that Ministers wished us to implement the Natura 2000 programme 'with a light touch'. Anyone familiar with these Directives and the enforcement procedures available to the European Commission, and with failure to comply activating involvement of the European Court, will know that this injunction was an excuse or even an oxymoron given that the Directives were the strongest habitats and species protection measures in the host countries, and indeed anywhere in the world. Despite all of this pressure, SNH staff nationally and locally did a brilliant job in working with owners, occupiers and managers in implementing the Directives. Part of the reason was that owners and occupiers had such a low regard for the SSSI system, particularly as it had to be renotified in the 1980s. Partly, it was also because we attached positive management agreements to the largest areas, such as the Flow Country of Caithness and Sutherland and the Lewis Peatlands and other locations. Owners and occupiers could see, therefore, this double incentive to go along with the system.

Management agreements had always been an important element in the arrangements with owners and managers of nature sites. Our approach was to develop an incentive style, so that the recipient knew what was expected of them and we could monitor compliance with the deal. Considerable sums of money were given to large estates of high natural heritage value. One we continued from NCC was with Rothiemurchus Estate on Speyside. This was an exemplar arrangement because of the high natural value of the habitats and the positive attitude of the owner, Johnnie Grant. In our renegotiations leading to a Nature Reserve Agreement in 1998, we eventually agreed that there should be no compensation element, and the focus of the arrangement was on the protection of species and habitats and on management of access for informal recreation. A new agreement was made with the Earl of Strathnaver for management of the Balblair woodlands on the northern shores of Loch Fleet in eastern Sutherland. It was an area of planted Scots pine which was the habitat of some rare indigenous plants, the One-flowered Wintergreen *Moneses uniflora,* and the Twinflower *Linnaea borealis.* Not unreasonably, the owner wished to fell the trees which were mature, but was persuaded to retain them through a management agreement. We were able to persuade a sceptical Minister, Sir Hector Monro, that these grants and associated agreements were worthwhile to protect natural heritage interests.

Inventories and Guidance Documentation

I am a great exponent of the need to produce documentation of what we know about all aspects of the natural heritage, how it is performing and what the trends are. Only then will we have a basis for informed debate and decision-making about action by ourselves and other authorities. I know this is an old-fashioned view because it is very resource intensive, and the world moves so fast. I disagree. I consider that the work which our predecessors did, which we did with local authorities, and which we did with the other nature and countryside agencies provided us then and for the future with a fundamental basis for assessing bids for change and development of whatever type.

We developed inventories and accompanying guidance covering many areas of our remit. I provide examples of these in the following paragraphs.

Inevitably with my early career as a geomorphologist and Earth scientist, I was keen to ensure that we considered all of the natural heritage and natural processes. Fortunately, we had inherited from NCC a group of Earth scientists. In the new organisational structure, I made sure that this expertise was elevated to the same level as the biological scientists. The Earth science team was tasked with demystifying the subject for the benefit of Area staff who had to look after sites of 'geological and physiographic interest' as the statute stated, and to use ordinary language in communicating the Earth sciences and the features, forms and processes. Ironically, improving communication by the Earth science community to other professionals and the public is an issue I have been campaigning about within the international Earth heritage community over the last decade with some modicum of success. Fortunately, the appointed head of the Earth sciences team, Alan McKirdy, was a good communicator, and the head geomorphologist, John Gordon, was a leading figure in aiding colleagues, classroom teachers and others in understanding the intricacies of the landscape. Staff produced Site Documentation Reports on each SSSI with a geological and/or geomorphological interest. In addition, staff led the production of key volumes of the Geological Conservation Review, a series which ran to 52 volumes covering every site in Britain classified by age or by formation process. *Quaternary of Scotland* was a notable volume in this series led by John Gordon and a consultant colleague, Donald Sutherland. It may be of no surprise to readers that Alan, John and I combined to produce *Land of Mountain and Flood: The Geology and Landforms of Scotland* in 2007.

We had a poor inheritance from CCS on landscape characterisation, as I have noted earlier. This was an incredibly important issue to be addressed given the lack of effective statutory protection for landscapes other than the weak legislative provision for National Scenic Areas in the Town and Country Planning Acts. This work was led by Rebecca Hughes, a qualified landscape architect with a strong academic pedigree, ably assisted by the landscape specialists we hired to work within our Area teams to help local staff deal with this part of our remit. Landscape Character Assessment was carried out jointly with local authorities, at a detailed map scale of 1:50,000, to ensure that they were useful documents to aid local authority planners in their work and to help SNH Area staff in their advisory role. All of Scotland was covered and reports produced. We used the same methodology as colleagues in England, led by the Countryside Commission and developed by academics at Sheffield University. This massive inventory was as essential to our work as the NCC's Nature Conservation Review in the 1980s and the aforementioned Geological Conservation Review.

Another aspect of this inventory work was the completion of the assessment of changes in land use and land cover over the postwar period. The Countryside Monitoring Scheme used air photography from the late 1940s, the early 1970s and a new purpose-built land cover survey funded by the Scottish Office Environment Department in the late 1980s. These datasets provided the perfect database for assessing the type, rate and spatial distribution of changes. Maps and explanatory documentation were produced. More important was the ability to use this information to seek to influence government policy towards changes in the landscape and land use. One classic element was the continuing loss of hedgerows, and trees within them, in the lowland agricultural areas. This resulted from the use of larger machinery which was more economical to use in bigger fields. However, we knew from scientific assessments that the removal of trees and hedgerows meant the loss of protective microclimates that hedges are known to produce and the loss of habitats for invertebrates and birds that are created. Their removal also had the negative effect of creating large open fields which in turn increased exposure to the wind and led to subsequent loss of soil.

Additionally, we collaborated with the sister nature agencies, through JNCC, to produce inventories of estuaries and coasts.

CHAPTER 4

Delivering the Agenda

'This Concordat (on access) is a major achievement. Two years ago, few would have believed that we could sit down and agree such a positive and forward-looking document'.

Magnus Magnusson on the signing of the Concordat on Access, 1996

'I believe that national parks are the right way forward for Scotland. The major gap we have identified in the current system of natural heritage designations relates to the management of a small number of relatively large areas of natural heritage importance, of which Loch Lomond and the Trossachs is a prime example. What we require in these areas is an integrated, rather than sectoral, approach to their management.'

Donald Dewar, Secretary of State for Scotland, September 1997

'I would like to offer my sincere appreciation for all the good work that SNH have done to protect our natural heritage through the Natura 2000 programme. … It is a tremendous accomplishment.'

Rhona Brankin, Deputy Minister for Environment & Rural Development, 2001

THE REMIT of SNH was broad and many elements required attention to tease out the policy agenda and what was needed to be done. There were many matters of national importance where either we felt that action was needed or that the government in power at our inception or after the 1997 general election wished to promote. This chapter tells the story of our role in delivering all of these elements of our remit.

The majority of these matters were on the countryside part of our remit. These tended not to be in contentious areas, such as environmental education and access to the countryside through footpath development. Specifically, the government decided to establish national parks and to resolve the long-standing issue of the rights of access to private land for the public. In both cases, we were formally tasked by the Secretary of State for Scotland, Donald Dewar, to take these two matters forward and provide advice to government. He made the announcement at a special conference at Balmaha on Loch Lomond, where he was accompanied by his key colleague and *de facto* leader on countryside matters, Sam Galbraith, even though he was at the time the Health Minister, such was the high regard that Dewar had of his close friend and colleague.

Environmental Education

Before our inception, Ministers decided to establish a Working Party on Environmental Education to back up the commitments emerging from the Brundtland report and the developing thinking leading to the Rio Earth Summit in 1992. It was chaired by Professor John Smythe, an eminent environment educationalist, with expert input from Ruth Grant who ably led the environmental education function in CCS and in SNH. Both of these people had an international reputation and were able to bring in the best advice from the international community. They were also helped by the outgoing Deputy Director of NCC in Scotland, Jim McCarthy, who was a thoughtful and respected colleague.

The report *Learning for Life: a national strategy for environmental education in Scotland* was published in April 1993. This was a comprehensive and detailed review of the situation with recommendations to take matters forward as a national strategy for environmental education. SNH was rather negative in its response. The Board felt that it was a disappointing report with many missed opportunities. We made clear that our priorities were environmental education as part of the school curriculum, and specifically including outdoor learning, even recognising the practical problems of gaining approval within schools for taking pupils into the outdoors. Our other target was to engage with land managers to foster their role in environmental education, which we could do through our management agreements where there were opportunities, such as at Rothiemurchus. We were particularly keen to emphasise the role which the refurbished Battleby premises could perform as a centre for environmental excellence.

Based on our response, we developed our own strategy early in 1994. A central element of this was the development of Environmental Education Initiatives which the Earl of Lindsay, as Environment Minister in the Scottish Office , launched for us in autumn 1995.

We placed particular emphasis on helping schools develop community grounds as education resources. This *Grounds for Learning* approach was funded through our grants scheme. We were particularly keen to work with schools in deprived areas, such as in Wester Hailes in west Edinburgh and in Alloa. In the former, we helped the pupils to plant wheat in boxes in playgrounds to allow teachers to demonstrate to them that the grains were an essential component for making bread, rather than bread merely coming from the supermarket. At the latter, we joined forces with Scottish Enterprise under their environmental renewal programme. We hoped that these projects would make a tangible difference to the pupils and to their parents in these areas. We also had many other projects, such as at a school on Islay. We made close links with geography teachers through the Scottish Association of Geography Teachers (SAGT), with Lynette Borrowdale as our lead, with support from Ruth, another geographer, and also from myself as an Honorary President of SAGT. A novel element was the development of our Environmental Community Chest: an education resource pack in the form of a wooden chest which could be lent out to schools and communities. Adrain Fenn led on this initiative. This was further developed into a second version: the Sea Chest.

We also developed our environmental education work on our NNRs. For example, in the redevelopment of the Knockan Crag NNR in Wester Ross, our environmental education team and our Earth scientist advisers worked to produce easy to understand displays and interactive devices to aid understanding of this important but complex geological site.

Meantime, the impetus seems to have been lost at Scottish Office level with the environmental education strategy for Scotland being taken forward by the Secretary of State's Sustainable Development Advisory Group.

Access Provision and Reform

A major element of our remit and therefore our work was on access. It had two basic components: improving the provision of public access and dealing with the legal basis for access. To do both of these, we had to work in partnership with many bodies across the sectors and interests.

We had inherited the well-considered work CCS had undertaken on access. The results of their consultation on access, *Access to Scotland's Countryside: A Consultation Paper*, was published in their final year of operations. This was a very useful starting point, but with our wider responsibilities we needed to look afresh to make sure we were taking an integrated approach to all elements of the natural heritage and to work in partnership as our operating principles demanded. We immediately set up an Access Task Force chaired by Alan Blackshaw on grounds of his great knowledge of the subject, supported of course by the great expertise inherited from CCS, Richard Davison, and especially John MacKay who had an amazing depth and breadth of knowledge which he used to such great effect. He was rightly recognised for his contribution by the award of an MBE. Our rubric was to seek to find local solutions to local problems, to look at better provision for urban and peri-urban communities and to consider charging for access. We knew that the legal issues were difficult and there was no prospect of legislation on legal rights as the Conservative administration would never get it approved in the House of Lords given the landowning interests represented there. We launched our consultation early in 1993 and also commissioned eight research papers from external experts, including on statutory rights of access. The issues emerging were of no surprise: public right of access to uncultivated land and to open cultivated land and the effect of increasing access on the natural heritage. There were also the historical views to consider way back to the 1890s when James Bryce sought unsuccessfully on a number of occasions to obtain the UK Parliament's approval for formal statutory access rights. There remained, in our view, the feeling of 'being in a state of trespass' on private land and the unresolved question of the 'rights of owners'. These had been vexed issues for years, with for example the Secretary of State for Scotland, Tom Johnstone, opining in 1942 that there was no such offence as trespass and the campaigning journalist Renee McCowan being clear that there was a traditional right of access to the open hill. At the very least, we needed to resolve these differences of opinion.

Extremes of views were inevitable on this vexed subject We recognised that a 'Concordat' style of approach was necessary, and the idea of an Access Forum led by SNH was actioned in 1994. Alan Blackshaw chaired the forum with representatives of the Association of Deer Management Groups, the Scottish Landowners Federation and the Mountaineering Council of Scotland. Later that year, we published our policy paper *Enjoying the Outdoors: A Programme for Action* reflecting the independent review we had commissioned of the 500 responses to our consultation and our further thinking.

Progress was slow, but was being made due to the willingness of the parties. A concordat, *Scotland's Hills and Mountains: a Concordat on Access* was signed by ten bodies: ADMG, COSLA, MCS, NFUS, Ramblers Association, Scottish Countryside Activities Council, SLF, SNH, Scottish Sports Association and the Scottish Sports Council. It was launched early in 1996. Magnus reflected on the views of the organisations that had achieved this agreement saying, 'This Concordat is a major achievement. Two years ago, few would have believed that we could sit down and agree such a positive and forward-looking document'. 'Quite right', we all said.

The work continued but with a significant change in emphasis with the announcement by the newly-elected Labour administration in September 1997 that it intended to bring legislation forward to the Scottish Parliament, once it was established, to legalise the right of access and the responsibilities on all users, owners and managers. This signalled a new impetus in our activities as we were given the lead role in the development of proposals and the accompanying countryside code. We received proposals from the Access Forum soon after the ministerial request - a clear sign of the detailed work and debate within the Forum over the years since its inception. Basically, it proposed a 'legal right of access to land and water exercised responsibly for informal recreation and passage' backed up by codes of behaviour, education of the public of their rights and responsibilities, a positive approach towards and by owners and managers of land with safeguards on their rights and safeguards for conservation. The Forum argued for more funds to be devoted to access through existing budgets of public authorities. The obligations on local authorities were spelt out, specifically the establishment of local access forums, the use of mediation in disputes, a duty to plan and to facilitate local access networks, and to have provisions for access in Local Plans, including *Paths for All*. We knew that the consensus in the Forum was fragile, but applauded what they had managed to achieve, and the very effective role played by Roger Wheater, who had taken over as chair, in bringing this about.

We concurred with the Forum's advice focussing particularly on the owners' rights to manage their land, the responsibility of those seeking access, the need to ensure that the natural environment was protected, that public education was essential and that additional resources were needed. We calculated the latter at around £6.5 million per annum from our budget, including our support for Ranger Services and local path networks. We also flagged up other issues requiring attention, such as owners' privacy around the curtilage of their properties, rights and responsibilities on water, access to nature conservation sites, liability, and the need for mediation and adjudication where there were disputes. In the spirit of openness, and despite the fact that our advice was directly to the government, we published it in late 1998 as *Access to the Countryside for Open-Air Recreation: Scottish Natural Heritage's Advice to Government.*

We supported the provisions of the draft Land Reform (Scotland) Bill when it came to First Reading in 2001, especially as the principles identified by the Access Forum, which we agreed with, were in the Bill's provisions. The key ones were a general right of access taken responsibly, safeguards on privacy, on land management needs and on conservation needs, new powers and duties for relevant authorities and additional resources to make the package work. This was all encapsulated in our briefing to MSPs so that they could, we hoped, not misrepresent our position for their own purposes and that it would properly inform the various committees debating the provisions of the Bill. In fact, this was a double win, compared with the ambiguity of the existing system: for the public as access users and for the owners and managers as providers.

We were clear throughout that there was no general common law right of access based on the advice of legal experts, especially Jeremy Rowan-Robinson. Equally there was the difficulty for an owner or their representative being able to secure the removal of someone from their land.

We were fortunate in having Board members who could bring the parties together, initially Alan Blackshaw, then Roger Wheater and finally Jeremy Rowan-Robinson. This was no mean feat given the potential polarisation on the issues by the diverse parties to the Concordat and later the recommendations for legislation.

After my retirement, clearly a deal of good work by SNH led by John Mackay and by colleagues in the recreation and access bodies, especially Alan Blackshaw, Dave Morris, Bob Reid and Jeremy Rowan-Robinson, helped to secure the approval by the Scottish Parliament in 2004 to the access provisions in the Land Reform (Scotland) Act and to the approval of the Scottish Outdoor Access Code. It is testament to a changed political climate, but also to the preparatory and ongoing work that my colleagues had done at executive and board levels over many years. It is a clear case of what I call 'strategic opportunism' – plan for the future to be ready when the opportunity arises.

Footpath Creation Programme – Paths For All

The other element of our access work was to initiate a new programme of path creation. We knew there were many paths in the lowland areas, but our respondents told us they wanted more, and we knew the educational, environmental and emerging understanding of health benefits for increasing provision. We were well aware of the responsibilities, but local authorities had limited resources and there needed to be more incentives to provide paths. Early in 1994, a Paths for People initiative emerged, a restyled *Paths for All - The Scottish Way*, which we launched in September 1994 at Battleby supported by the Earl of Lindsay, our Minister, and Gus MacDonald, the Chair of Scottish Television, which had adopted Paths for All as its Millenium project. Gus was President and Magnus, Chair of the Partnership. Alan Blackshaw represented SNH on the new partnership, and we appointed staff. Our aim was simple: 'to help improve local access for walkers, cyclists and horse riders, whatever their ability, age or skills'. It was a grassroots approach to create networks of local paths, signed, mapped and promoted to meet local needs. We had a vision of 200 networks over the next decade, 40 by 2000 - A Millenium Project. We wished to link these to the existing longer distance routes already in place and those others intended. We needed national leadership and had the support of all the key national government agencies. We also had the support of local user groups and local authorities, as well the farmers and landowners.

However, raising other funds proved unsuccessful. First, our bid to the Millenium Fund in partnership with ten bodies in 1995 was rejected on grounds that it was not sufficiently distinctive, whatever that was supposed to mean! Second, Magnus and I presented our project to the Chair of TESCO, Lord MacLaurin, but he did not find it specific enough for their interests. Nevertheless, we got the initiative up and running, allocating with Ministerial approval, £400,000 per annum from our budget together with £100,000 from a legacy given to us. We had calculated that to create 1 km of path would cost on average £3,000, with a total cost over the decade of £20 million. We failed to achieve that level of funding. By 1998, we reviewed progress with our partners to reinvigorate commitment. The fact that, 30 years after it was established, the partnership is still working on provision and maintenance is testament to the initiative itself, to the partnership collaboration, to the commitment of staff in partner organisations and to the charity's own leadership. The one sad note is that Ian Findlay, who moved from SNH to take over the leadership and did an outstanding job, died in a tragic accident in 2021. In his memory, there is a new fund to stimulate more access.

In addition to local path networks, there was commitment to maintain the Long Distance Routes initiated by CCS. Given their role in increasing economic benefits, we considered that other government agencies, such as the Scottish Tourist Board and the two Enterprise Agencies, should contribute resources during our policy review in 1995. As a result, we decided that our funding to local authorities should be reduced from 100 per cent of costs to 75 per cent. The West Highland Way was a great recreational success with good commercial spin-offs, which is more than could be said of the Southern Upland Way which, frankly, has proved to be an uninteresting and little-used route. However, extending the West Highland Way to Inverness in the form of the Great Glen Way and other longer distance routes, such as the Speyside Way, have been accomplished and proved to be successful for walkers and for local communities.

We knew we were still behind the level of path provision in England and the cultural approach in the Scandinavian countries, but I believe that Scotland was in a better position on access provision and on the prospects of clarifying the ambiguities in the legal position by the end of my term than we could possibly have expected at the outset.

National Parks for Scotland

The idea of national parks in Scotland has had a long history following the commission of inquiry led by Sir Douglas Ramsay in 1949. The fact that they were not approved by the government of the day, despite similar provision for national parks in England and Wales, was a result of resistance from landowners and from local authorities in Scotland. CCS tried to argue the case on a number of occasions, but there was no political mileage by either of the parties in government in their time. However, with the publication by CCS of its report on *Popular Mountain Areas in Scotland*, Ministers were persuaded by their officials, led by me as Head of Division, in 1991 to establish special committees to review the issues of recreation, access and nature management in both the Cairngorms and in the Loch Lomond and the Trossachs areas. Two working parties were established. The government asked SNH to give priority to the working parties' efforts. There was no political chance of legislation, but at least there was movement to look at the issues. Another example of 'strategic opportunism'.

The Loch Lomond and The Trossachs Working Party delivered its report in 1993. The outstanding questions were who would pay for implementation of its findings, including the development of a management strategy, and what sort of management structure should be put in place: a Joint Committee or a Joint Board. There was no agreement between the local authorities on which they preferred as the Joint Board would mean giving up some of their powers and responsibilities. The possibility of National Heritage Area status was also raised in the report. The SNH response was in the 'yes, but' category. We expressed concerns about the safeguarding of both the natural and cultural heritage, how to achieve improvements in the management of recreation activities and, more broadly, how the practice of a 'working Countryside' could be maintained and how community development could be achieved.

There seemed to be a loss of impetus partly because there was no political will nationally or locally to take matters forward and partly because the Chair resigned on his appointment as Chair of the Forestry Commission. One positive outcome was the establishment of the water-borne ranger service on Loch Lomond. This came about for two reasons. There were uncontrolled behaviours on the loch, particularly by motorised craft users. And there were concerns about increased pressure on the loch as a result of restrictions being imposed on the water bodies in the English Lake District, and the allied codes of practice and restrictions on vessel speed and types of activities there.

The Cairngorms Working Party, chaired by Magnus Magnusson, produced its report, *Common Sense and Sustainability: A Partnership for the Cairngorms*, in 1993. It was based on the voluntary approach as the landowners did not wish to have restrictions imposed upon them. Governance was an issue with the overall preference for a Partnership Board. This was agreed and established by the government. With Magnus Magnusson stepping down as chair, David Laird took over. Outstanding issues remained to be resolved, for example who should pay for the costs of the body, how a strategy could be successfully developed and would the local authorities be allowed to retain their development control responsibilities. The momentum was maintained, and the Partnership produced its strategy late in 1996. Most of the issues had been resolved through an integrated approach and all parties, both public and private, were prepared to meet their obligations. Resource shortages were noted. In the event, the Scottish Office made additional provision in the SNH grant-in-aid to support the Partnership, and the money was ring-fenced for this purpose.

Overall, the Cairngorms work made more progress than the Loch Lomond and The Trossachs work. A great deal of discussion and debate had taken place which was the necessary prerequisite for what was to become new policy with the change of government in 1997. This preparatory activity over some years was one of the lessons we learned from reviewing best practice around the world in setting up new processes to protect and manage areas for the public benefit.

The scene changed politically in 1997 with the election of the Labour administration. Following the aforementioned announcement of the plans to establish two national parks, SNH was tasked to lead on the development of the proposals and provide advice to the government. This was a new role for us, and we were determined to undertake it thoroughly and effectively. Ian Jardine was given the lead role accompanied by Peter Rawcliffe and aided by all those who had experience of the two working parties, and the lessons learned from approaches in other countries. We decided to undertake a sounding consultation in late 1997 and we followed this up with a full consultation later in 1998. The majority of respondents were in favour of national parks, but were unconvinced about the details. Loch Lomond and The Trossachs received strong support, but that for the Cairngorms was more muted. We followed these consultations with many meetings in the two areas. We produced our advice recommending that the development of a Park Plan to be approved by the government was an essential early step. We expressed concern about the lack of effectiveness of the voluntary principle and made it clear that transfer of statutory town and country planning powers would be challenged by the local authorities. As a result of our advice, draft legislation was produced early in 2000. Our response was to request stronger powers for all public bodies to actively support the national park authorities. Rather than the standard and relatively weak 'have regard to the national park' provision, we made a plea not to weaken nature protection. One particular feature we argued for successfully was the inclusion of a provision to enable the establishment of national parks in the marine environment. The reason for this was that most national legislation in other countries separated out the establishment of terrestrial from marine national parks. We felt this was an anomaly given the possibility of recognising national park status from the seabed to the mountain top in certain areas of Scotland in the future.

I will not summarise the debates in the Scottish Parliament, they can be read online. I sat in the public gallery for the Stage Three debate and final decision. The National Parks (Scotland) Act 2000 was approved by unanimous applause rather than by a vote reflecting support for the overall concept. It was apparent to me that there was still not a consensus among MSPs of what a national park was for and what it should achieve. The duties on the park authority included economic and community development as well as care for nature and landscape. This in spite of the fact that the Act had a provision which stated quite unambiguously that if there was a conflict between the five objectives as set out in the Act then protection of nature must prevail. I doubt if this message was registered by the MSPs in giving the approval to the Bill. Curiously, having been told informally but firmly by the Minister of State in 1997 that Scotland should not have national parks like those in England, the legislation approved by the Scottish Parliament was not significantly different from the long-standing measures for England.

The passing of the primary legislation paved the way for the work on establishing the two national parks and the preparation of a Designation Order for the approval of the Scottish Parliament. SNH was now formally designated in the Act as the Reporter for preparing the case and consulting with all interests and making recommendations to the Scottish Government. We undertook the largest consultation that we had ever done about the proposals for the Loch Lomond and The Trossachs National Park. We reported that the park authority being given powers under town and country planning legislation was the most effective way of fulfilling the conditions in the Act;

this was agreed. The result was very strong support for the core area, but debate about other areas, such as Glen Fruin, the Argyll Forest Park, and the Lochearnhead/Ben Vorlich/Glen Ogle areas. These were all included in the park. Thereafter, there was a good deal of political toing and froing about the boundary, particularly the inclusion of the Cowal areas, seemingly as a political expediency to the junior partner in the Labour/Liberal Democrat coalition. The park was formally established in July 2002.

We undertook a similar exercise for the proposed Cairngorms National Park. The Open Meeting of the Board, held in Aviemore, was an interesting experience for us as staff and for the public attending. Some of the latter seemed to think that staff should not have any role, but it so happened that collectively we had more knowledge of the area and how it met or otherwise the objectives of the designation and this was a surprise to onlookers. We submitted our advice in August 2001.

In concluding this section, I felt that we had done an outstanding job in our formal advisory role to the Scottish Government which was given an excellent basis for drawing up the primary legislation and the designation orders for the two parks. It was truly a team effort, helped also by the reviews we had commissioned from external experts on how the national parks operated in England and Wales, and also in other parts of the world. We used our extensive contacts and our personal knowledge through our involvement in key European and international bodies, such as IUCN, Eurosite and Europarc, from whom we learned so much from colleagues.

Designations

Successive governments took the view that there were too many designations to protect nature and landscape, and that the system needed to be both reduced and rationalised. This view was reflected by many who found the layer upon layer of different labels for slightly different purposes confusing. Were they all needed and what would a purpose-made solution to meet Scottish requirements and circumstances be, were all pertinent questions we were faced with. Two things were clear. The system had grown as a result of different requirements through different statutory opportunities over time without taking an overview. The other was that no one was adequately explaining the system as a whole and what it was trying to achieve.

We set up our own Designations Task Force in 1992, which reported in 1994. Its main conclusion was that the system had developed cumulatively, and that each designation had its own legitimate purpose to satisfy Scottish, UK or international requirements and responsibilities. It was important to ensure that everyone in SNH, and more particularly our partners, understood the purposes, as well as the strictures and opportunities behind each of the designations. Guidelines were produced to this effect. We knew that there was a need to look again at the NNRs to determine which were fulfilling the original purpose set out in the 1949 National Parks and Access to the Countryside Act and also to review the role and purpose of the UNESCO Biosphere Reserves. The former led our own internal group to propose changes (see below), whereas the latter needed to wait for the outcome of UNESCO's global review.

We did have a particular concern about informal designations for sites and areas of local relevance that had no statutory backing. One of these was SWT's Listed Wildlife Sites. We recognised, however, that these had a legitimate purpose in raising the profile of nature protection locally. As we were providing substantial funds to help SWT recover its financial position to manage its own reserves and to deliver valuable conservation work, we decided that the best approach was to ensure that there was an accredited process for identifying and labelling these sites.

The Scottish Office undertook its own review in 1996, presumably as it was not satisfied that their notion of rationalisation had been achieved through our review. Curiously, it concluded that the two Scottish designations with no statutory basis, the Forestry Commission's National Forest Parks and the SWT's Listed Wildlife Sites, should be safeguarded from any changes. Curious in that on the former they had control as the lead Forestry Ministry and on the latter could influence SWT indirectly through our annual grants. They raised concerns about NNRs, NSAs and Natural Heritage Areas. The Scottish Government undertook a further review in 2001 as Ministers in the new administration had concerns about the 'plethora of designations' as they termed it. Their consultation paper was entitled the *Nature of Scotland*. We were critical of both of these reviews. We felt that the real issues of nature and landscape protection were being ignored. Our understanding stemmed from our local experience and from our knowledge of international best practice. In particular, we were very critical of the lack of attention in the government's report on ways of protecting large areas. This had been obvious for some time, for example, from the misuse of the SSSI mechanisms in the Flow Country and for underpinning the notification of Special Protection Areas and Special Areas of Conservation under the EU's Natura 2000 programme. Added to this was the lack of serious consideration of the means of protecting the core of designated sites where the greatest natural interest occurred. We considered that the use of zoning to recognise different management objectives in different parts of a site was the way forward, as clearly defined in the IUCN Management Categories for Protected Areas, which was the best international guidance available. We remained particularly concerned about the use of the voluntary principle and whether there were sufficient incentives for it to work and, more particularly, whether there were workable enforcement mechanisms to stop unscrupulous damage to sites and areas. Needless to say, the government review died a death without any changes. However, our local and international experience meant that we wished to evolve the Scottish approach, especially for nature sites and areas.

National Nature Reserves

NNRs have always been regarded as the *crème de la crème* where nature is the primary management objective. They were either on land owned by the government through NCC and its successors, such as Beinn Eighe, the first NNR in Britain, or on land owned by charitable environmental bodies such as the NTS, or on selected privately-owned estates such as Rothiemurchus. Each Reserve had a Management Plan. I was disappointed to find that they were a comprehensive inventory of the Reserve, but virtually nothing about the real management issues and what it would cost to rectify the position. Hence, looking more fundamentally at NNR management through our Area teams was another task. This process was, of course, helped by the fact that some of the Area Managers were previously NNR managers.

We undertook two reviews. One was to settle the purpose and to identify the role of other partners as owners. The second was to redefine the purpose more clearly, to identify Approved Bodies who owned and managed sites and to determine which sites should remain, which could not fulfil the redefined purpose, and which sites should be added to the list. The new purpose was defined as:

> To be a selection of those areas that characterise the very best of Scottish nature, where the natural interests will be put first, exemplifying the best standards in the way they are cared for and which can together and, in

most cases, can create special opportunities for people to learn about and appreciate these outstanding qualities and to be inspired by them.

At the end of this process, there were 71 NNRs, that matched the revised purpose. They were owned either by SNH or by Approved Bodies, such the Forestry Commission, NTS, RSPB, SWT and some privately owned estates.

SSSIs

SSSIs were always the bedrock of nature conservation, both flora and fauna, and geological and geomorphological features. NCC in Scotland had completed a major re-notification task in the light of changes to the legislation approved in 1981 and modified in 1985. There was a great deal of criticism of the use and purpose of the designation, the process, the use of Permitted Development Rights and what was meant by Operations Requiring Consent. The system was based on the 'voluntary principle', which meant that owners could only be formally challenged through the courts about actual or threatened actions which would significantly damage the scientific interests in the site. NCC and later SNH were not prepared to pursue this approach, given the cost and the uncertainty of the outcome. We decided that clarification for everyone was needed, so we produced a booklet in 1994, supported by Sir Hector Monro, our Minister, the NFUS and the SLF.

The main problem was that this mechanism was being used way beyond its original intent: to protect small habitats and specific species in lowland Britain. No wonder SSSIs were termed 'islands of protection in a sea of devastation' (no one knows the source of this very accurate phrase!). I decided, with the chairman's approval, but to the consternation of some of my colleagues, to up the ante about the failures of the SSSI system in a speech to the Crofters Union conference in Portree in 1997. Ironically, the speaker before me was my Joint Accounting Officer, the Head of the Agriculture and Environment Department and the one after me was one of my Board member bosses. My comments hit the headlines in every rural newspaper from Shetland to Kintyre. It began a debate, but eventually we were hidebound by the position of the UK Department of the Environment and the concerns of the voluntary environmental bodies, so no changes were made.

National Scenic Areas

As the only statutory basis for protecting Scotland's landscapes of the highest national importance, National Scenic Areas were significant, but their statutory basis was poor and there was little political support for securing a stronger and more effective system. They were first established under planning legislation in 1980. We were asked by Lord Sewel in 1998 to undertake a review. We issued our consultation paper early in 1999. Our advice to government was the need for a much stronger statutory basis for protecting scenery. This was not achieved until much later as I shall discuss in Chapter 10.

We used the system to argue for the protection of the national scenic interest in a number of cases. For instance, we successfully argued that the proposed super quarry at Lingarabay on Harris was unjustified on grounds of fundamental damage to the NSA for South Lewis, Harris and North Uist. We successfully argued against the proposals for a barytes mine at Duntanlich in highland Perthshire because of its effect on the Loch Tummel NSA. It was also clear in developing the two national park proposals that incorporating the NSAs for Lomond and for The Trossachs, and for both the Cairngorms and the Deeside and Lochnagar NSAs, would enhance their status and secure improved protection of the scenic heritage.

Natura 2000 Areas

These designations represent the strongest form of nature protection in Scotland as part of an EU regional system and extended to the countries in the European Economic Area. However, it is by no means a perfect system as we discovered in our role of the government's implementing body in Scotland.

There are so many idiosyncrasies in the selection of species and habitats in the annexes to the EU Species and Habitats Directive that a consistent approach was not possible. Two spring to mind to exemplify my point. The detailed classification of coastal dunes and cliffs was in marked contrast to the broad descriptions of upland vegetation. This led to great detail on the former and insufficient on the latter. The identification of priority species did not consider the great variation in occurrence and abundance through the EU territory so that magpies, for example, were scarce on the European mainland but were rightly regarded as a natural pest species in the UK. Additionally, the identification of priority habitats, such as peatland and heather moorlands, did not always make sense as the latter in Scotland is almost exclusively an anthropic manifestation of management rather than a natural feature as expert uplands ecologists, such as John and Hilary Birks, have pointed out. In addition, it was designed to assume that plants and animals will stay where they were when a site was identified. We knew that this static approach was fallacious in the real world and was, obviously, becoming even more so as the effects of climate change became apparent.

We were also supposed to undertake the work without a formal consultation process. We raised this within government but got nowhere. Fortunately, we had a visit from Bruno Julien, the Head of the Natura programme in the European Commission, who was sympathetic to our approach. We consequently carried out formal consultations. Ironically, as this was the most stringent protection scheme for nature so far used in Britain, the response from owners was for the most part favourable. We were also able, successfully, to make the case for not using SSSIs for protecting the stems of rivers and for coastal sites.

There were some sites which were not readily supported by the Scottish Government. One was the River Tweed. Although the UK Government, from the England perspective, was supportive, clearly the Scottish Government was being lobbied hard by the fishing interests.

All of this had raised in my mind the need for a broader more comprehensive approach. This in part came about from my two day visit to the Flow Country in 1989 with NCC. No progress was made and latterly SNH staff were instructed to use the SSSI mechanism for protecting the most important areas of the 'flows'. This meant that the intervening areas were not protected and over the boundary negative effects could occur. A broader envelope approach was needed.

Applying the Natura programme to the marine environment proved to be more difficult. We had had little experience apart from the battle in the latter days of NCC in Argyll, particularly in Loch Sween and in Loch Creran, where an alliance of recreational boating and the different fishing interests came together. The NCC approach was leaden footed in seeking to deal with their legitimate concerns.

What we also had to contend with was the tension between species protection and dealing with the protection of whole habitats and even ecosystems within which species lived and survived. Internationally, the debate was moving towards larger scale areas and the development of corridors to link protected areas within the wider landscape. There was little enthusiasm in Scotland, apart from within SNH, for learning from these approaches.

Politicians were also annoyed about the implementation of these Directives. I recall, for example, being summoned to meet the Conservative group of MSPs in 2000, most of whom I had met previously. They were concerned that we had lost support because of our insistence on designating Natura 2000 sites and demanded to know why we were doing this. I had to explain to them that the Conservative Government under Margaret Thatcher had signed the two Directives, and we were only acting under the direction of both the UK and Scottish Governments as their implementation body. They were unaware of the origin, were satisfied with my explanation and agreed that they would take the matter up with government. In the event, quite reasonably, nothing changed.

The resource costs in staff time and money to implement the Natura 2000 system were very considerable and meant that without the added resources requested from the government we would have to drop other work. The imperatives of designation were emphasised by the role of the environmental NGOs challenging the UK Government through the European Commission and threatening to put their case for the tardiness and narrowness of the UK response to the European Court. This was something which the UK Government wished to avoid.

I am convinced that our development of management schemes for major habitats, such as peatlands and moorlands for example, aided the progress we were able to make. The Caithness and Sutherland Peatland Management Scheme and the Lewis Peatlands Management Scheme received rapid and positive responses from the rights holders, as did, in 2001, the Moorland Management Schemes for Muirkirk and North Lowther Uplands, the Arran Moors and the Glen App and Galloway Moors. This changed the complexion from imposition to one of partnership and at a much lower cost to the public purse than compensation style arrangements.

One final and crucial point has to be made. The commitment of staff to delivering the Natura 2000 was immense. Special mention needs to be made of the leadership of Ian Jardine, the organisational skills of John Burlison and

Sandy MacLellan, the dedicated work of the scientific staff to develop the site definitions and especially the Area teams at the coalface to deliver, most especially, the huge areas in Caithness and Sutherland led by Terry Keatinge and in Lewis led by David MacLellan.

UNESCO Biosphere Reserves

One of the outcomes of the Man and the Biosphere Programme (MAB) in 1968 was the development of Biosphere Reserves. Their purpose was to recognise the interconnection between humans and nature as a positive partnership using a three-fold zonation system. Core Zones were for strict nature protection and research, outer or Development Zones were where people lived and undertook activities in an environmentally friendly manner, and intermediate or Transition Zones were to act as buffers. Scotland had nine Biosphere Reserves. They were ahead of their time and more than any other designation, they applied the sustainable development ethic to people and nature working together to deliver a better future for both. But their name created confusion. Following the UNESCO review in 1995, we reviewed the Scottish sites, along with colleagues in England and Wales through the UK MAB Committee in 2000. We concluded that none of the nine met the revised criteria, either they were too small, had no one living there, or were being managed through other mechanisms.

Rationalisation was achieved in a systematic manner through changes in the definition and purpose by the approving body. This is a lesson maybe for other reviews?

UNESCO World Heritage Sites

Little progress was made on achieving listing of Scotland's sites of 'Outstanding Universal Significance' for nature heritage on the UNESCO World Heritage List during the decade. In 1989, the UK Government had agreed with the proposals to add both the Cairngorms and the Flow Country onto the UK Tentative List, as proposed by myself and colleagues in the Scottish Office Environment Department. In other words, they were in the queue for consideration nationally before putting a full case to the World Heritage Committee of UNESCO. We managed to retain this status for these two propositions during my time in SNH, but no substantive progress was made. Informally, we knew that the chief adviser on natural World Heritage Sites in IUCN, Jim Thorsell, was not supportive of either case and we were unlikely to make progress until a more objective process was in place in IUCN.

St Kilda was on the World Heritage List for its cultural history. Our marine team, ably led by John Baxter with David Donan, had used our remote-operated vehicle with its camera to undertake some photography around the archipelago. I remember a call from them one Monday morning asking me if I could come down to our Bonnington Bond office in Edinburgh to see the results. The excitement was palpable on the phone and no wonder. Instead of the wave and current scoured sea bed we had expected, the camera showed a rich flora and fauna down to at least 50 m depth. Sea pens, starfish, anemones and many other species along with a kelp forest were there in abundance. Additionally, the area seemed to be the eroded caldera of a volcano with ledges of the eroded lavas evident. This stimulated us to seek government approval for an extension of the St Kilda site into the marine environment. This included ensuring that its geological significance as an element of the opening of the North Atlantic Ocean around 60 million years ago and, therefore, of the same era as the Giant's Causeway in Antrim, was added to our arguments. We were fortunate to have a visit to Scotland by the head of the Natural Heritage section of the World Heritage Centre in Paris, Mechteld Rossler, not long afterwards. She strongly encouraged us to put forward the marine and geological extensions. Subsequently, the first terrestrial and marine World Heritage Site in the world was formally listed.

Natural Heritage Areas

A great deal of work was undertaken within SNH to develop the NHA proposition. Criteria were devised and consulted on and were approved by the Board in mid-1993 following assessment of the results of consultation. We submitted our proposals to the Scottish Office early in 1994, but I do not recall any response. It seemed to be a classic case of what I call 'Not invented here', meaning 'it was not our idea, and we do not wish to consider it', as well as opposition from other parts of the Scottish Office.

Politically, the concept made no progress beyond its inclusion in the Natural Heritage (Scotland) Act. The focus of Ministers in both administrations was in reducing the number of designations, in simplifying the process, as indicated above, and also delivering the requirements of the Natura 2000 programme. For these reasons as well as the drive for national parks under the Labour administration, there was little enthusiasm for NHAs. Lord Sewel told me that they should wither on the vine in name and in statute and that he did not want to resurrect them. He did, however, recognise that the thinking behind them might have a future role in developing the current suite of designations. That helpful comment was never translated into our approaches on the ground as we were hemmed in by the strictures of the EU on the Natura programme and by the insistence of the UK and Scottish Governments on the use of SSSIs to underpin those two designations: SACs and SPAs.

CHAPTER 5

Working With Government

'Roger, you should know that there will be times when SNH annoys us, but we have to put up with this as that is how we set you up'.

Malcolm Rifkind, 1991, and Separately Lord Sewel, 1997, as Scottish Government Ministers

'Scottish Natural Heritage has made notable achievements in many areas of its work... The most notable of these is that the Government is clear that SNH should pursue the full breadth of its remit in an integrated manner. We also want it to retain the operational principles of working in partnership and delegating authority to the local level...I wholeheartedly commend SNH for its achievements to date and look forward to seeing its continued success into the new millennium.'

The Earl of Lindsay, Minister for Agriculture and Environment, 1996 in The Scottish Office, *Natural Priorities*

'This award (CBE) is well deserved recognition of the significant contribution you have made to the environment and, in particular, the way you have steered Scottish Natural Heritage from its conception to is present respected position. Well done!'

Lord Sewel, Minister for Agriculture, the Environment and Fisheries, The Scottish Office, 1999

IT HAS always been clear that the government of the day is in pole position. It determines the budget, formally directs the organisation through an annual Grant-in-Aid offer letter, can send specific Directions when considered appropriate, appoints the Chair and Deputy Chair and all of the Board members, and approves the appointment of Chief Executive on a recommendation from the SNH Board.

Looking back over recent years since I retired from SNH, I note that we are in an increasing period of the government knowing the answer and increasingly holding the NDPBs to account. This is legitimate for publicly-funded bodies. However, there is a resistance to these bodies developing new approaches and being creative. Too often the advice from the government was old-fashioned and did not move matters forward. I will give examples of the type of instructions given and why they were wrong. In SNH, I had to live with some of them, but certainly not all of them.

There was a changing political environment. It began with the highly positive stance across the political parties to the establishment of SNH as evidenced in speeches by the then Secretary of State. Since then the climate has chilled considerably with a few positive periods in between.

The Honeymoon Period

Ian Lang MP, Secretary of State for Scotland, stated categorically in the Second Reading debate in the House of Commons that SNH would have another vital role: to advise the government or any other party on any aspect of policy or activity which it considers has an effect on Scotland's natural heritage. He said, 'We expect this task to be carried out with objectivity, rigour and integrity, but most of all effectively' (Hansard, 11 February 1991, col 626).

One critical piece of advice was given to me by successive Ministers of different administrations. Malcolm Rifkind, the originator of SNH, said to me personally when congratulating me on my appointment as Chief Executive, 'Roger, you should know that there will be times when SNH annoys us, but we have to put up with this as that is how we set you up'. Ironically, after the 1997 election of the Labour administration, the Minister of State, Lord Sewel, responsible for environment, agriculture, fisheries and forestry, called me into his office and used almost exactly the same words to me. These two statements, given sincerely and honestly, did give SNH the political endorsement of the freedom of action which the Act of Parliament had stated. Ministers and their officials did not often accept this working practice which created difficulties for us in our working relationship, and meant that the public often became frustrated by us apparently not doing our job.

Ian Lang led the celebration event at Battleby for the formal launch of SNH on 11 May 1992. Sir Hector Monro, the Minister for Agriculture,

Forestry, Fisheries and the Environment hosted a reception for SNH and its partners at Edinburgh Castle on 1 June 1992.

Later in the year we had feedback from the Head of the Scottish Office Environment Department when he visited the Board in November 1992:

> He said that both the Department and Ministers considered that SNH had got off to a tremendous start having set itself clear objectives which embodied the Secretary of State's key operational principles of partnership and delegation to the regions. He said that Sir Hector Monro had been impressed by the SNH regional structure and the way it is working in practice and by the fact that SNH is clearly making positive efforts to develop partnerships. Ministers were also impressed by SNH work on developing the Government's Citizen's Charter policy in the Natural Standards format. He impressed on SNH the need not to be discouraged by the lack of immediate results but to continue the dialogue with Government and with other partners in order to achieve long term benefits. He acknowledged the importance of ensuring that Scottish views were fed into the development of the Common Agricultural Policy and the Common Fisheries Policy, both of which have enormous implications for the natural heritage.
>
> (SNH Board Minutes, 3 November 1992, para 26)

Half a year later, Sir Hector Monro paid the Board a visit. He was given presentations on our progress and specifically on red deer, forestry, environmentally-friendly farming, geese and the implementation of the EC Directives. In response, the Minister indicated that:

> He was delighted with SNH's performance in its first year which was just as had been hoped for. He said Scotland has taken to SNH. In particular, he commented on the way the regional set up had got over the problem of remoteness; difficulties had been resolved at a personal level generally without confrontation. He stressed the need to continue with an approach based on coordination and cooperation and mentioned the work on the Cairngorms as an example of a meeting of minds. On Loch Lomond he suggested it might take longer to get an agreed conclusion.
>
> (SNH Board Minutes, 19 May 1993, para 7)

Sir Hector said that he preferred the voluntary approach to deer management. He recognised that there was an issue about access to forested areas. On agriculture, he said there were changes of views in the Department of Agriculture, but stressed that it was important for SNH to maintain its pressure on increasing awareness of these environmental issues.

At a dinner hosted by the Secretary of State, Ian Lang, in September 1993, he made it clear that he was impressed with SNH's breadth of thinking, the wide range of issues which we had tackled in our first year, and the different approaches we had taken to each.

As Time Progressed

Despite the Scottish Office being the policy progenitor of SNH and the organisation being given a statutory basis of being an independent adviser, relationships were not always positive with many areas of tension. Outsiders maybe wondered about this, but they were rarely, if ever, exposed in public. There were a number of occasions when we, to paraphrase, did annoy Ministers. Quelling SNH's statutory advisory role on any matters that were likely to affect Scotland's natural heritage became one of the most contentious issues. I recall many examples of the tensions.

Conservative administration Ministers who were closely involved in nature conservation challenged SNH when it produced a statement on the relationship between agriculture and the natural heritage. We were told that SNH should not be commenting on the second Forth Estuary crossing from the perspective of environmental sustainability, despite the fact that this was our statutory responsibility. We were instructed to implement the toughest wildlife legislation, the EU Habitats and Species, and Birds Directives (collectively known as Natura 2000), 'with a light touch' as if they did not really matter. We were instructed by UK Department of the Environment Ministers and officials to use the SSSI mechanism for implementing Natura 2000 for wide-ranging species and for large areas. We were frequently warned off commenting on the environmental effects, both positive and negative, for example of salmon farming, wind farms, ski development and large scale industry. We were told to lay off a police boss over potential interference with a bat roost in his loft, although he threatened illegal activity. We were instructed that the Mull Sea Eagles scheme should be compensation based not activity based.

In our early days, we dared, in the view of the Minister for Transport in the Scottish Office, to stray into roads and transport matters by giving an opinion on sustainability in relation to the natural heritage for a new crossing of the Forth Estuary at Queensferry. This was the Minister who had so ably taken the draft legislation through the House of Commons Committee. The same person was not too pleased about our commentary on seeking to develop the proposed upgrading of the A77 from Glasgow to Ayr to motorway, We had suggested for sustainability reasons that the government, as Trunk Roads Authority, should use waste materials from mining operations, which were readily available in the Central Belt of Scotland, as the road bottoming, and that the line of the road should follow that of the current road so as not to lose valuable agricultural land if an entirely new course was used. In the event, both of these suggestions were adopted in the design of the road. We also challenged the proposed route of the enhanced electricity transmission line to Northern Ireland on landscape grounds. We were not against this vital improvement to upgrade the infrastructure, but we were concerned about the design of the transmission towers and the route proposed. We did not formally object, but wished the issues to be fully aired and a compromise achieved through a Public Local Inquiry. The resultant ministerial decision was satisfactory from the landscape perspective, as I consider is evident when one visits the area.

The Secretary of State who had introduced the Bill in the House of Commons was soon negatively influenced against us with comments that SNH is 'the pariah of the countryside'. He demanded that a review of our work be undertaken prior to the Public Expenditure Survey in 1993. It was a worrying challenge to our approach, but we were not required to make any changes.

One recurrent theme was that the rhetoric of the 'silver bullet' solution for local economic development was not to be challenged as 'the market knows best'. This philosophy meant that consideration of possible untoward consequences to the natural heritage, for example, was not a material factor in decisions as the economic benefits of a particular type of development, such as fish farming or skiing, were obvious. This rhetoric survived the change from Conservative to Labour administration following the 1997 election.

I recall a specific example of this 'market must be left to operate' rhetoric about wind turbine locations for electricity generation. We had held discussions with the industry, with other parts of government who were involved in assessing the effects of the substantial increase in applications for wind turbines and with the communities around Scotland whom we worked with and where many staff lived. We considered that a sensible approach was for the development of a locational strategy which would identify those areas where restrictions should be imposed because of the effect on air traffic control, as indicated to us by the National Air Traffic System controllers, and, for example, where military low flying for training pilots was essential to be safeguarded as was made clear by the Ministry of Defence. In addition, we knew from the all-Scotland survey of landscape character and sensitivity where the most sensitive landscapes were. And, of course, we knew where the most sensitive wildlife areas were, especially those where ground nesting birds and the diurnal and seasonal flyways of birds occurred. We took our case to the government on my very last meeting with officials before retirement in March 2002. I was accompanied by Ian Jardine, my successor, and Bill Band, our well-respected expert on planning and development, to meet the Head of the Environment Group and the Head of the Industry Group. To cut a long story short, despite arguing our case for developing with other partner bodies a locational strategy for identifying 'go', 'no-go' and 'maybe' areas for wind turbine installations, we were told summarily that the market must decide on the location. In consequence, a great deal of time and money has been expended by wind turbine and electricity generation companies, by statutory bodies and by volunteers representing community interests in arguing case by case at Public Inquiries into development. What a gross waste of time and money by all with little discernible benefit!

There was one *cause célèbre* where I was told that we should back off by the head of department in the Scottish Office which was responsible for SNH. It was about the protection of bats which have strong legal status under the Wildlife and Countryside Act 1981 (as amended) and latterly under the Conservation of Habitats and Species Regulations, especially in the wintering and breeding seasons. Basically, it is illegal to disturb bats in their roost in any way. Bat roosts can be shut off from formal access only after the bats have vacated them. The case in point was the threat by the Chief Constable of Central Scotland Police. The tabloid press had a field day attacking SNH and also the Chief Constable. My response to the department was to say that we were doing our job 'without fear or favour' as the statute demanded.

In the 1990s, strategies with long timescales were not the order of the day as they have been in more recent times. Despite the long vision emanating from the Rio Earth Summit, which Ministers had subscribed to, there were two pieces of work which did not find favour with Scottish Office officials.

The first was setting out our vision and promotion for how our sustainability duty should operate. In developing this work, we recognised that there were many impediments to progress through the strong sectoral approach in policies and financial instruments throughout government, with many unsustainable developments being approved, and the lack of integration of information. We sought to clarify the position by producing papers on transport, water and sewage, and waste management, for example. Nevertheless, the Scottish Office officials were concerned with our approach and wrote a critical letter to us later in 1994. The Board reviewed the criticism and categorically rebutted its contents. Part of the reason was that a group of officials in the Ministry were seeking to set their stamp on this area of public policy. This ultimately led to the establishment by the Secretary of State of the Sustainability Working Group chaired by the well-respected lawyer and business person, Sir Charles Fraser. However, the group had a short existence of no more than three years.

Grants to support the purchase of land and water for conservation were always a hot potato. We sought ministerial guidance, rather than waste time on speculative cases. We were advised in late 1994 that 'SNH should be more selective in grant offers for land purchase'. That was sufficient guidance, and we revised our land purchase grant policy accordingly by the end of the year. At the same time, the Scottish Office refused to approve our request to support the John Muir Trust for purchase of land at Strathaird, near Elgol on Skye. Our selectiveness was obvious in our later cases, for example providing £50,000 to the Brasher Trust for purchase of land on the Knoydart peninsula, but with the condition that a management plan was produced for our agreement. We also gave £7,000 to the community of Valtos in west Lewis.

One particular case annoyed the Secretary of State at the time. We had paid *c*£1.8 million to purchase the peat-cutting rights at Flanders Moss. It was the largest raised bog in Britain and its hydrological integrity had been badly damaged in the past through drainage and peat cutting. Put simply, it was a wasting natural asset and our role in seeking to reverse the situation on a site of international importance was clear. The local MP, who was also

Secretary of State for Scotland, thought that the money would have been better spent on schools or hospitals. We gained the approval of our Minister, and the purchase went ahead. As a result, the slow recovery of the site was able to develop.

An earlier case was the proposal by the NTS to be given an endowment to purchase the Dunbeath Estate in eastern Caithness from its US owner. The Board approved a grant of £700,000, subject to Scottish Office approval. In the event, the sale fell through because of legal difficulties between the seller and the potential purchaser. Whether we would have been given Scottish Office support we considered necessary is a moot point. The lesson was that providing an endowment was a much more effective way of ensuring that resources were available for long-term conservation and restoration of a site.

More significant, perhaps, was our approach to dealing with real cases of conflict between wildlife and local people. A classic example was how we proposed to deal with a dispute on Mull between some farmers and their claims about Sea Eagles taking live lambs in the spring. We sought to move away from the traditional compensatory approach, beloved by the Department of Agriculture to placate farmers, to a more positive one which engaged farmers as partners sharing in resolution of these issues. We fashioned a scheme with the RSPB to invite affected farmers to do a number of tasks: monitor the food remains in the Sea Eagles' eyries to determine the animal remains there and by placing pregnant ewes during the lambing period in parks near to the farm steadings. The total cost per annum was around £12,000, compared with significantly more if we had used the compensation route. Most affected farmers went along with this approach and did put pressure on those of their fellows who did not join in.

I must admit that this approach did not always work. One case was on South Uist where crofters were really annoyed about hedgehogs eating the eggs of their chickens and, therefore, reducing their availability for consumption by the family and the local community. At the same time, the crofters were concerned about the predation by hedgehogs on ground nesting birds, as the latter attracted tourists to the area and brought income to the crofting community. This was a classic example of the needs of the local community and the national nature conservation agency coming together. Unfortunately, the hedgehog protection supporters, many based in southern England, were not at all receptive to the hedgehogs being killed, to the extent that Board members were warned to check any suspicious post addressed to them for fear that it might be booby-trapped. Through pressure by these activists the government forced SNH to translocate the offenders off the island.

Petty at times were the challenges from the Scottish Government as well. I remember being challenged one day for SNH giving a gift costing £70 to a visiting dignitary from one of our sister agencies in central Europe. My response was twofold. The gift was in recognition of the importance of making links with sister bodies around Europe so that we could learn from each other and build partnerships for ideas and their implementation. My other retort was to recall that the National Audit Office had just formally rebuked the Ministry of Defence for wasting £700 million on mismanagement of facilities at Coulport!

Another challenge was why we were publishing brochures about Scotland's natural heritage as that was really for a commercial organisation to do. Officials seemed to have forgotten that we charged for these brochures. What a narrow-minded perspective, I thought, when we had a clear and vitally important educational role and experts well capable of writing brochures in the *Naturally Scottish* series about key species such as Red Kites and Sea Eagles which now grace our skies to the enjoyment of all who see them. We also published a *Living Landscapes* series so that the public would have a better understanding of, for example, kelp forests, boglands, machair and soils, all key elements of Scotland's natural assets. And we partnered with the British Geological Survey to produce our series on *Landscape Fashioned by Geology* to illuminate readers on how the land was formed over millions of years and what was happening to it now. We resisted the demands.

One thing that was disrespectful to Board members, and therefore to SNH, was the tardiness of decisions on appointments and re-appointments to the Board by the Scottish Government. All too often Board members did not know whether they had been re-appointed or otherwise by the end of their term on 31 March of the year in question. Who was to blame, officials or Ministers, I was never sure despite many calls from SNH to officials asking when and by whom decisions would be reached. It struck me that this situation also reflected a lack of equitable administration by the Scottish Government of its many NDPBs.

Following up this inconsistency of treatment of NDPBs by different groups of officials in the Scottish Government, a group of NDPB Chief Executives, at my instigation and with the help of Margaret Ford and David Bolger, the heads of Eglinton Management, decided in 1997 that we should get together. We collectively wished to see what we could learn from each other, what were the common issues we faced, what solutions each body was bringing into practice. Specifically, we also wanted to make connections with the Scottish Government at the top management level to express our concerns and seek solutions to the different attitudes and approaches of our 'sponsor division' staff, those responsible for the particular area of policy such as tourism and the Scottish Tourist Board, or housing and Scottish Homes. We had a collective feeling that officials operated on the basis 'make up as we go along', rather than there being any central coordination of the administration's approach to the effective relationship with its NDPBs. A dozen or so Chief Executives met together and collectively found this helpful in many ways. Sadly, the top officials in the Scottish Government perhaps felt threatened by this, instead of realising that if they set up a central NDPB coordination unit there would be a more equitable approach. When eventually we had a meeting with the Permanent Secretary and other senior officials, they seemed apprehensive, but we sought to allay their fears that all we wished to achieve was consistency of treatment amongst us all, as that should be the basis of good administration. We were clearly listened to as an efficiency scrutiny of the Scottish Government's sponsorship of its NDPBs was undertaken aimed at achieving more internal consistency and more coherent guidance to NDPBs. The outcome was a more strategic approach based on a Management Statement accompanied by maximum delegation, publication of the NDPB's Corporate Plan and agreement on Performance Targets with monitoring of inputs and outputs. This was all welcomed by our group of CEOs. However, it failed to stop the desire of officials in the Ministry to interfere and question at a low level what and why, presumably at times on the basis that the Minister had picked up some gossip from others.

I cite these as examples of the inevitable tension between the government and its agencies. It is typical of the situation between the officials in the Ministry who are, to a degree, envious of the power, resources and influence which their 'sponsor body' can have. It is typical of the relationship between the sponsored body and the sponsor department. I was all too familiar with this tension having had both the gamekeeper and poacher roles as noted earlier in Chapter 3. All 'the taxpayer' should ask is that these relationships are performed professionally without grudge and in the full spirit of co-operation. It is therefore very important that the lines of communication between the officials in the Ministry and the staff in the government agency are open, honest and effective. To foster this, I made sure that Ministry colleagues should visit offices to meet staff and understand our work. I did that myself by annually taking my opposite number, whom I had known from the day we had started as Scottish Office officials in 1974, on visits to meet staff and see projects on the ground. It was time very well spent.

Funding Natural Heritage Work

There was a continual battle between SNH and the Scottish Government about the level of funding needed. We had to undertake all of our statutory responsibilities, to deliver the commitments the government gave to us and to respond to the ever-changing external environment which had both positive and more negative effects on nature and landscape.

This matter formally lay with the Secretary of State for Scotland. Contrary to earlier indications that there would potentially be more money given for the additional tasks that SNH had been given compared to its two predecessor bodies, the then Secretary of State, Ian Lang, informed SNH that the level of resources would be much less. However, we had support from the environmental NGOs, in particular WWF Scotland as Simon Pepper, its outstanding leader and a great colleague and friend behind the scenes, was determined to raise the issue politically. He did so through a paper in October 1991, *Scottish Natural Heritage – Paying the Bill* with a series of recommendations for staffing and funding activity on the ground at a total cost of £41.2 million. This would only be adequate, he argued, with cessation of compensation payments and additional funds being given for management agreements. This was helpful in arguing our case. Magnus Magnusson was furious with the government's attitude. He regarded this as the government reneging on a promise Ministers had made to him personally on his appointment as Chair. He went to see Mr Lang and laid his cards firmly on the table that unless the additional money was forthcoming he would resign and do so publicly. On this occasion Magnus's threat worked and the additional resources were provided in the budget for the first year of SNH. In carrying out this threat, Magnus well knew that such challenges do not go down well with Ministers and the threat could not be carried out again.

The annual Public Expenditure Surveys were, therefore, key areas where we needed to be adept at arguing our case at executive and board levels. It was not just a case of saying we needed more resources; all bodies and all departments within the Scottish Government machine did that as a matter of course. We became skilled at arguing the 'what and why', and the results additional resources would achieve. It was particularly difficult to identify the effects of partnership working and reducing conflict in monetary terms as it was in many respects intangible unless there was a new accord or deal or unless a new programme funded by all of the parties emerged. We did our best to argue this case, along with all of the other elements of the budget.

At times, we were successful, particularly in the early days and when we were given additional responsibilities by government. At other times we were not, and forward budgets were reduced in line with expenditure cuts throughout the government with the accompanying demand for delivery of the infamous Three Es: greater effectiveness, economy and efficiency. Of course, we made efficiency savings in many ways to the extent that the outcome of the Financial Management and Performance Review I report on later in this chapter gave us a clean bill of health in 1998. This was achieved by improved information systems led by our excellent IT team of Colin Brown, Scott Lindsey and Kenny MacLean. We also reduced office costs by more efficient use of space and in some cases changing offices to obtain a more favourable financial deal. We did try to co-locate with, for example, the Scottish Agricultural College but there was a reluctance by their management to do deals. We had no support from the Scottish Government despite the fact that in my last role there, I worked with the Minister and other officials to drive forward office sharing in rural areas. We also made sure that all of the many pockets of information held around SNH, in effect as personal data of individual staff, were properly identified and digitally recorded to allow access to all users. This was a step forward led so effectively by Malcolm Lowry and his review team staff.

SNH Grant-in-Aid from Scottish Government

Financial Year	**Total Grant-in-Aid £ Millions**
1992-93	34.229
1993-94	36.892
1994-95	41.178
1995-96	38.615
1996-97	36.850
1997-98	37.005
1998-99	37.203
1999-2000	38.979
2000-01	41.303
2001-02	51.142

Source: SNH Annual Reports

[Figures are money of the day. Includes capital and operating elements.]

In the mid-1990s, still under the Conservative administration, the Minister, The Earl of Lindsay, came to see us in our Hope Terrace office. He said he was very pleased with our work and performance, but he was going to cut our budget by 10 per cent. We knew that this cut was occurring on many other budgets and Magnus was clear that he could not play the resignation card again. On this occasion, it did not greatly harm the relationship with the Minister who we knew was frustrated at his inability to reduce other budgets in his portfolio, such as agricultural support. Indeed, he and I were able to jest over time about 'I support you but here's a 10 per cent budget cut'.

We argued for increases in our budget to deliver the additional work from the Scottish Government: for example, work arising from the three government working parties on environmental education, Cairngorms and Loch Lomond and the Trossachs, and later the demands for implementing the Natura 2000 programme and the Biodiversity Action Plans. With the development of our Paths for All programme, we were given additional resources which we passed on to the Partnership. We also obtained some financial help from other government bodies for our Paths for All initiative, but it was not sustained, nor increased in quantum.

The greatest increase in our grant-in-aid occurred in the Spending Review of 2000 when we received a £21.8 million increase over three years from 2001-04, with the greatest increase being in the first year, as shown in the table (see earlier). Part of this was a result of our concern about the lack of pay parity for SNH staff compared with staff in government and in other government funded bodies. We argued that this was really affecting our ability to recruit and retain staff and inevitably led to low morale. Our case was accepted and our new pay system with parity was implemented in 2001. This had a very beneficial effect throughout the organisation.

One aspect which became of increasing concern was the cost of pensions for staff who had retired. We knew that it was ethically correct and legally necessary to pay for these as the first call on our budget, as we did not have a funded scheme. The Scottish Government recognised this issue as well and, following successful negotiations with the Treasury, it was agreed that the pension fund would be transferred into the Principal Civil Service Pension Scheme at no cost to SNH by March 2003.

A long-standing argument with the government was the need to ensure that other programmes, such as agriculture and forestry, did not have a deleterious effect on the natural heritage and, more positively, contributed to its improved management. Despite many discussions at ministerial and official levels and tacit agreement in strategy documents, I have to conclude that we made very little headway. Even when the environmental portfolio of the Scottish Government was brought together with agriculture, forestry and fisheries under the same Minister and head of department nothing changed. It seemed that those administering these programmes, and the lobby bodies influencing them, especially the NFUS and the forestry industry, were far more powerful.

A particular case was the financial responsibility for payments to farmers for goose management. Despite many attempts to obtain a shift in responsibility to the government's agriculture budget, we were firmly told that it was for SNH to make the payments from within our own budget with no recognition that a tweak to the agri-environment programme would have been much more effective. Another issue was the funding of the Farming and Wildlife Advisory Groups jointly with local authorities. We strongly supported this initiative as without it there was little or no environmental management advisory capability to help farmers. We had farmer members on our Board who were leading figures in the FWAG movement and throughout my decade in charge we supported the group and helped the central office to become more effective and efficient. We tried latterly to come to an arrangement with the Scottish Agricultural College, which ran a very effective Farm Business Advisory Service and was gradually moving into environmental advice, but its chairman scuppered a new arrangement, Interestingly, I challenged him on this soon after my retirement at my interview for membership of the SAC Board. He accepted the criticism, and despite my challenge, I was appointed to the Board.

Funding of local authority activity had been a significant part of the expenditure inherited from CCS: ranger services, countryside in and around towns initiatives and long distance routes. We knew that in the longer term we could not continue this. The government was not keen about one part of the public sector funding another - a very fair point. However, we knew when, for instance, we reduced our funding for the local authority ranger services there was a high likelihood that local authorities would not find resources from their own budgets to continue the work at the same level. Central government was not prepared to intervene for the perfectly good reason that it did not wish to prescribe how local authorities allocated their resources. In fact, the practice of Special Grants to local authorities was hardly ever used. I was well aware of this mantra from my time dealing with local government finance in the Scottish Office .

We were expected to raise money for our work. We certainly charged for the purchase of the many booklets we produced in various series. After the refurbishment of the Battleby education and conference facilities in 1994, we hired it out to other users, provided that it did not restrict our own use. We had high hopes of gaining funding from the various lottery funds: the Millenium Fund and the Heritage Lottery Fund included. The only bid I can recall that was successful was £210,000 for the upgrading of the visitor centre and redevelopment of trails at our Beinn Eighe National Nature Reserve in Wester Ross. Some bids with partners for land purchase and management were successful which did reduce the strain on our budget We were never given the real reasons for the unsuccessful bids; a great ability by funding bodies to use weasel words was all too evident.

Government Reviews of SNH

Magnus met me with a very serious and unusually worried look on my return from my annual leave in summer 1995, a walking holiday in Corsica. The Scottish Office had decided to undertake a fundamental review of SNH he informed me and assumed that I would be very concerned. These scrutinies are never easy for the organisation under review, as I well knew from having been on the gamekeeper side when responsible for the Highlands and Islands Development Board in the old Industry Department for Scotland in the second half of the 1980s. Suffice to say, it is vital that the Chief Executive sees these exercises not as a threat, but as a means of leading changes to improve the performance and operation of the organisation. That is what happened. To Magnus's surprise, I said that will be a great opportunity for us in SNH to take the organisation forward. I had in mind at the outset of SNH, and told the trade unions so, that within five years we would change the structure fundamentally; especially by stripping out the regional tier and giving the Area teams more responsibility and by devolving more roles and resources to them. I also had in mind to change the spatial basis of our operation and to develop a new strategy which I had previously outlined to the Board in a private session, as described in detail in Chapter 7.

A number of outsiders, such as Peter Marren who started from the premise that the high point of nature conservation was in the 1960s and 1970s, have suggested that SNH was always being reorganised as he opined in his *New Naturalist* series book *Nature Conservation* in 2002. They are grossly misinformed. A measured pace of change, yes, but I knew I could never meet the aspiration of some staff who wished a period of no change, as no leader could ignore what was happening in the world around them. Going back to my earlier point about 'strategic opportunism', any leader worth their salt should be prepared when the opportunity arises. That arose with the Scottish Office's Quinquennial Review of SNH in 1995/96 with the view to implementing changes for the second five years of SNH. These five-yearly reviews of government bodies had begun under the Thatcher regime and, as I recall from my civil service days, they all too often sought 'to pull an organisation out of the ground' so to speak to see if it was still alive. What was the ambition of the Scottish Office civil servants in this review? This is an important question, as unless the leaders of the body under review can see the likely line of attack, they will not be in control. And yes, it is in effect a battle for control between the central government and its 'sponsor' body. Having been the 'gamekeeper' for four bodies in my administrative roles in the Senior Civil Service, I had a good idea of how the 'poacher', which is what I now represented, might position themselves.

To put all of this in context, Quinquennial Reviews comprised two stages. The Prior Options Review was to test rigorously whether the functions of the body in question are required to be performed by the public sector at all and whether these should be discharged differently or by others. A second stage, termed the Financial Management and Performance Review, focusses on financial management and control. I will deal with this stage after assessing the first stage process and its outcome.

The Study Group was chaired by the Secretary of the Scottish Office Environment Department accompanied by the Under Secretary for Environment in the Environment Department with Magnus and me representing SNH. The secretariat comprised an official from the department and Ian Jardine for SNH, whom I selected for this role because of his tactical nous and his ability to work with government officials. We had commissioned a review of our efficiency and effectiveness from Ernst & Young in 1995 which helped to identify actions and also laid the ground for the later second stage exercise. The resultant *Report of the Study Group on Scottish Natural Heritage* was published in November 1995. It paved the way for the second part of the Quinquennial Review with the invite to Ministers 'to consider the implications of the pressure on discretionary spending' and requested a new policy document to be produced early in 1996. The summary statement was telling in the pressures that the UK Government was under to deliver the requirements of the EU Birds, and Habitats and Species Directives through the Scottish Office and SNH for Scotland. It stated:

> SNH policy has been to spread its resources across the range of its functions, and in particular, to move away from the previous focus on nature conservation in designated areas and to spread its resources more widely throughout the countryside

Having reviewed the trends since 1992 and recognising the decline, in real terms, in its grant-in-aid from the Scottish Office, the Study Group report went on to state:

> The result of this will be a reduction in SNH's ability to undertake discretionary work and a greater concentration on statutory work, and work related to the Directives and other Ministerial priorities such as the Cairngorms, Environmental Education, Loch Lomond and the Trossachs, and the Biodiversity Action Plan.

The report set out the dilemma of reverting to a more nature conservation focus and reducing effort on the discretionary work on understanding and enjoyment. In other words, downgrading the inherited work from CCS and refocussing on the NCC inherited work and ignoring the innovative work which SNH had developed. The Study Group agreed that the options were limited. Five options were identified:

First, was to disproportionately reduce the discretionary items on conservation measures, such as less work on NNRs, less support for positive management on SSSIs, less support to voluntary bodies for conservation projects and cease grants for habitat and landscape enhancement.

Second, was to scale down the impacts of Natura 2000 and the Biodiversity Action Plans.

Third, and at SNH's suggestion, was the reconfiguring of SNH's decision-making processes and organisational structure, as that was a major element of our plan following our own internal review.

Fourth, was to change SNH's operating principles basically by abandoning the partnership approach.

And finally, as is the norm in these types of exercises, to consider transferring responsibilities to other bodies within the Secretary of State's portfolio.

Wisely, the Study Group concluded that whilst there was some scope to reduce expenditure, it was modest at less than £1 million per annum and 'none of the options could be chosen without attracting opposition or causing significant damage to nature conservation and enhancement'. SNH was well pleased with this wording, in effect the wringing of hands by the Scottish Office officials.

More significantly perhaps was the section entitled 'Other issues for Ministers to consider'. Here the Study Group returned to the hardy perennial of the extent and breadth of SNH's advice to others, whether the research effort was effectively focussed and whether there was effective interaction between the Policy and the Research and Advisory Services Directorates.

We did not accept this point as we thought it was part of the Scottish Office's discomfort about our scientific work and the earlier concerns of Ministers about daring to comment on government policies which could and did have a profound effect on the natural heritage. Curiously, the Scottish Office had instituted a Special Grants (Environmental) Programme with Ministerial approval. We thought this was merely finding something for one of the Environment Department Divisions to do and really did overlap with our work. The Study Group agreed that overlaps should be eliminated, but, inevitably, not in which direction. The Scottish Office were also concerned about our small grants schemes, but we considered them an effective way of working with, for example, schools and community groups. The most important element of 'other issues' was grant assistance to local authorities and other public bodies. This was particularly significant for the Countryside Ranger Programme and Long Distance Routes. There was a clear dilemma here as the Scottish Office officials agreed with SNH that if we withdrew support from these schemes, Local Authorities were most unlikely to fund them with the resulting reduction in activity of benefit to the public. There were more detailed conclusions and recommendations we could live with, but I see from my marginal annotations on my own copy those listed were where we would want to resist. There was therefore still a lot to play for.

The early 1996 target for conclusion of this phase was not achieved. There followed the best part of a year of negotiation on the terms of the Scottish Office's new strategy for SNH. The outcome document published by the Scottish Office *Natural Priorities: Aims and Objectives for Scottish Natural Heritage in the Medium Term*, was published in November 1996. In the foreword, the Earl of Lindsay, the Minister for Agriculture, Forestry and the Environment said:

> Scottish Natural Heritage has made notable achievements in many areas of its work...this new statement now takes account of changes both at home and outside the UK in terms of obligations and aims for the natural heritage, and its enjoyment, and will provide a medium term framework for the next stages of SNH's work. It does, however, retain many important elements from the previous document (*Scotland's Natural Heritage: the Way Ahead*). The most notable of these is that the Government is clear that SNH should

> pursue the full breadth of its remit in an integrated manner. We also want it to retain the operational principles of working in partnership and delegating authority to the local level...I wholeheartedly commend SNH for its achievement to date and look forward to seeing its continued success into the new millennium.

The document concludes with the following statement:

> In this document the Government has endorsed their wish to see SNH continuing to adopt a broad-based multi-functional approach to all of its work, operating in a devolved manner in partnership with other organisations founded on the voluntary principle.

Significantly, it went on to state:

> There is also scope for closer integration with the work of other bodies, for example SOAEFD and SEPA, and the Government will continue to ensure that all bodies within their sphere of influence play their full part in delivering the priorities for the natural heritage set out in this document.

Whether that meant more effective working relations particularly with other parts of the Scottish Office especially SOAEFD, the Scottish Office Agriculture, Environment and Forestry Department, remained to be seen.

One particular statement was of great significance. The government stated that implementing EU obligations and the biodiversity agenda stemming from the Convention on Biological Diversity and the ensuing UK Action Plan 'place inescapable obligations on SNH'. 'The Government's policy is to meet these obligations in full, but to implement the relevant Directives and commitments with a light touch.' This caveat highlighted the dilemma of a Conservative administration in fulfilling these obligations, which they were uncomfortable with, and they felt that while the obligations would have to be implemented, not too much effort should be put into doing so.

The outcome of this review process was the following statement on SNH's priorities for the medium term:

- To promote biodiversity in accordance with the UK Biodiversity Action Plan, and the commitments made by the Government in response to the Biodiversity Action Plan Steering Group report.

- To manage special natural heritage sites, particularly the Government's Natura 2000 programme to implement the EU Habitats and Birds Directives.

- To facilitate the integrated management of the Cairngorms and Loch Lomond and the Trossachs in line with the Government's decisions following the two Working Party reports on these key areas.

- To improve environmental education in Scotland in line with the 'Learning for Life' report which the Government have endorsed as the basis for their policy on environmental education.

- To assist land managers to care for the natural heritage and manage the public's enjoyment of it, including improvements to access to the countryside and in Scotland's hills through a co-operative approach, support to land managers to facilitate the enjoyment and conservation of the natural heritage, and continued co-operation with the Scottish Office and the Forestry Commission on agri-environment measures, woodland networks and other land uses.

- To protect marine and coastal areas through agreed management strategies for Scotland's main estuaries through the 'Focus on Firths' initiative and work with other coastal authorities.

- To work with local authorities to achieve natural heritage and access objectives.

- To support the Central Scotland Forest Initiative.

- To deliver special nature conservation functions at the GB/UK and international levels though the Joint Nature Conservation Committee.

- To advise on the development of polices that affect the natural heritage through the provision of well-focussed and constructive advice to other public and private bodies whose policies and programmes are relevant to the natural heritage.

The Scottish Office, *Natural Priorities: Aims and Objectives for Scottish Natural Heritage in the Medium Term*, 1996

My view was, and remains, that this was a ringing endorsement of what we had done and how we had done it, and what we proposed. It reconfirmed the broad remit, retained the important discretionary functions on environmental education and support to others, the policy advisory role, and the ability to inform and educate through our programmes. It laid to rest many of the issues that had been simmering in the mind of some Ministers and their officials from our establishment. It is a tribute to the input of all staff and, in the case of these reports, to Ian Jardine, in achieving a much greater and objective understanding of SNH by the civil servants than they often liked to have. Being given the green light to pursue the whole remit was an excellent outcome; in other words no salami slicing off of bits that the current politicians or officials did not like.

One of the specific outcomes was the appointment of a new Board member in April 1997, Professor Fred Last, a specialist in ecology and environmental management who had taken an interest in our earlier days through the Royal Society of Edinburgh. This was supposed to strengthen the scientific basis of SNH at Board level, and maybe lessen the role of Michael B Usher. The opposite happened in effect.

Last quickly recognised the scientific capability within SNH and the quality of its advisory output. He also built a good working relationship with Michael Usher to the benefit of SNH. In the meantime, we focussed on the revision of the operation of SNH and the consequential changes to the management structure. Later, Last wrote:

> I write to congratulate you on a job very well done...little did I think that the coming together in Scotland would proceed so smoothly – congratulations.

I turn now to the second part of the Quinquennial Review, the Financial Management and Policy Review. In the light of the earlier exercise reported above, the Scottish Government decided that a very restricted review should be undertaken in 1999. It should focus on performance management covering efficiency measures and the performance indicators, targets and measurements in SNH and the funding relationship and value for money of two programmes - the Cairngorms Partnership and the Central Scotland Countryside Trust. Scottish Government officials took the lead, and we had our top scrutineer and advocate, Lindsay Montgomery, to look after our interests. In the event, we found the findings and recommendations very positive and posing no difficulty for us. The funding arrangements and value for money of CSCT were given a clean bill of health. However, the conclusions on the operation of the Cairngorms Partnership were rather critical in terms of decision-making responsibility, priorities and performance management. One of the outcomes to be resolved was the pension costs to SNH, as this could have a serious effect on our capacity to fund our work, as pension costs have to be the first call on our annual budget; I have noted the successful outcome earlier in this chapter.

Readers might wonder why I have written so many words about these reviews. Basically, they can make or break an organisation, and it is the Chief Executive, in their formal role as Accountable Officer, who is the responsible person in the organisation rather than the Board. I hope readers will find this section illuminating in how the government scrutiny system of its bodies, like SNH, works and in particular how the body itself invests the time of the most appropriate senior staff in steering and contributing to these vital exercises.

Speculation About Mergers

There were many occasions when external interests suggested that other areas of government business should be merged with SNH or *vice versa*. One of the perennial ones was the possibility of merging the Deer Commission for

Scotland, partly as the deer numbers of most species were increasing with proven negative effects on habitat health and recovery. Indeed, successive chairs of the Red Deer Commission for Scotland, and its successor the Deer Commission for Scotland, told me privately that they had never been able to control the population expansion. The idea of merger really came from deer interests. The idea was fuelled quite deliberately by the long-standing Chair of the Deer Commission, Patrick Gordon-Duff-Pennington, who seemed to play a look-both-ways game saying that he agreed with us that this was not an SNH responsibility and then going to the Agriculture Department head and saying that SNH wanted to take over his commission. I always felt, to put it bluntly, that the idea of merging the two functions was a ridiculous idea in theory and practice.

At a time of frequent calls for the 'abolition of QUANGOS' or at least mergers, there was always speculation about merging SNH and SEPA. This was never more than a political totem by political parties in their election manifestos. It was a fundamentally flawed notion as their statutory responsibilities and functions are totally different: advisory for SNH and regulatory for SEPA.

I end with two points on the merger issue:

First, politicians never seemed to consider the implications for the staff in the organisations of their notions for mergers and, therefore, the continuing effectiveness of the running of these organisations. My line to my colleagues was always that it is the functions that are most important, and no government will hand those over to the private sector. Precisely how they are brigaded in one or more bodies is a second order issue. This was precisely the issue about merging CCS and NCC after all: the functions remained but the organisational configuration changed.

Second, the debate was always at the facile level of reducing the number of public bodies as a virility symbol rather than examining the functions that needed to be performed by the public sector and then determining the most effective and efficient way of discharging them organisationally.

External Reviews

Parliament

The Scottish Affairs Committee of the UK Parliament was undertaking a review of Scottish public bodies. We sent in some voluminous evidence as the basis for the oral session which Magnus and I were invited to in London on 20 May 1998. We were questioned for a considerable time by six MPs representing Labour, Conservative, Liberal Democrat and Scottish National Parties and chaired by David Marshall. The record is available as Minutes of Evidence on *The Work of Scottish Natural Heritage*. I just record the closing remarks of the Chair at the end of the evidence session:

> On behalf of the Committee can I say what a pleasure it has been for us because this morning has been a most interesting, informative and enjoyable session, and that is not always the case on these occasions. I would also like to thank both of you for the very frank and full way in which you have answered our questions because that has benefitted the Committee greatly, and I am sure the wider audience will have learnt a lot from this session this morning. On behalf of the Committee, I thank you both very much indeed for your attendance this morning.

If that is not a ringing endorsement of our written evidence and our response in the oral session on behalf of the whole of SNH, I don't know what is. We recorded the session and used it for staff training on how to handle such occasions.

This was the only occasion in ten years when we were invited to give evidence on our work to either the UK or the Scottish Parliaments. I thought it was necessary for us to be asked on more occasions, but that is perhaps an unusual view. Ironically, when Sam Galbraith, the Scottish Environment Minister (all too briefly unfortunately) came into my office on a visit, the first thing he did was to apologise that the MPs had given us a hard time at the oral hearing. I had to say that neither Magnus nor I thought it was hard and that we had enjoyed the opportunity to interact with MPs.

Dealing With External Views

Newspapers, local and national, are always ready and willing to criticise government and its agencies. SNH was frequently a victim. Sometimes maybe we had got things wrong, not consulted effectively and were regarded as a negative force in rural Scotland. Much of this was because of the job we had been given to do on the designation Natura 2000 sites and areas on behalf of government and the inadequate amount of resources provided for undertaking the task. It was in our offices on Skye and in the Western Isles that the weekly publication of the *West Highland Free Press*, masterminded by Brian Wilson, gloried in the headline cartoon of SNH as 'See No People'. I will leave readers to discern the oddity in the phrase and to ascertain what evidence there was of depopulation caused by what we were doing. Rather, we were helping to create jobs by publicising the natural heritage and its wonders through our literature and through our meetings with local communities and with the tourism promotion authorities, all lubricated by our network of local staff.

It is never good practice for the head of an organisation to be forever responding to misreporting by the press. It is best to leave one's powder dry for the few occasions when it really matters to challenge the record and state the organisation's case.

Lest this chapter gives readers the impression that there was always tension between SNH and the Scottish Office and, later, the Scottish Government, I should say that the relationship for the most part worked in practice. However, too often it was left to the discretion of departmental officials as to how it was handled. Perhaps in saying this, I am recalling my own role in the Ministry as the 'gamekeeper' of four NDPBs maybe wishing they were at the sharp end of delivery. Finally, it was fitting that when I had the honour of being presented with a CBE by Her Majesty Queen Elizabeth II at Holyrood Palace, two of the key Ministers from the early days of SNH, Malcolm Rifkind and Sir Hector Munro, were present as members of the Queen's Bodyguard in Scotland, The Royal Company of Archers, to shake my hand in congratulation!

CHAPTER 6

Developing the Organisation

'It is time for change.'

Professor Seaton Baxter, SNH Board member, 1996

'SNH has undertaken useful work in the development of Natural Heritage Zones, and the Government encourage continued development of this work. This zonal system will provide a further basis within which SNH can plan and identify priorities and targets. The production of strategies for each zone could provide a way for SNH to deliver advice to partners with increased consistency and economy.'

The Scottish Office, *Natural Priorities*

'A bold and imaginative way of establishing some high level objectives for the natural heritage of Scotland'.

SEPA Chief Executive commenting on the Nature Heritage Futures Programme

THERE COMES a time in the life of an organisation when it is ripe for making changes in approaches, and consequent adjustments to structure and operations. This is what we did after four years of experience and led to the Organisational Development Programme of SNH in 1996–97 and the development of the Natural Heritage Futures Programme. In this chapter, I describe the initiation of these two programmes which fundamentally changed our frame of reference, the reasons for these changes, the methods we used to develop and implement them, how we organised ourselves internally, how we presented our work and how we engaged with partners.

When the SNH Board invited me to present my future plans for the organisation in late 1995, I described a two-pronged approach: the adoption of a bioregional planning approach and the refocussing of the operation into local delivery and national influencing with the rest of the organisation –

financial and human resources, scientific advice and guidance, providing the service functions. The Board was somewhat taken by surprise as they thought that this was their test of me coming to the end of my five-year contract in March 1997 and deciding whether they should recommend my reappointment. Their surprise was that I was proposing something fundamentally different, by mimicking the best international thinking alongside the pragmatics of delayering the organisational structure and especially giving more power and responsibility to the Areas. On the latter, I had been consistent from the outset that the regions structure inherited from NCC was a necessary bridge from the past to the future. I had made this clear in discussions with the trade unions at the outset of SNH, specifically that within five years the Regions would be abolished, and the Area teams would be given much greater responsibility for delivering our work, fully in tune with and alongside local partners.

This is a long story, but I hope it demonstrates that in approaching external reviews and getting the overseeing Board to understand the blending of international thinking to organisational delivery on the ground, one should have a clear view of the future. Needless to say the senior Scottish Office officials driving the five-yearly review of SNH were distinctly uncomfortable and tried not to have any reference to this thinking and to the changes in the operation, approach and organisational structure in the review report. With Magnus's help, we won the day, as discussed in Chapter 5.

The Organisational Development Programme

Staff, quite reasonably, asked why we needed to change anyway after all of the turmoil of the merger. There were a number of pressing internal and external reasons for change. Internally, our work with Colin Eden and Fran Ackermann at the Strathclyde Business School, our own audit and review work and the development of our Management Strategy gave me and my Management Team colleagues a clear insight of the issues needing to be addressed. I was concerned that the working relationships between the research and advisory services functions and the two points of delivery – national policy and Area delivery – were not working as well as we needed, and the tension between the Resources Directorate and the rest of the organisation called into question who was in charge. In short, we had real issues about where authority lay with too many pulling against each other rather than corporate working together. We had a top-heavy senior management structure, nine was too many now and around five made more sense. Allied to this, the Regional Boards were not quite as effective as they were originally and were taking too much staff time rather than pursuing the external role we needed from them. I also felt that the organisation was ready to devolve roles and responsibilities to be more effective, particularly locally, around Scotland. Last, but by no means least, the workloads carried by staff were getting greater and more intolerable as time passed.

Externally, there were clearly pressures on our funding with public expenditure cuts and demands for efficiency savings from the government, which showed no sign of relenting. The recent pay award made staff very unhappy. There were, rightly, concerns that our pay was lower than that in the government, and that included the Chief Executive! However, we were not our masters in these negotiations. At the same time, the outcome of the SNH Joint Study and the Interim Review led by the Scottish Office, made it clear that we needed not only to fulfil the government's priorities of delivering the results of the three working parties, but also continue to operate across our broad remit and deploy the same operating principles, most especially the staff intensive partnership working. In addition, the external perceptions of SNH were not all that positive: no priorities, too many objectives and plans, always says no, not enough effort in applying statutory duties, and especially insufficient resources on recreation and access, and on protected sites. As Michael Scott reported in *British Wildlife* following interviews with undisclosed environmental NGO leaders:

> As a placeman from the Scottish Office, there is more concern about the pragmatic approach of chief executive Roger Crofts. He is seen as trying to second guess the wishes of his political masters, but this compromising has often served merely to make SNH look ineffective and inconsistent, winning it allies neither in the NGOs nor, it seems, amongst the senior civil servants who have to deal with it.

That was their view, off beam in many respects as the outcome of the Joint Study demonstrated, and showed a total lack of perception of my character. *C'est la vie*!

We were not idle and commissioned our own independent studies in 1996: *Perceptions of SNH's Performance by Partner Organisations* by Deloitte Touche, and *Perceptions of SNH's Performance in Relation to Local Authorities* by the Planning School at Heriot-Watt University. (I discuss these further in Chapter 8.)

The Deloitte Touche study reported in April 1996. It gave a quite different perspective from in-depth responses by 25 bodies across the whole spectrum of our engagement. Staff were regarded as helpful in dealing with partner bodies who also liked doing business with SNH. The publications availability and quality were rated highly, as were consultation procedures, and our work on access and environmental education. There was criticism of the inconsistency in our procedures, for example grants advice, lack of effective programming of research, and the slow response on licensing and management agreements. There were more positive responses on contacts with local staff than centrally-based staff. There were inevitably divergences between those in the environmental NGO sector who were more critical than private sector owner and managers of land. There were concerns about our ineffectiveness on landscape work. In short, there were many useful pointers to feed into our organisational change programme to improve our performance with key partners.

Something needed to be done, but it must not be forced upon us. I was absolutely clear that as Chief Executive I should lead in the development and implementation of a programme of positive change. In reality, this was not change for change's sake. To put it another way, as one of my more perceptive Board members, Seaton Baxter, said, 'It is time for change'.

The key objectives of our revised Management Strategy were to build an effective and credible organisation by providing effective leadership, developing effective and efficient management, developing skill potential of staff, improving job satisfaction, reducing excessive work pressures, improving collaboration within SNH, developing our remit in an integrated way and improving collaboration with key stakeholders. We set up a special unit staffed by volunteers and were supported by three Board members who volunteered to act as a sounding board.

I must underline that I do not believe in structural change in organisations for the sake of it. I have seen too many Chief Executives in government agencies and in charities move the furniture round without thinking what are the strengths and weaknesses of the organisation and what needs to be done to improve the situation. That is what happened in English Nature under its second Chief Executive, and frequently under successive Directors at the NTS, for example. However, I did have discussions with the Chief Executives of English Nature, the Scottish Agricultural College and Historic Scotland, to learn about their approaches to organisational change. Changing the organisational structure is not a purpose, but a consequence of changes in direction and approach, and so should come last rather than first. In SNH, when asked for an organisation chart of the new structure, I produced a diagram with local delivery and national influencing as the two fundamental purposes with the other functions in supportive roles.

I should explain the new structure and new roles which were a consequence of the Organisational Development Programme and, in particular, the new ways of working.

First, the Management Team would be reduced from nine to five Directors. This was aided by the retirement of Duncan Campbell, Chris Fox and Peter Tilbrook and the return of Jane Dalgliesh to the Scottish Office. Lindsay Montgomery remained as Director of Infrastructure Services – personal, finance, IT, audit and review, health and safety, buildings and graphic services. On Lindsay's appointment as Chief Executive of the Legal Aid Board for Scotland, Ian Edgeler was appointed and joined us from the Royal Botanic Gardens of Edinburgh. In addition, Jeff Watson was promoted to the vacant Director role.

Second, the Regions were disbanded as management units, and Areas became the sole focus of local delivery. For more effective working geographically, they were reduced from thirteen to eleven with the amalgamation of Fife, Lothians and Borders to form the Forth and Borders Area and the amalgamation of Speyside with Inverness-shire and Easter Ross to form East Highland. These changes and some early retirements also gave us the opportunity to appoint some new Area Managers. As a result, the four Regional Boards were replaced by three Areas Boards to provide continuing interaction between SNH and interests around the country.

Third, we made the fundamental decision not to continue the separation of policy from local delivery at director level, giving three Directors a combination of national and local directing possibilities - another measure to bring co-ordination across the organisation.

Fourth, we were determined to ensure that staff in the two main delivery areas had all of the data, knowledge and information to undertake their functions effectively. Colin Galbraith, recently arrived from the JNCC in Peterborough, took on the leadership role as Head of Advisory Services. We assigned four staff as Client Services Managers to oversee the provision of these services. In addition, we took the decision that there were staff with great knowledge and expertise and whom we no longer wanted to encumber with managerial responsibilities, so we created Special Advisers on Freshwater, Uplands and Landscape.

Fifth, we retained our National Strategy group of specialists with a co-ordination manager, Jane Clark, whose work was overseen by the three Directors.

Sixth, we decided to create a small Chief Scientist Unit headed by Michael B Usher to lead on our scientific programme, as well as maintaining the lead on the annual thematic conference programme and the production of the proceedings. With Michael's retirement in 2001, this unit was reassigned into the Advisory Services Directorate.

Seventh, the office of the Chair and Chief Executive retained the secretariat, internal and external communications and corporate planning and reporting.

Including staff based at NNRs, we had 37 offices which retained our broad distribution around the country. Finally, and most importantly, we gave guidance and training for all staff on how to improve teamworking throughout the organisation.

When it came to implementation, there was a clear decision to be taken: Do we do it ourselves or do we invite in the help of external consultants? We discussed this with the trade unions and with our middle managers and the answer was unequivocal: we do it ourselves. Champions put themselves forward to help articulate the purpose. A more cohesive organisational spirit emerged as we decided to actively engage the middle managers. Malcolm Lowry, the head of Audit and Review, Moira Monro, the head of the Graphics Section and Roddy Fairley, from the Policy Directorate, all took leading roles. The Board helped with the establishment of a time-limited Advisory Group of four members knowledgeable about running organisations. The objectives were quickly agreed: improved speed and effectiveness of decision-making, increased empowerment, reduced workloads, greater teamworking, increased opportunities for staff development, reduction in staff costs, less effort on administration, reorientate the role and reduce the size of the top management and increase the managerial role of middle managers.

To increase engagement, I established the Management Forum comprising all of the Directors and the middle managers. We met off-site, at the Stirling University Management Centre, bi-annually with an overnight as part of developing a more collegiate style. We simply wanted to encourage staff in all parts of the organisation to get to know their colleagues better, to share their commitment to the same cause irrespective of their role, and to explore how each could help the other. This may sound far-fetched and rather late in the day to readers, but the time was ripe for this to occur. The fact that the Management Forum continued to exist for the next fifteen years at least is support for the importance of this approach. No longer were the Management Team of Chief Executive and the Directors the bogey folk for everything that went wrong or were perceived to be not to the liking of the rest of the staff.

For the early sessions, we had input from David Bolger, an outstanding consultant, who with his wife, Margaret Ford, in Eglinton Management, played an influential role in helping us and other government bodies develop their cultures. Importantly, we invited key external speakers so that we all had a clear view on external thinking and their perception of us. These included the Head of the Agriculture and Environment Department, the Auditor General for Scotland, and heads of the Institute for Customer Service and the Scottish Constitutional Committee.

We agreed what our approach should be as managers in SNH, including leading and directing staff, working as a team, setting an example and improving internal communication.

We held a series of staff conferences around the country with over 90 per cent of staff attending. These were another means of helping staff to feel part of the whole and to get to know their colleagues face-to-face. At each one, my role was to walk round and listen, but also to inculcate our role in providing solutions. I did this through a slide show focussing on our work: protecting the special areas and sites, retrieving the lost species, repairing the damaged areas, repairing the access routes, improving the farmland, developing in harmony with people and business, improving everyone's understanding, working with nature and working with others.

Getting staff over their concerns about change and worries about loss of their job and uncertainty about roles and locations was vitally important, alongside the obvious decline in real terms of our funding and the poor pay deal from the government. It was not just a matter of putting out explanatory notices from the Management Team. It was about the Chief Executive doing the rounds to address these legitimate concerns and seeking staff buy-in. It was about holding seminars for staff focussed on the issues they were most concerned about. But it was also about changing the culture from what I called the vicious triangle of Me/You/Them to the virtuous Circle of Us. Being blunt about behaviours which were unacceptable and converting them into acceptable ones was part of my mission.

No Thanks	**Yes Please**
Blame somebody else	*Shared responsibility*
Not invented here	*Together agree good practice*
Not my idea	*Share good ideas*
Only we are right	*Yes, you are right*
They are wrong	*We get it right jointly*

The number of staff in SNH rose from the 465 at the outset to around 800 on my retirement. Some would argue that this was a profligate use of government money. But that was to misunderstand the largely advisory and influencing role which SNH had by statute and by government edict, and the importance of working in partnership to drive changes in approaches both nationally and locally. I make no excuses for this increase as it was both necessary if we were to be effective in discharging our responsibilities and in taking the many initiatives at our hand or with others. It would have been easy from the narrow-minded perspective of 'efficiency savings', a long-standing government mantra, to reduce the numbers of staff and to close offices around the country. But this was against our principles of operating and would have made us more remote and detached as the predecessor bodies had been, compared with our area-based approach which had been successful in engaging with local issues with both friends and protagonists. Or we could have reduced our research and advisory services, but would we then have increased our expenditure on consultants as many parts of government had done? I never regarded this as good value for public money, unless it was to ensure that we had independent advice on specified issues.

Most important was the ability to recruit new blood to fill the gaps in our expertise. We recruited Land Agents to negotiate with owners of land, nature conservation experts to implement the Natura 2000 programme to tight government timescales, and landscape experts to deal with the many bids for development in the countryside. We also recruited staff who were knowledgeable about energy and climate change so that we could address these growing areas of public policy and development which were only just emerging on the public agenda. Competence and experience were important, but equally so was creativity and commitment to making a difference in the job.

It is important that a Chief Executive has in mind the need to provide career opportunities for staff. One aspect that I really welcomed was the ability to make a number of temporary staff permanent as a result of the roll-out of the Organisational Development Programme and the money, totalling £1 million, that the government had given us to allow early retirement or 'voluntary severance'. In total, 33 cases were approved. Also, I was always keen to hear from staff who wanted to develop their careers, for instance by being given some time to complete an MBA or simply to switch career within SNH, for example, from scientific advice to training, or from area roles to trade union duties. There is a well-known mantra of poor management of 'square pegs in round holes'. That is why I was always keen to support staff movement by encouraging line managers, with the help of personnel staff, to avoid this stupid syndrome. Creativity to meet personal aspirations and sympathy and support to deal with health and domestic issues had to be the guiding mantras, although at times our personnel team were reluctant to aid this humancentric approach which I both espoused and demanded.

Was the programme a success for staff? The findings from a staff survey undertaken by DK Research, led by Douglas Kerr and produced in 1998, were generally positive on understanding aims and objectives, internal relations and communications, coping with workloads and with managers being more approachable. More attention was needed to articulate the Organisational Development Programme. There was criticism of internal recruitment systems, training, and development. A further survey by the same external consultant in February 2002, indicated further positive changes from the previous survey. It showed that there was a more positive atmosphere and staff felt less stressed, better paid, with a greater sense of leadership from managers. They also felt more in touch with what was going on, that their work was more valued, that training and development were taken more seriously and were generally more positive about staff development. Significantly, staff recognised that SNH needed to change, and that organisational development was well understood. Both reports were given to all staff so that no issues were hidden. The survey results speak for staff reactions without any commentary needed from me.

All of this work enabled us to progress our bid for Investors in People status. This was a necessity at the time for all organisations, but the amount of effort for all staff was substantial. At least, we could build on our earlier work on Natural Standards. Eventually, we gained the status in February 2001. The assessors praised staff for their positive attitude and commitment to the work of the organisation and for their ability to implement plans into practical action.

Scottish Natural Heritage Futures Programme

Apart from the further development of an organisational togetherness, the most important initiative I developed was the Scottish Natural Heritage Futures Programme.

I had been in the USA on a busman's holiday looking at national parks and talking to senior staff in the US Parks Service. This led me to think about the relevance or otherwise of different categories of wildlife and landscape protection and, in particular, the placing of boundaries for administrative convenience which did not have a natural rationale. I had recently met Hal Eidsvik, the previous head of Parcs Canada. In a talk at Battleby, he laid out a new spatial framework for Canada's National Parks in the form of bioregions. I had also met Kenton Miller, of the World Resources Institute in Washington and by then the Chair of the IUCN World Commission on Protected Areas, and totally understood his arguments for setting protected areas within their landscape setting of the bioregion. I had read WWF's report on the world's 200 bioregions as a new framework for international conservation. I had also been concerned for some time that the basis of SSSI identification, the Areas of Search, was based on administrative units, counties, which did not provide a rational basis for the distribution of plants, animals or geological and geomorphological features. At the same time, I was becoming increasingly concerned about the amount of our work, in resource terms, which was devoted to the special places, especially nature sites, compared to the insufficient resources given to 'the wider countryside'. Although the EU's adoption of a bioregion approach for the identification of sites to be designated under the EU Habitats and Species Directive was the right approach conceptually, the definition of the regions left a lot to be desired.

The original purpose of this work was to develop a new spatial basis for protected areas to replace the SSSI Areas of Search. I felt that these were anomalous for achieving effective conservation., but it proved not to be feasible to make such a fundamental change after the re-notification of SSSIs in the 1980s and their use to underpin the Natura 2000 designations. It was one of those issues where the Chief Executive was well known for flying a kite to stimulate a debate without a clear outcome, other than to move matters forward. Changing Areas of Search would have meant potentially the removal of some sites and the notification of new ones. The consequent renotifications would have been diverting for SNH and owners and occupiers.

I did not wish to lose a forward-looking positive change, influenced by the best international thinking and practice. Basic work was undertaken by Michael Usher and his team of data experts, aided by review reports by academic colleagues at Aberdeen University. They used the information on biodiversity, geology and geomorphology, soils and topography as the key determinants of biodiversity distribution to come up with a series of bioregions for Scotland. We then added the detailed information on landscape. After a number of iterations, there emerged a series of areas of similar biogeographic characteristics. The approach was data led, even though this was patchy in places. But there had to be a degree of pragmatism in the choice of regions: too many would be too cumbersome to use as a basis for strategy and action, too few would be too great an oversimplification in a country of great natural and landscape diversity. We published our report the *Biogeographical Zonation of Scotland* in 1996 authored by Michael B Usher and David Balharry.

The Scottish Office had given a green light to the Natural Heritage Zones work in *Natural Priorities*. Specifically, this document states:

> SNH has undertaken useful work in the development of Natural Heritage Zones, and the Government encourage continued development of this work. This zonal system will provide a further basis within which SNH can plan and identify priorities and targets. The production of

> strategies for each zone could provide a way for SNH to deliver advice to partners with increased consistency and economy.
>
> The Scottish Office, *Natural Priorities*

When presented to the Head of the Department of Environment and Rural Affairs, I was told firmly that we should not be doing this work. In other words, forward-looking, strategic assessment and developing a programme of partnership activity nationally all around Scotland was regarded as not what we should be doing. I ignored the injunction, maybe because I had just been reappointed as Chief Executive, albeit for only three years, and the Board had strongly supported the programme, and felt it essential to carry on. The real motivation, however, was the strong support of and commitment by staff around the organisation. For us to be allowed to actively think about futures 25 years on and talk actively to partners about them was a release mechanism from the treadmill of designation, management negotiations and responses to planning casework.

We did a great deal of internal and external consultation to ensure that there was support for and buy-in to our proposals and that they reflected local and national views. We also sought international input through a seminar with IUCN colleagues from Canada, the USA and Switzerland and from the Royal Holloway, University of London, Environmental Research Institute (where I had a long-standing honorary position). We led a formal consultation process and amended the documents accordingly. The whole set was launched at a seminar in the Royal Society of Edinburgh in March 2002. As Ian Jardine, my successor as Chief Executive, said in his statement in the SNH Annual Report for 2001-02:

> It is fitting that we were able to publish, shortly before Roger retired, our Natural Heritage Future reports setting out a visionary way how we would wish to see the management of the natural heritage taken forward over the next 25 years.

It seemed to the Board and senior staff that looking forward a quarter of a century was an appropriate matter for SNH to be considering, in full consultation nationally and locally with key partner bodies and communities. This programme really galvanised staff throughout the organisation as I realised when I did my periodic rounds of visits to offices throughout the country and when we met for our twice-yearly Management Forums. The fact that it formed the basis for the strategy of SNH for many years after my retirement is testimony to the outstanding work of colleagues who put flesh on this skeleton and used it as a working tool in their interactions within and outwith the organisation.

The Natural Heritage Futures programme was encapsulated in a suite of documents - reports covering each of the 21 Natural Heritage Areas, together with seven overview documents - Coasts and Seas, Farmland, Forests and Woodlands, Freshwater, Hills, Moors, Settlements, and seven National Assessments - Earth heritage, Freshwater, Habitats, Landscape, Physical aspects, Recreation and Access, and Species.

It is interesting to read, twenty years on, the staff reactions to the publication of all of the documentation which they had achieved:

> 'I enjoyed working on this.'
>
> 'What a concept.'
>
> 'A job well done appreciated by those externals who have seen it so far.'
>
> 'An appropriate testimony to ten years of integrated efforts.'
>
> 'This should help to ensure the forest resource continues to improve.'
>
> 'Bringing the fragments together led to a more substantial whole than I dared to imagine.'
>
> 'It is already receiving praise from many of our local clients.'

And the head of another government agency said publicly, 'A bold and imaginative way of establishing some high level objectives for the natural heritage of Scotland'.

Refreshing Our Approach

There is a danger in always tinkering with words to satisfy the current rhetoric. By 1999, we decided that it was time to refresh our corporate aims and operating principles. We did this in the light of the outcomes of the earlier government review (discussed in Chapter 5) and the Organisational Development Programme, and the new demands placed on us by the government elected in 1997.

Our updated aim was agreed as follows:

> Scotland's natural heritage is an asset locally, nationally and globally. We promote its care and improvement, its responsible enjoyment, its greater understanding and appreciation and its sustainable use now and for future generations.

At the same time, we refreshed our Operating Principles:

> We work in partnership by co-operation, negotiation and consensus, where possible with all relevant interests in Scotland - public, private and voluntary organisations and individuals.
>
> We operate in a devolved manner, delegating decision making to the local level within the organisation to encourage and assist SNH to be accessible, sensitive and responsive to local needs and circumstances.
>
> We operate in an open and accountable manner in all of our activities.

The more difficult aspect of this type of work is how to assess its effectiveness in a particular case or to take an overview of those factors and areas that are more significant than others. We certainly struggled with the assessment part for the landscape.

A New Context: Devolution For Scotland

The devolution settlement with the establishment of the Scottish Parliament and greater ministerial control meant that decision-making was physically closer to Scotland than in Whitehall and Westminster. During this period, there seemed to be a constant change in the Minister responsible for the environment portfolio. This was difficult for the incumbents having little time to make a real difference and for us to build up a relationship with them. Nevertheless, we had very good working relations with Lord Sewel, Sarah Boyack, Rhona Brankin and Sam Galbraith.

We immediately set about refreshing our strategy to reflect these changes. One outcome was the launch of our new agenda *Scotland's Environment for Scotland's People* in October 1999 to reflect the inclusive people-orientated and sustainable development approach of the new administration. Fourteen practical propositions were made to improve Scotland's environment for its people. These included greater integration of policy and action to achieve sustainable development, promotion of good environmental stewardship of land, improving public access to the countryside, enhancing urban environments, securing sustainable use of the marine environment and updating natural heritage designations.

The new administration meant new policy initiatives which we had to address. In addition, we articulated our scientific understanding and developed our policies on issues including Genetically Modified Organisms, climate change, and land reform. On land reform, our approach was more focussed on wise stewardship of land rather than who owned it. In our responses to the Scottish Government's White Paper in 1999, for example, we argued for community involvement rather than necessarily community ownership, for enabling increase in the capacity of communities to manage land, and to be able to work alongside other owners such as environmental bodies. In later responses on the draft Land Reform Bill, we expressed concerns about the lack of attention to the responsibilities and duties placed on owners and on the public. Increasingly, we recognised the need to expand our focus on urban communities. In addition to *Scotland's Environment for Scotland's People*, we continued and augmented the *Countryside In and Around Towns* programme we had inherited from CCS. To this we added a *Greenspace for Communities Initiative* in 2000.

CHAPTER 7

Dealing With Contentious Issues

'Many difficult areas primed for conflict have been dealt with and defused.'

John Goodfellow, CBE, Former President
National Farmers Union Scotland, 1999

'Skeins mean strife – incoming flights of geese will bring a gaggle of problems to Islay.'

Headline in *The Herald*, 13 October 1997

'Jobs versus nature in battle for mountains.'

***The Independent*, 6 May 1996 (on Cairngorm funicular proposals)**

THERE ARE always debates about how to resolve contentious issues when it comes to the interaction between local communities, economic development and the care and management of species, habitats and landscapes. Invariably, these can become highly polarised and set back relationships that have been built up and can take inordinate amounts of time by all concerned. In the end, only time, willingness to listen to and engage with opposing interests, identifying areas of common ground and shared objectives can provide a way forward to addressing them.

In doing our job we had to face criticism in the media on many occasions. Sometimes it was well wide of the mark and extremely hurtful to staff locally. It sought to undermine us and damage our reputation. Here are just a few quotes to illustrate this point:

> 'Every pound allocated to SNH is a pound less for education, health and regional councils.' Lochcarron Community Council, 16 July 2001.

> 'SNH is a tyrannical bunch of lunatic environmentalists.' Councillor Manford, Barra, 21 October 2001.

> 'SNH is a state organisation that is effectively back door nationalisation of the land.' John Scott, MSP.

> 'SNH are becoming intolerable in the way they are operating. They are becoming the bureaucratic eco-warriors. If SNH keeps trying to stop development and regulate crofting, Harris will become wilderness.' Councillor Angus Graham, Harris.

> 'Magnus Magnusson has masterminded a buck passing operation to the Cairngorms Partnership. I suggest he and SNH have opted out of responsibility and leadership . The two organisations SNH inherited must be turning in their graves.' Roger Carr, former chair of CCS, letter to press, 10 May 1996.

> 'SNH do not want deer or stalking as a dynamic business.' Max Hastings, *The Field*, December 1998.

Fortunately, we worked with many people farming the land, fishing our waters and living in rural communities who made their positive views of our work and our relationships with them abundantly clear to staff. They were the silent majority with a considered view, but did not often get a hearing in the media. Even the West Highland Free Press, one of SNH's most vociferous critics in their weekly columns, did flatly reject some of the criticisms. In relation to fencing of the machair on Barra to keep out rabbits to protect the habitat of value to nature and to the crofters, the newspaper stated categorically:

> it is not SNH nor the Barra bunnies which should now be the object of public ridicule but the Councillor for Barra.

Here are some positive examples to give a more balanced picture.

> 'Island's geese lay golden eggs.' *Sunday Mail*, 1 August 1993.

'Red Kite soars back after successful breeding season.' *The Scotsman*, 5 January 1996.

'Scottish Crofters Union relaxed about Peatland Management Scheme.' *West Highland Free Press*, 15 October 1999.

'25 year vision for a greener Scotland.' *The Scotsman*, 19 March 2002.

'Keeping feathers unruffled – partnership is best way to resolve Hen Harrier dispute.' *The Herald*, 15 November 2000 (referring to Arran).

And. finally a classic example of blaming the messenger and failing to understand where the formal decisions lay:

> 'Happiest press release of the week across my desk was one from Scottish Natural Heritage. In God's absence, our land's nature is looked after by the mega quango. After decades of delay and years of consultation they have finally given permission for beavers to be released in Knapdale.'
>
> Peter Clarke, *The Scotsman*, 2000.

There were many such issues affecting the state and use of the natural heritage that required the attention of the SNH Board, senior management and staff locally and nationally. Some were tendentious locally and had national ramifications for decision-making and policy. In this chapter, I will deal with many of these that were concerns during my time in SNH, including the Lingarabay super quarry planning application on Harris, the protection of the peatlands in Caithness and Sutherland and on Lewis, the protection of the Cairngorms plateau in the context of ski development in the Northern Corries and the proposals for a mountain railway, the ownership and management of the island of Rùm, and the reintroduction or translocation of species. Readers will no doubt have their own views for whatever reasons. All I aim to do is to expose the issues as I recall them during my time as SNH Chief Executive.

Agriculture

Early on, SNH decided that it should produce a statement on agriculture and the natural heritage. The Board, including its farmer members, all felt that this was essential given the extent of agriculture in Scotland, over 80 per cent of the land surface under its various forms of practice. A warning shot came over the phone from one of my colleagues in the Department of Agriculture to tell me that the Minister for Agriculture was very annoyed at SNH undertaking this work as agriculture was none of its business. Ironically, it was that Minister who had been on the Council of the old NCC and was well versed in its work. At least, I had a friend in the Ministry to privately say, 'A word in your shell-like ear'. Despite his help, we were generally disappointed with the approach by the Department of Agriculture and their lack of engagement with us.

We produced our substantive report, *Agriculture and Scotland's Natural Heritage*, in late 1994. We expressed concern about overgrazing by sheep, backed by the results of joint research with the Macaulay Land Use Research Institute and the Scottish Agricultural College. We argued for an incentive scheme for the management of the natural heritage on farms through a partnership programme for conservation and enhancement.

In 1995, the House of Commons Scottish Affairs Committee was undertaking an Investigation into the future of Scottish Agriculture. We sent in our substantive written evidence placing the environment as one of many factors influencing the agricultural industry. We argued the importance of developing farmers' roles as environmental stewards in the hope of achieving a switch from the intensive practices that had a detrimental effect on the natural resources of the farm, most particularly the fundamental resource - the soil. We argued the need for codes of practice to provide sustainability standards. John Thomson, Peter Pitkin and I gave oral evidence on 27 March 1995. We gained a fair hearing and got over some key points: on developing tailor-made agri-environmental schemes, developing longer term set-aside with more environmental benefits, supporting the role of agriculture practised carefully in maintaining the natural environment, the role of farm conservation plans and the importance of advisers such as FWAG. This was a sea change from our early years when the Minister had complained about us having any views on, or role in, agriculture.

We continued our agricultural work. One particularly important element was developing a project to harness new technology into improving agricultural practice from an environmental perspective. Joyce Tait and Peter Pitkin led on this initiative - TIBRE (Targeted Inputs for a Better Rural Environment) was the result. A manual of possibilities was produced, and we held demonstration and training sessions with farmers. The work attracted a great deal of interest among farmers, advisers, consumer organisations, and the agrochemical and biotechnical industries. This approach changed the dynamic of our relationship with the farming industry. We were not seen as a threat but a helpful partner. This project was also an example of how to play to the strengths of colleagues, as Joyce Tait who had joined us from an academic institution, had a track record on how to use technology for environmental benefit.

Throughout the decade, we promoted and supported conservation advice to farmers through substantial funding to the Farming and Wildlife Advisory Groups (FWAG). The farm advisers were key to this work, alongside the more business-orientated advisers from SAC. It did seem logical to increase effectiveness and to provide a more integrated approach that FWAG and SAC should be merged into one operation. Unfortunately, the SAC leaders were not supportive, and tried to take over the FWAG functions in a cack-handed manner. Following a joint review we undertook with the Agriculture Ministry, it was agreed that we would continue to fund farm conservation advice directly through FWAG.

Despite our representation, through our Chair, on the Forward Strategy for Agriculture group chaired by the joint Agriculture and Environment Minister, Ross Finnie, from 2000 onwards, we saw little change. Environmental measures remained as no more than a peripheral element of agriculture, whose primary purpose remained to produce food.

I conclude that despite our continuing interaction with the farming community, the funding of farm conservation advice and application of innovative thinking, we made little progress. Even though ministerial portfolios usually brought together agriculture and environment, and many Ministers were more than sympathetic to our arguments, the agricultural lobby in Scotland and more widely in Europe ruled. So there was little forward momentum for changing the EU Common Agriculture Policy to fundamentally recognise the dual role of farmers in producing food and being stewards of the soil and other natural resources of their land.

Deer Management

There was, and still is, a perennial problem of increasing numbers of deer, especially Red and Roe Deer, and the detrimental effect they have on the regeneration of woodlands and degraded habitats in the uplands. How best to resolve this was a recurring question. Reorganising the agencies, for example by switching the functions, a typical idea of those wishing to move difficult tasks somewhere else, was invariably made without detailed consideration of how to resolve the issues. In this case, it was perfectly clear what action needed to be taken - use all of the powers in the legislation to force a reduction in the deer population. The boundary lines between SNH and the Red Deer Commission (RDC) were clear and reinforced by the Minister responsible for both matters: the RDC takes the lead and SNH provides scientific input. Interestingly, as the Minister made clear late in 1992, via his officials, both the Commission and the Deer Management Groups needed to place more focus on reducing numbers to achieve a better ecological balance with their habitat. The problem has always been that the system is run on a 'voluntary basis' so that landowners individually, and collectively through the Deer Management Groups, should voluntarily reduce numbers. However, the land-owners did not see the high numbers as a problem, rather they wished to retain them as part of their sporting estate credentials and as the valuation of their land was based on the number of shootable stags. This position ignored the evidence emerging from the longest-running and scientifically-accredited study of red deer led by Tim Clutton-Brock and his colleagues at Cambridge University on Rùm.

We produced our report *Red Deer and the Natural Heritage* in September 1993, a mark of the urgency we placed on moving matters forward. It was a good example of joint Board and staff working together, with the Earl of Strathnaver chairing the group, supported by Des Thompson and Peter Reynolds. It was our first policy paper supported by a robust evidence base. Our arguments were that management of deer needed to be improved by persuading all Deer Management Groups to draw up management plans. We suggested a demonstration project with dissemination of the scientific results through the deer management networks. The East Grampian Deer Management Group agreed to the pilot, influenced, no doubt, by David Laird, one of our Board members, who was deeply involved in deer management in the area.

We also recommended that changes were needed to the deer legislation. Inevitably perhaps, the response of the RDC was negative, and they ensured that reservations were also expressed by the government agriculture department. We, therefore, amended our paper, and with the help of Sir Hector Monro, the Environment and Deer Minister, launched it in June 1994. We followed this up with a costed action plan later that year. Our arguments had evidently found favour as the new Deer (Scotland) Act came into force in December 1996. In turn, we produced a manual on how to assess habitat damage. We remained concerned that there was insufficient commitment by the renamed Deer Commission for Scotland (DCS) to management plans for all of the Deer Management Groups. The name change did, however, recognise that the 'deer problem' was not only the Red species, but also Roe and the increasing spread of the Sika and Muntjac species, including the fact that hybridisation between the smaller species was increasing.

There were powers in the legislation to compel owners of the deer range to reduce numbers if there was a case for doing so because of the damaging effect on protected habitats. We put forward two cases at the beginning of the new millennium, one on Glas Maol at the head of Glen Isla and the other in the Inchnadamph area of Assynt. Needless to say, these were not pursued by the government or the DCS!

We had tried an entirely different approach in the mid-1990s. How could the consumer be persuaded to eat more venison? With the help of the Prince of Wales, following our meeting with him at Sandringham, we began discussions with the supermarket chain Safeway. They agreed to a trial of selling venison in target stores in Scotland. Unfortunately, the approach did not work commercially for them. There is a long-standing myth amongst consumers that venison has a strong flavour and is difficult to cook. Whereas, in my experience, it is mild in flavour, there are many ways of cooking it without necessarily strengthening the flavour using juniper berries, and it is a very healthy red meat as the animal is an herbivore with no medical additives in its diet.

Commercial Forestry

We inherited clear thinking from both CCS and NCC on the effects of commercial forestry on nature and on landscape, respectively. Our forestry review concluded in 1993 that there needed to be a greater focus on management of commercial forestry as well as on the management of native woodlands. We also argued for changes to the financial support regime to recognise the need for tax adjustments to support new plantings in their early years. There was a great deal of case work to which we had to respond via the Regional Forestry Advisory Groups. All too frequently the commercial perspective won the day in decisions about grant aid for new planting. In our position statement on forestry in 1999, we made it clear that more attention needed to be placed on safeguarding the natural heritage interests and on the role of communities in decision-making on planting. We did not give up our advocacy, based on the expertise of woodland staff and the knowledge of staff around the country, but it was always an uphill battle against the commercial forces of the timber industry.

We had played a more effective role in supporting the various native woodlands initiatives around Scotland. For example, we provided financial support for Highland Birchwoods for planting, for management and for promoting the use of birchwood in the construction industry. On our own land, particularly on Rùm, we attempted to demonstrate the value of native wood, such as pine and birch, for commercial purposes.

Birds of Prey and Grouse Moor Management

It was obvious from the surveys undertaken through JNCC for all of Britain that there was a serious problem of raptor persecution in certain areas of Scotland and northern England. These seemed to coincide with areas where the land was primarily used for grouse shooting. Far too many owners and their staff regarded raptors, such as Hen Harriers, Merlin and Golden Eagles, as vermin, especially as they claimed that these birds ate grouse chicks to the detriment of the sporting business of their estate. It was, therefore, regarded by them as fair game to kill raptors. It was a particular problem on estates in the Angus Glens, in the Monadhliaths, and in southwest Scotland. Our meetings with the Scottish Landowners Federation (SLF) were not at all productive in our early days as their leaders felt that they were in the right, even despite the clear statutory protection of these birds and their habitats through the Protection of Birds Act 1954.

What was a way forward? We held conferences and commissioned research with other bodies, such as the Game Conservancy Trust. However, there was no meeting of minds. A breakthrough came with the endeavours of Colin Galbraith and Des Thompson, our own accredited experts on raptors and moorland management, aided by Ian Newton, the internationally-recognised expert on raptors, with the Duke of Buccleuch as a major owner of grouse moors. There was an unresolved issue on Buccleuch's Langholm Moor about the decline in grouse bags and its causes. Some of us felt that this was the result of overgrazing by sheep and poor muirburn practice over many decades. This was certainly evident to me when I paid a visit to the area with Ian Newton and the Duke, and noted the steady decline in grouse bags since the 1920s depicted on graphs in the estate office. However, the estate and certainly some of its employees took a different stance. The Duke, always a thoughtful and conscientious manager, felt there was a possibility of some trials. Colin and Des, with the input of other experts, developed an experiment of supplementary feeding whereby laboratory mice and day old chicks were fed to Hen Harriers as a substitute for wild food. These trials were at considerable cost to the estate and to the statutory partners, English Nature, JNCC and SNH. Certainly, the research resulted in a diminution of grouse chick predation, but it was helped by an instruction by the Duke that no illegal activity would be tolerated on his estate. There remained, however, disagreement between the experts on the interpretation of the results. A further study was commissioned, with substantial financial contribution from the Duke. This work certainly brought the different sides together and placed SNH in the leading role of seeking solutions.

One of the outcomes was agreement of the parties to establish a Moorland Forum in 2002 to succeed the Moorland Working. It was chaired by Lady Isabel Glasgow and included a wide range of member bodies around the table to seek practical solutions to upland management, including the vexed issue of raptor persecution. It was backed by the formation in the same year of the Scottish Raptor Monitoring Scheme, including key NGOs and the Scottish Raptor Studies Groups.

This matter demonstrates two essential truths. First, that trials of different approaches using the best scientific knowledge and expertise is a necessary part of seeking solutions. Second, and more fundamentally, getting the disputatious parties around the table is a necessary mechanism to tease out common ground, isolate the sticking points and achieve solutions for the future. It is then for recommendations to be made to government. It will only act when it is expedient for them to do so, for political and/or financial reasons.

Rùm

The island of Rùm was sold to the Nature Conservancy by the Bullough family in 1957 for the sum of £23,000. It is an amazing example of the diversity of natural heritage and made it a key place for SNH to care for. Its mountains were formed when the North Atlantic began to open and are examples of the volcanic activity still seen in that geological province, for instance in Iceland. These formations provided the laboratory for greater understanding of the formation of rocks in the magma chamber of the volcanoes erupting at the time. The Rùm Cuillin is also an excellent ridge walk, not quite on a par of difficulty or length with the Cuillin Ridge of Skye, but, nevertheless, a memorable experience that can be done over a long day. The western hills exhibit probably the best range of landforms produced by periglacial activity in Britain at the end of the last glacial period. The island is the breeding ground of many birds protected under the EU Birds Directive, including Red Throated Divers, and a very large colony of the burrowing Manx Shearwaters. The herd of Red Deer, introduced from southern England in the nineteenth century, has been the source of groundbreaking and internationally recognised research on these ungulates led by Tim Clutton-Brock of Cambridge University and his colleagues, including Fiona Guinness, and Josephine Pemberton of Edinburgh University. This work has provided a greater understanding of the animal ecology of the species which has been used in their management. The island is also the location for the original attempts to reintroduce the White-tailed Eagle (Sea Eagle) to Scotland in the 1970s. Unfortunately, it never worked for reasons which are still not apparent despite the best efforts of staff, led by the late John Love, the amazing naturalist and author of many books about the island. More recently, the disappearance of trees on the island due to overgrazing and felling for human use has begun to be reversed by planting of native species grown from seed in the tree nursery. All in all, therefore, Rùm is an entirely appropriate island for SNH to own and manage on behalf of the nation. It is truly 'Nature's Isle' as Magnus Magnuson called it in his excellent book of that title.

However, the ownership comes with two difficulties - the maintenance of Kinloch Castle and the management of the human community. The castle was built in the late nineteenth century by the owners, a wealthy family producing machinery for the Lancashire cotton industry. It contains many unique and probably priceless features, such as an orchestrion complete with all of its 'bells and whistles', a hydro-electric plant - probably one of the first in Britain built not only to heat the house but also to allow tropical plants and animals, including alligators, to be kept there. The plumbing in some of the bedrooms were early versions of what we might call a jacuzzi. There is a fully-fitted billiard room complete with its own air extraction system from the days when male snooker players smoked cigars during the game. I tell this so you will realise that maintenance of this building and its artefacts is not the responsibility of a natural heritage agency. But nevertheless, we had to maintain the property and its contents at the considerable cost of at least £0.25 million a year to our budget.

The ownership of the castle is a moot point. Previous attempts by my predecessor, Morton Boyd, to broker a deal with the NTS to take over ownership only failed at the last moment because of the likely costs to NTS. Our attempts to persuade Ministers that it should be handed over to Historic Scotland were rebuffed. Nevertheless, we were still blamed for the cost of maintenance on our budget. We looked at many options for its use, including a high-quality hotel for foreign visitors, an environmental education and training centre, and a museum. But none of them was financially viable. Even the interest of the then Prince of Wales through the BBC TV series *Restoration* to protect cultural assets did not result in much-needed resources, as Kinloch Castle did not get the public vote in the final round. He later told me of his disappointment at not being able to help us, especially given his track record, for instance, in the Dumfries House renewal project and the programme of local employment it has achieved there.

We made the mistake of inviting experts from the National Museum of Scotland to assess the castle's contents. I say mistake because they concluded that nothing should be changed, the threadbare furniture coverings should be left as they were, the photograph albums of the Bullough's family visits on their motor yacht around the globe were not to be made available for the public to examine. Any ideas we had of the fabrics being repaired or replaced or the precious items being taken to a museum were thwarted by their intervention, and, more particularly, our preferred option of converting it into a high-quality hotel and field studies centre were negated. I regard this as a failure of my tenure. Interestingly, only now are moves being made towards the possibility of selling or even demolishing the castle.

SNH staff lived on the island. One family, the MacIvors, had an intergenerational presence. However, it was difficult to recruit families to live there for more than a few years. Although there was a single teacher school, paid for at great cost by Highland Council, there were never more than a handful of pupils. Once children reached secondary school age, they had to go to the school in Mallaig and stay there during the week. Hence any staff recruited to the island with young families stayed for only a short time until their children reached secondary school age.

In effect, there were two communities living on the island, the Cambridge University researchers at Kilmory and SNH staff in Kinloch village. For the most part relations were fine, but there were times when, should I say, unfortunate liaisons occurred and jealousies built up. On occasion, we had to summon the police from the mainland to sort matters out, in one instance to confiscate a rifle from someone not normally resident on the island.

Another, more fundamental, issue arose in the later 1990s, stimulated by the demand for community development and ownership of land and property in remote areas of the Highlands and on islands like Rùm. With the successful community buy-out on Eigg, there was pressure from local councillors and some members of the North Areas Board to release land to people who wished to live on the island. I thought this was taking conformity of approach to community ownership to an extreme extent and would make it very difficult to manage an already difficult situation. Why, in any event, should Rùm not be managed as Nature's Island rather than a community buy-out? After my retirement, I recall visiting Rùm with John Love in 2010, during the course of a lecture cruise we were undertaking for the NTS. We were disgusted at the mess around Kinloch village, totally out of keeping with a naturally and culturally important island, although fitting with the rhetoric of politicians without thinking of the consequences.

My conclusion is that government does not always act to resolve a problem by assigning the responsibility to the appropriate body. It then blames the lack of change and the consequential financial expenditure on the body left with a burden, neither of its own making, nor at all relevant to its purpose.

Landownership and Management in the Cairngorms

Another issue regarded the Cairngorms from the points of view of maintaining and upgrading ski infrastructure on the north facing slopes and who should own and manage the land in Glenfeshie and on Mar Lodge specifically.

First, I'd like to remind the reader of the international status of the Cairngorms natural heritage. In 1989, when I was responsible for nature and countryside in the Scottish Office Environment Department, we successfully put forward for the Cairngorms to be placed on the UK Government's Tentative List for World Heritage Site status. The reasons for its Outstanding Universal Status were clear: the ancient remains of the magma chambers from the volcanic part of the Carboniferous period being exhumed and uplifted and later planed by processes we are still not entirely sure about into a plateau surface. Thereafter, on numerous occasions, the valleys were deepened by the action of glaciers within the Cairngorms icecap, but surprisingly the plateau remained largely untouched, as originally described by David Sugden in his PhD thesis on the glaciation of the Cairngorms. Either the overriding ice, or periglacial activity, resulted in the exhumation of the tors on some of the tops revealing also the process of chemical weathering. Added to this, in the straths and glens are remnants of more extensive shrub and pine woodlands. It was the geological and geomorphological features that we thought scored highly, also recognising the high biodiversity interest from the valley bottoms to the mountain tops. However, the nomination was never taken forward, partly because the UK Government had other priorities and partly because of concern that it was not as unique as we thought given the existence of similar features and genesis in Baffin Land. Whatever the outcome, the area is vitally important as a place for the natural heritage in all of its forms and dimensions.

One particular aspect of the Cairngorms was the naturalness of the River Feshie. This had been studied intensively by the expert fluvial geomorphologist, Alan Werritty, and his research team at Dundee University, as an example of a gravel-bed river system. He and his research students, two of whom, Ness Brazier and Cath Lees, we were fortunate to recruit to SNH, advised us on the problems of extraction of gravel from the river, particularly from the depositional fan at the confluence with the River Spey. The local landowner had been extracting gravel and disturbing the natural system, and not unreasonably, SNH wanted this to cease given the SSSI protection status of the site. We placed a Nature Conservation Order on this activity, basically a stop notice. This eventually led to a Public Inquiry which concluded that the *status quo* should remain in view of the scientific importance of the river, but there should be allowance for maintenance work. In other words, an uneasy compromise was reached.

One long-standing issue has been the level of deer numbers and the effect that this has had on the regeneration, or otherwise, of the natural vegetation most affected - Caledonian pine on the lower slopes, willow and other mountain species on the plateau and the two types of juniper *Juniperus communis* - prostrate and vertical on Speyside. We had known for years that restricting herbivores by erecting enclosures, for example on Mar Lodge Estate around Derry Lodge and in Glenfeshie near the Lodge, was proving that shrub and tree level regeneration would occur. We took the SNH Board and the North East Regional Board to see the former site in spring 1995. Seeking to reduce deer numbers was not just about the ineffectiveness of the local Deer Management Group, but also about the attitude of the landowners and their staff. This raised the questions of who owned the land and what chances were there for changes. This proved to be a very vexing issue, albeit the outcome for the natural heritage was soon very positive and has remained the case. Let me tell the reader more of the SNH involvement.

We had been told quite bluntly by our Minister, Sir Hector Monro, on more than one occasion in our early years, that we should not own land nor become involved in funding landownership by environmental charities, nor indeed have any involvement in influencing landownership. We accepted the injunction on the former two points, but we could not ignore the later point because ownership and the stewardship of the natural heritage are usually linked. In the Cairngorms, there was a mixed pattern of ownership. We owned a small area of land, Inshriach on Speyside, and we had the aforementioned long-standing management agreement with Rothiemurchus Estate. RSPB was undertaking large-scale habitat management on its Abernethy estate. But other areas were, to say the least, poorly managed with too many deer leading to overgrazing and arresting the growth of the natural vegetation. Of particular concern, was the position on two co-joining estates – Mar Lodge and Glenfeshie.

The latter had been in the long-term ownership of the Dulverton family whose base was in Devon. It was heavily overgrazed, but the management seemed to have no intention of positive action. As the owners aged, their enthusiasm seemed to wane. Also, environmental NGOs, led by Ramblers Scotland and its campaigning Director, Dave Morris, started a public campaign for change and established a consortium to bid for the estate. This prompted some of my Board members and myself to consider alternatives. A possible consortium with the right motivation and the resources was put together, Will Woodlands, with reduction in deer numbers as a priority, and a potential bid for forestry grant aid, but with the contentious possibility of fencing to protect the young trees from browsing by deer. This did not please the eNGOs as it was not known publicly who the consortium was. A journalist started to probe into this and, unfortunately, a conversation between myself and one of my Board members was tapped by a journalist with a threat to publicise this. Needless to say, that was stopped by the journalist's bosses, but it did demonstrate the need to be careful on the old style mobile phones. More particularly, it demonstrated the level of public interest about achieving ownership of estates that would be beneficial to habitats and to public access. The particular arrangements failed and, out of the blue, the estate was bought by a Danish retail magnate who was not known in Scotland.

By this time, the Labour administration had taken over the government and the Minister of State responsible to SNH, land and other issues, Lord Sewel, felt it was important that the new owner understood his responsibilities to the public in taking over this land. He, therefore, sent the Head of the Environment Group in the Scottish Government and me to Copenhagen to meet and brief the new owner, Klaus Helmerson. He and his business partner, Jørgen Smidt, were surprised at this, as clearly his agent in pursuing the purchase transaction had not briefed him on the issues of management of habitats and access. He listened, but was perplexed. He realised that he had taken on a responsibility that had not been anticipated as his intention was to run this as a private estate with no interference on management and with limited access. He was more interested in sporting estate management, particularly deer stalking and salmon fishing, with limited deer culls. He did not see any habitat degradation that others were claiming or the need for woodland restoration. The ambiguities which we detected in the owner's views about the role of government and the vociferous lobbying particularly by Ramblers Scotland, maybe put him off and, after a while, the estate ownership was transferred to another Danish businessperson and then, later still, to the current owners, Anders and Anna Povlsen.

The Povlsens have an amazing 200-year vision for the land and have, with their estate managers led by Thomas McDonnell until recently, significantly reduced the deer numbers to the extent that the natural vegetation of the herb, shrub and tree levels has grown at a rapid rate. I conclude this story with a visit that many of those involved, in one way or another, with demanding change in access and land use on Glenfeshie, gathering for the award of the Royal Scottish Geographical Society's Geddes Environment Medal to Dick Balharry just before he died. We were celebrating his outstanding and charismatic environmental advisory work to estate owners and on improving natural habitat management. The Povlsens were our hosts with me, as the then Chair of RSGS, having the privilege of presenting the Medal to Dick.

The story of the ownership of the Mar Lodge Estate followed a slightly different course in the 1990s and early into this millennium. It marches with Glenfeshie on its west side and stretches from the high ground to the south of the Dee valley to the High Tops of the Cairngorms. Its ownership had a somewhat curious passage. In the 1960 and 1970s it was owned by two Swiss brothers who decided, in keeping with ideas of the times, to establish a ski development. Snow surveys during that period showed that snow retention in the corries of Beinn a' Bhùird were good, but before moving into the mountains the two brothers developed a small ski tow on the south-facing slope behind Mar Lodge. The remnants of the buildings can still be seen. Needless to say, this did not work. But in preparation for the Beinn a' Bhùird development, the owners created a vehicular track onto the summit plateau. I mention this because it was one of the most successful and early interventions in restoration at high altitude undertaken by the NTS when it took over the ownership later on.

A wealthy businessman from the USA, Mr Kluge, took over the ownership, ostensibly to satisfy his wife's wish to have a base near to the Royal estate at Balmoral. Magnus Magnusson, David Laird and I met him for a discussion in June 1992 about how we hoped the estate would be managed and what type of management agreement we envisaged to achieve this. This was all news to him, and we left him in a perplexed state. It was no surprise that not long after our visit, he called us to say that he had decided to put the estate on the market. Many manoeuvres then sprang into action, The eNGOs wanted to ensure that they had a key role. RSPB showed a strong interest in purchasing the estate as it would give them ground on the southern side of the Cairngorm massif to match their Abernethy estate on the north-west side. A consortium of eNGOs sought to fashion a bid, but no agreement was reached, and we were concerned that this would lead to lack of clarity on the management. There was a stronger preference for a single owner or single body. We could see the advantage of ownership by an environmental charity and worked behind the scenes to raise interest in the NTS. This did not please other eNGOs. Interestingly, a private charity, the Easter Trust, which later we discovered was funded by the Salveson family based in mid Aberdeenshire, were prepared to contribute to the purchase.

The most important funding sources by far, however, were the National Heritage Memorial Fund (NHMF) and the Heritage Lottery Fund (HLF). Unusually, the Trustees of these two bodies were prepared to provide a capital grant for the purchase and an endowment fund to support the operation of the estate. I say unusual in that the norm of lottery bodies, and indeed government agencies, was to provide money for purchase and leave the new owner to fund the operating costs. This was very evident when colleagues from the other nature and countryside agencies and I gave evidence to the House of Commons Culture, Media and Sport Committee on 12 November 1998. There was a clear difference of opinion between us and the committee about endowment as they just were not prepared to understand that the offer of capital grant did not secure the perpetual care of heritage assets, irrespective of whether it was land, buildings, art works or whatever. I argued that all lottery grants should be given with a reasonable set of conditions and, more fundamentally on endowments, I stated in my oral evidence (as reproduced in the published transcript):

> Everybody seems to think that the endowment to the NTS for Mar Lodge was a mistake.....but I happen to think this was the right way round in the funding package, Why is there such reservation...about giving endowments compared with capital grant? I can see the difficulty of providing ongoing revenue funding whereas endowments can secure the future.

Fortunately, we won the argument in this case with NHMF/HLF providing the two elements of financial support for purchase and for management. SNH indicated that it was prepared to offer a long-term management agreement. So the deal was done. The consequence was, however, not easy in terms of turning round the management of the estate. The Easter Trust appeared to be the tail that wagged the dog despite the fact that their financial contribution was significantly less than that from the Lottery sources and the cumulative grant from SNH. They insisted on the estate having a sporting management objective alongside a conservation objective. Although this applied specifically to the Dalvorar beat on the south side of the River Dee, it influenced the whole attitude to management. Unfortunately, this situation dragged on for years, sadly, I have to say even after my retirement from SNH, throughout my tenure as a member of the Council and then of the Board of NTS. Despite various reviews to resolve the situation, it was not until the second decade of this century that resolution was achieved. I am quite clear that NTS, of which I am a Life Member and former Chair of its Conservation Committee, has the prime responsibility for caring for the cultural and natural heritage and that it should not run Mar Lodge Estate as a sporting estate. Not long before writing this section, I revisited Glen Quoich, and was delighted to observe that the Scots pine was regenerating rapidly and climbing up the valley slopes. Clearly the deer numbers had been reduced to allow this to happen, and it is testimony to the current management and the effective working of the SNH/NTS management agreement.

This proves that long-term visions do indeed take a long time to be developed, agreed and implemented especially when there are countervailing forces of traditional estate management involved in the decision-making process.

The Cairngorms Ski Developments

The reader might begin to think that this book is turning into a story about the Cairngorms. Suffice to say that there were so many issues which SNH became involved in. One very significant one was the ski developments at Coire Cas and Coire na Ciste on the northern slopes overlooking the Spey valley. I will not go into the long history of argument about the development, in particular the divisive Public Inquiry about the proposals to extend the ski development westwards into the remaining Northern Corries on the one hand and the argument for protecting the Northern Corries, particularly Coire an t-Sneachda and Coire an Lochain on the other. Just to note that as a civil servant with responsibility for Highland Development, I was party to a number of financial rescue operations for the ski development on public land overseen by the former HIDB.

The contentious issue for SNH was the proposal by the Cairngorms

Chairlift Company and Highlands and Islands Enterprise (the successor to HIDB) to construct a funicular railway up Coire Cas to the summit of Cairngorm. Our responsibility was for the protection of the plateau area which the government had agreed should be designated as an area of European significance under the EU Birds and Species & Habitats Directives. Most observers had known for a long time that the old chairlift was well past its use date, and international experts had advised HIE on the alternatives. A funicular railway was the preferred means of improving skier uplift. Our concern was to ensure that this did not result in more visitors onto the very fragile plateau, creating erosion and resulting potentially in the UK Government being challenged by the EC for not protecting the designated area to the extent which the Directives required. We held meetings with the Cairngorms Chairlift Company. To our surprise they offered 'a closed system' - users of the funicular would not be able to access the plateau from the top station. We probed them on this realising that their ability to deliver such as system would mean that our concerns to protect the European sites would be overcome. However, we would need to be assured that there was a legally-binding Section 50 agreement under the planning legislation and that there was a Visitor Management Plan to our satisfaction and one that Highland Council, as the planning authority, could also agree to. The Board decided by a majority vote early in 1996 to sustain its objection as there was no guarantee that the European nature interests could be protected. It took another year to obtain agreement to the terms of the Section 50 Agreement and the Visitor Management Plan. It took a further year before the Board felt able to formally confirm that SNH was lifting its objection in the light of the two agreements guaranteeing to safeguard the requirements of the European Directives. However, this was by no means the end of the argument.

The eNGOs, led by WWF Scotland and RSPB Scotland, objected to the proposals and sought a Judicial Review against the SNH decision. The judge threw out the case and SNH successfully pursued the contestants for its costs, and an agreement was made. The eNGOs followed this up with court action against HIE as the owners and developers, Highland Council as the planning authority and SNH as the nature conservancy body. This was a difficult time for those staff leading for SNH, especially Ian Jardine and those staff who were living on Speyside. We were significantly helped by a visit from Bernard Julien, the senior official in the European Commission responsible for

Natura 2000, who determined that the closed system would be acceptable to the Commission. There were prolonged proceedings in the Court of Session. Ultimately, Lord Nimmo Smith, a Senator of the College of Justice who presided over the case, found in favour of the development on the grounds that the operators would operate a closed system and had to abide by the terms of the Section 50 Agreement and the Visitor Management Plan. The Visitor Management Plan and its detailed Monitoring Scheme were finally agreed at the end of 2001. In concluding this story, I merely note that the funicular railway has not been a technical success, but is now operating after considerable public expenditure to overcome its operational problems.

The main point on the ski developments from the SNH viewpoint is that matters are never black or white, but that legally-binding agreements, providing that they are enforced, do enable development to go forward. The answer lies in the willingness of the parties to secure such a binding agreement. Equally, it is right and proper for the eNGOs to advocate their position and seek an outcome that is in the best interests of the natural environment.

Mineral Extraction

We began our work on the effect of mineral extraction on the natural heritage interest by responding to the Scottish Office Planning Guidelines in 1992. We also produced our own policy paper on *Mineral Working in National Scenic Areas*. We stated a presumption against mineral working in NSAs. Our main conclusion was the need for an overview approach by government rather than a focus on individual applications dealt with in isolation. We proposed the establishment of a Planning Inquiry Commission to consider the overall policy in the full knowledge that it was most unlikely to be accepted. Whilst there was statutory provision for such an approach, the town and country planning system, since its establishment, had been based on dealing with individual applications for development. This approach was to remain the case throughout with strong resistance to reviewing the basis for different types of development and their spatial, environmental, social and economic effects, such as renewable energy installations and forestry. We produced a policy statement on minerals in 1994 to help guide staff in dealing with planning applications and advising local planning authorities.

The super quarry proposals at Lingarabay in south Harris were very divisive locally and nationally. We took a different stance from NCC or CCS and requested that the Secretary of State call it in based on the landscape effects of the proposals on the National Scenic Area. On reflection, later in 1993 we made a formal objection on landscape grounds, although we recognised the potential economic benefits to the area if the development went ahead. The landscape impact would be devastating, as the photomontage developed by Alison Grant, our landscape architect, cleverly demonstrated. The decision-making process from the establishment of the inquiry until the ministerial decision turned out to be a long-drawn-out saga lasting six years from October 1994 until the decision in November 2000. We added concerns about irreparable damage to the habitats on the summit of the hill to our objections at the Public Local Inquiry. The Findings of Fact only emerged in early 1998 and were so biased that we challenged them, and changes were made. Eventually, the Reporters' Report was submitted, and it then lay in the Scottish Government for a long time, until Sam Galbraith was appointed as the Environment Minister, when within a matter of days, he rejected the quarrying proposal entirely on grounds of its effect on the landscape.

This was not the first of our objections to mining proposals. A barytes mine was proposed for Duntanlich, near Aberfeldy, in Highland Perthshire. Barytes is a key clay mineral in oil well pressure control and there were no other deposits on a commercial scale in Scotland. However, our responsibility was clear: to assess the likely detrimental effect on the scenic value of the Loch Tummel NSA, rather than to judge the national significance of the mineral. In the event, the Reporter recommended refusal, and the government accepted that advice in early 1995.

These cases and other Public Inquiries demanded resilience and forbearance of staff leading our evidence. It was essential that they got the full backing of expert colleagues in providing material. Most of all they needed support throughout the process from managers, including myself, and Board members during these arduous and confrontational hearings.

Reintroductions

The material I quoted earlier on the loss of native species, including some which are the ecological keystones, needed to be addressed by SNH. There was some expectation raised by the terms in the EU Habitats and Species

Directive about reintroductions, which states at Article 22 (a) 'Member States study the desirability of reintroducing species...that are native to their territory where this might contribute to their conservation'. It is an advisory rather than mandatory provision. Those wishing to see more reintroductions misused the Directive to argue their point that action had to be taken. Others, not unreasonably, argued from an ethical perspective that because human actions had resulted in the extinction from Scotland of some species, then we had a moral duty to repair the situation. These matters were not straightforward ecologically. The debates in the SNH Board were also coloured by the attitudes and opinions of the various interests which had an important effect on what some Board members considered was the right thing to do.

Sea Eagles

It made no sense to leave the reintroduction of the Sea Eagle in an incomplete state. Despite the best efforts of all of the parties involved, the reintroduction on Rùm had not been successful. The combined efforts of the NCC team, led by John Love, and the expertise and experience of Roy Dennis, the willing cooperation of the Norwegian authorities and their lead expert, Harold Misund, and the support of the RAF who readily brought the chicks from their breeding area around Bodø in Nordland, Norway, to RAF Kinloss, Moray, demonstrated that there was a basis for a further programme of re-introductions. The programme devised was to bring the chicks to various locations which were regarded as suitable ecologically. What we did not know at the time was how successful the reintroduction programme would be or, more particularly, where the birds would breed most successfully.

Mull became the bird's favoured location. This led Chris Smout, our Deputy Chair, to opine in a Board meeting that Mull should be described as 'the Isle of the Eagles' as it also had successfully breeding pairs of Golden Eagles. Given the stout resistance by some farmers on the islands, this did not seem to be something to trumpet at the time. However, Chris's epithet for Mull proved right as over the following years Mull residents adopted the idea as they saw it put the island on the map as a visitor destination and that the threats of predation on lambs could be to a large extent avoided.

The secrecy of the programme and the precise location did lead to some curious behaviour by some of my colleagues in SNH. As a frequent visitor to Mull due to family relations having moved there, I asked colleagues in the Oban office where I could best observe the birds. They said that they could not tell me as this was a well-guarded secret. In frustration, I rang the lead staff member in the Oban office who gave me the answer of where to look without hesitation. This incident brought home to me a concern that wildlife watching was for the specialists rather than those of us who would like to have the same experience without any detrimental effect on the species. Interestingly, on the ferry from Oban to Craignure, after a meeting with the Scottish Crofters Union, I met many of the Mull crofters and farmers who, with one notable exception, privately said how pleased they were for the Sea Eagles to be breeding on the island without detriment to their activities. On the other hand, I was taken to see cages in another part of Scotland where the young Sea Eagles were being fed without any contact with humans to prove the point that every precaution was being taken not to intrude on the behaviours of the chicks.

The Barn Door-shaped bird has now become a positive symbol of this reintroduction programme in Scotland, with successful reintroductions in other areas of the mainland, although there remain concerns where the birds are newly establishing.

Red Kites

The sight of the Red Kite effortlessly manoeuvring its forked tail, and the sound of its mewing call is now commonplace in Galloway. It has successfully bred in the area. I now see the bird every day flying over my village and I know it gives a fillip to all those who live in The Glenkens area of North Galloway. Its reintroduction has not been without problems. Research has shown that the main prey of Red Kites is carrion, dead animals in whole or parts, as a result of natural mortality or accident. I recall a visit to the Black Isle with Board members and staff and meeting a farmer who had got the message that he could give a helping hand to the new arrivals by placing the afterbirth of his cattle onto the roof of the byre. Not everyone accepts this as a known fact. Persecution has been, and remains, a problem on the Black Isle, whereas elsewhere the reintroductions have been successful.

Beavers

By far the most contentious of the proposals for reintroductions was for the European Beaver, *Castor fiber*. Everyone on the Board had a view: some positive, some very cautious, some entirely opposed, and some representing the views of confidants. How to resolve these, not unnaturally, different perspectives was a dilemma. We could, of course, have decided not to pursue the matter at all. However, many European countries were undertaking beaver reintroduction programmes and why should Scotland not at least consider it was a reasonable argument. There was also strong pressure from some wildlife interests to undertake the reintroduction, and they had good contacts with experts on the European mainland. A telling argument was the fact that beavers are natural river engineers and could help to regulate water flows in rivers, maybe help in reducing flood peak water flows and create new habitats of benefit to other species.

When the Board first discussed the matter in February 1997, the main issues were how should we approach the matter: not too slow and not too fast, was it a scientific or a policy matter? We knew we should follow the IUCN Guidelines and that there should be full public consultation. We decided, therefore, that our scientific team, now led by Colin Galbraith, would start the process according to the *IUCN Guidelines for Re-introductions and Other Conservation Translocations*. We adopted a two-stage process: first, to get the science right, and second, to allow Board members to air their views and gain agreement on the way forward. I should note that SNH could only make a reasoned proposal to the Scottish Office, it was for Ministers to decide on whether a licence should be issued to allow the reintroduction to occur. Many reports were written, and consultations undertaken with experts, including at the UK level through JNCC. These are all available publicly. The ecological basis for reintroduction was sound, but it required the right conditions at the proposed reintroduction site.

The West Areas Board opposed the reintroduction in May 1998, as it was unconvinced about the scientific case and the potential negative effect on riparian interests. This latter point reflected those on the Board and those who had been lobbying Board members from a fishing perspective; not very impartial. The SNH Board expressed concern about the spread of disease from the lake behind the beaver dams in the light of experience in New Zealand of the spread of *giardia*, otherwise known as beaver fever which affects the stomach, but these could be allayed technically following consultation with government experts. The Board agreed in August 1998 to a trial reintroduction having addressed issues such as compensation for the effect on salmon and how to deal with the removal of beavers at the end of the trial. A Beaver Steering Group was established early in 1999 with Roger Wheater as Chair and including representatives of fishing, forestry and farming interests.

This is by no means the end of the story. A framework document was produced setting out the case for a carefully controlled field trial. Debating points were: Was this a core business priority? Was it value for money? What was the exit strategy and how could the threat of *giardia* be reduced? The disagreements within the Board meant that a vote was held, with a majority in favour of proceeding, but subject to a cost limit of £250,000 over seven years, seeking partner funding to reduce SNH's financial exposure, ensuring scientific rigour, determining an exit strategy and finding a suitable site. The Board could not have done its job without the rigorous analysis and assessment by staff led by Colin Galbraith, aided by first-hand experience in other European countries, for instance the visit by Michael Scott, with Michael Usher and Jeff Watson to Denmark, and the careful attention to the IUCN Guidelines.

One stumbling block was the choice of location. SNH staff worked with Forestry Commission Scotland staff and identified Glen Affric on state-owned land managed by the Commission as a suitable site. It is one of the most natural areas remaining in Scotland with an excellent natural vegetation succession. However, the then Chair of the Forestry Commission put his foot down on the basis that it was his favourite place within the Commission's estate, and he could not allow this location to be used. Hence, officials looked and identified another location on the west side of the Knapdale in Argyll. However, this brought opposition from the local landowners and fishing interests, which were strongly represented to the Board. There was also concern about the impact on native trees as the European beaver is well known for felling small and medium-sized trees to form its dam. I have subsequently observed this occurring in Scotland, and in the Donau-Auen National Park on the Danube downstream of Vienna and in the Čepkeliai Strict Nature Reserve in Lithuania. Whilst not ideal compared with the originally favoured site, the Knapdale site was on state-owned land managed by the Forestry Commission. It has proved to be a very successful site.

The Board's decision was not the end of the matter. The case was submitted to the Scottish Office where it got stuck, I think at official level, until staff were moved to other roles or retired and at ministerial level where Ross Finnie was leaned on by the farming and fisheries lobbies. Eventually, a positive decision emerged in 2008 with the Scottish Government granting permission to the Royal Zoological Society of Scotland and the Scottish Wildlife Trust, with SNH coordinating independent monitoring of the trial.

Frustrated by the length of SNH's decision-making and the lack of a decision from the government, a group of individuals decided to take the matter into their own hands. They arranged for the purchase and transfer of beavers from a zoo in Kent into west Angus, the Bamff Estate owned by Paul Ramsay, and at Aigas near Beauly, owned by Sir John Lister-Kaye. Lawyers can argue whether this was illegal or not. Suffice to say, it would be if beavers were imported from another country. However, Ministers were not best pleased and in the early 2000s Roseanna Cunningham demanded that SNH eliminate those that had spread from the Bamff site into the Spey river system without identifying the means of doing this. Needless to say, that was not carried out.

Others will no doubt have a different take on this account and the subsequent arrangements to pay compensation to farmers for areas of their land that have been flooded due to beaver dam building and on SNH later issuing licences for the removal of beavers from the upper Tay. My conclusion is that a clear process, using the internationally accepted reintroduction guidelines, which focusses first on the ecological case and then on the social and economic issues, should be followed. That is exactly what SNH did under the scrupulous and scientifically focussed leadership of Colin Galbraith. While it is accepted that Board members will seek the views of knowledgeable friends and colleagues, it is important that the best interests of the organisation and its agreed strategy take precedence.

Wolves, Lynx and Other Animals?

There was, throughout my time at SNH, an ongoing debate about the reintroduction of top predators such as wolves and lynx. There were two main reasons. The best way to reduce the deer population, other than the traditional sport shooting, was to introduce the two key predators, the wolf and the lynx. The first, and only question, that we addressed at the time, was whether there was sufficient habitat to sustain the population of these two animals. The advice was clear and unambiguous that there was not. Calls for reintroductions of wolves on Rùm were made, but even though the island is 10,000 hectares in size, it was regarded as problematic ecologically and would also disrupt the internationally significant scientific research on red deer.

The main point for a government agency on the issue is to scrupulously follow the international guidelines on reintroductions developed by global experts in IUCN.

Translocations

The possibilities of reinforcing species, plants or animals, by taking them from their current successful location to help in their return to locations where they used to exist was a thorny issue. As with reintroductions, there are carefully thought-out Translocation Guidelines developed by global experts working within the IUCN. Their use gave a degree of reassurance that procedures were rigorously followed, but it did not entirely take away the emotional perspectives of participants in the debates. My own view is quite simple. There are times when nature needs to be given a helping hand in the process of restoration of species and habitats. As I write, this is now a well-trodden path, but two or more decades ago it was rather more debatable to some interests. Fortunately, I consider that our debates and the actions taken following decisions by the SNH Board, informed by the best ecological science in the context of the international guidelines, were fully justified. The roles and expertise of Colin Galbraith and Michael B Usher were essential in ensuring the best possible scientific advice was rigorously provided from our expert staff. We were also fortunate in having the deep knowledge and experience of Roy Dennis to guide us throughout this process. His book of his translocation and reintroduction work makes excellent reading - *Restoring the Wild: Rewilding Our Skies, Woods and Waterways.*

Let me start by giving a relatively straightforward example: the translocation of the Sticky Catchfly *Silene Viscaria* back into Holyrood Park on the shoulders of Crow Hill from its seed germination point in the Royal Botanic Garden Edinburgh (RBGE). This was a joint project between RBGE and SNH. Not only has it been very successful, but it has spread down the slope to the foot of Samson's Ribs in recent years.

Not all of the translocations are successful. One case, again a joint project, initially with Plantlife and Historic Scotland, and latterly also with the RBGE, was the translocation from the Edinburgh Botanic Gardens to a wet area on the edge of the Bawsinch Nature Reserve in Holyrood Park of the Pillwort *Pilularia globulifera.* Maybe the area was not permanently wet enough, nor trampled enough by cattle to create an effective habitat. Anyway, one must ensure that the conditions are right.

An important translocation debate within the SNH Board was the proposal to take some osprey chicks to advance the return of this bird to the English Midlands. Ospreys were gradually moving southwards on their own account, for instance into southern Scotland. However, there was a desire to give nature a helping hand in speeding up the recovery process by establishing chicks in Rutland Water, a large reservoir in eastern Leicestershire, and, interestingly, the site for some years of the annual Rutland Bird Festival. Concerns were expressed that this was a step too far, but the reassurances that the chicks selected would not have a deleterious effect on the host population in Scotland, meant that both the SNH and Natural England Boards agreed. Here the scientific basis for translocation, together with the experience and proven track record of those involved in the project, gave the reassurance needed to the decision-making bodies. On the other hand, the case for translocating ospreys to Galloway was rejected by SNH as it would happen naturally – as occurred the following year!

Goose Management

Scotland plays an important role internationally in providing the winter home for geese which breed in the Arctic. Barnacle Geese from Svalbard and Greenland, White-fronted Geese from Greenland and Pink-footed Geese from Iceland, as well as Whooper Swans from Iceland, all overwinter in Scotland. They are a spectacular sight when seen arriving from their long flights. They are equally spectacular in the diurnal flights in the classic V-shaped formation between roosting and feeding areas. However, it is the feeding areas that proved the issue of contention between farmers and SNH. Put simply, the geese needed an autumn feed to recover their strength on arrival. More significantly, they needed to build up their energy for the flight to the breeding grounds in the spring. International agreements, including the wintering and breeding host countries, ensured improved protection and were resulting in population increases. This was important to secure the biological viability of each species. At the same time, it placed a greater demand for feed during the period they resided in Scotland, basically from September to March. We quickly developed our views with a paper on grey geese and agriculture in which we argued the need to defuse conflict, not to provide compensation but rather focus on management solutions, use scaring techniques to move the grazing birds on and seek longer term solutions.

At the outset, we were challenged to find a solution on Islay where, not unreasonably, the dairy farmers were concerned about competition for grass feed in the spring between geese and the dairy herd, which provided a very valuable source of income to the farmers and to the island economy as a whole. We approved the Islay Voluntary Goose Management Scheme in 1993 at a cost of around £300,000. We proposed to enhance the scheme with a three-year scheme from 1993 at a cost of £415,000, but The Scottish Office would only approve £285,000. This scheme was rolled forward for three years in 1996 and again from 1999. These arrangements did improve relations with the farming community to some extent, but it was never more than a fragile truce.

There was debate about licensed shooting of those goose species which were in a biologically positive state of health. However, there was reluctance on behalf of ourselves and of the farmers to proceed, the latter because they did not wish to get into a blame game, and us because we felt that this was not an enduring solution. We trialled scaring schemes. We used gas guns on Islay, but these proved ineffective. On Orkney, we hired people whose physical presence was meant to scare the geese. It had some modest success. We argued strongly with the Scottish Office that an agricultural solution was needed to deal with the problem. That never happened.

Other schemes were developed to address local issues. The Solway Barnacle Geese Demonstration Scheme was agreed for one year from autumn 1994. It had a number of unique elements to trial a broader-based approach. Norwegian input was provided as the birds' breeding area was Svalbard, an Arctic archipelago administered under an international treaty by Norway. Biological modelling of the populations using internationally accepted approaches was undertaken. Also, a stewardship element for grazing - The Merse Management Scheme - was introduced as the geese overwintered on the pastures along the north shores of the Solway. The parties were sufficiently satisfied with the demonstration project to agree a three-year scheme from 1995, and it continued thereafter.

These individual schemes were really only buying time. They took up a great deal of staff time and financial resources. However, they did not get to the root of the problem of devising effective longer solutions which met the legitimate demands of the farmers and secured the future of the goose species. We needed a broader policy. We developed our goose management policy early in 1994 focussing on short-term management schemes in particular problem locations such as South Walls on Orkney, Loch of Strathbeg in Buchan and along the Solway Merses. We were also clear about the need for robust scientific estimates of the population size and dynamics to ensure that the international agreements to provide for biologically viable populations were being honoured. We knew that working with the farmers had to be one way forward. An accord between the NFUS and SNH was negotiated in 1984 which, *inter alia*, recommended that the Scottish Office established a national working party on goose management. Eventually, as these matters take time to crank through the bureaucratic processes where protection of the *status quo* is the operative culture, a National Goose Forum was established in 1996. It ran for at least four years. To back up our approach, we produced a paper *Wild Geese and Agriculture* early in 1997 and presented it to the Minister for Agriculture and the Environment, the Earl of Lindsay, and to his officials. Needless to say, our main proposal for goose management to be funded through the government's agri-environment programme was rejected on the grounds that this was a nature problem and not an agricultural one. We were forced to continue with, and to fund, the various management schemes. Not giving up, we tried again under the new administration in 2000, but the answer was as before, that it was for SNH to pay for the goose management schemes out of our grant-in-aid from the Scottish Office as there were no funds available in the agri-environment programme.

I can only conclude that neither the farmers nor the geese got a sensible solution and the costs to the public sector of *ad hoc* approaches in particular locations was higher than it needed to be. One good outcome was that the populations of barnacle, Greenland white-fronted and pink-footed geese continued to increase as the protection in the breeding areas improved and winter feed was provided in Scotland.

CHAPTER 8

Working in Partnership

'Since the formation of SNH I have always admired the way in which you have steered the different interest groups towards a common goal for the general good of Scotland. I also very much enjoyed our contact during my term as NFU Scotland President.'

John Ross, CBE, Chairman,
Scottish Quality Beef and Lamb Association Ltd

AFTER OUR establishment there were new government agencies in Scotland and in other parts of the UK, and it seemed sensible to make links with them, to share experience, to learn about good and not so good practice, and how to work with partners and with the government at Scottish and UK levels.

Working With Equivalent Bodies in England and Wales

With the establishment of new bodies in England - English Nature (EN), Scotland - SNH, and Wales - the Countryside Council for Wales (CCW), the three Chief Executives decided it was important to meet periodically. The purpose was to exchange views, to identify good and bad practice from the past to build on and change, respectively. We also needed to determine how our organisations should perform our joint responsibilities through the Joint Nature Conservation Committee and the management of its staff, who were all seconded from one of our organisations. We met quarterly face-to-face, usually in York, and latterly with the head of the JNCC Support Group for part of the time. Ian Mercer, the Chief Executive of CCW, was a geographer by training and had most recently been the Chief Executive of the Dartmoor National Park. Derek Langslow, the Chief Executive of EN, was an ornithologist by training and research, having worked in the Chief Scientist Unit at NCC. It was very worthwhile as Derek Langslow said, 'I greatly enjoyed working with you and have appreciated your friendship, advice and support very much. You've built a fine organisation at SNH. Well done'. We quickly identified that there were some common problems from the way that NCC had been run in the past. For example, staff who looked after National Nature Reserves could use home as their office. This meant that managers had very little control on what their staff did. We decided that this arrangement should be phased out where possible, in discussion with the staff concerned and with their managers.

Another issue was travel overseas to undertake work which was not part of the postholder's daily job and not necessarily in the interest or to the benefit of the organisation. We decided that in each of our organisations all foreign travel must be approved by the Chief Executive to ensure that it was an essential part of the job of the individual and to the benefit of the organisation. One condition of approved travel was that on return the traveller must produce a detailed report of relevance to the organisation and, where appropriate, led a seminar on the outcomes. This decision was widely praised by staff, except for those few who had exploited the previous arrangements.

A further aspect was the relationship between NCC and the main international nature conservation organisations, of which there were many. This task was undertaken on a personal basis by one member of staff who rarely, if ever, reported back to colleagues and clearly regarded the role as a sinecure. We thought that this was unacceptable and had to stop. The solution we agreed was to allocate responsibility for each of the bodies on the list to one of our organisations. We did this on the basis of consulting with our colleagues who were knowledgeable about these bodies. In SNH's case, Sandy Kerr, our dedicated International Manager, advised that we should take the lead on IUCN, partly as NCC Scotland had played such a role when Morton Boyd was Director, as had John Foster the first Director of CCS, the former particularly in the Species Survival Commission and the latter in the National Parks Commission along with his colleague Malcolm Payne. It was also partly because it gave us the opportunity to play across our broad remit embracing nature conservation, community engagement and environmental education. We three Chief Executives agreed to this.

My two colleagues were supportive of rebuilding the relationship with IUCN in the UK, in particular to steer it from an environmental lobby group to one which properly reflected the membership basis of the Union as a whole, notably national governments and state agencies along with international and national environmental NGOs. We, therefore, made a working arrangement with the NGO members, with the support of the UK Government, to play an active part and, importantly, to rotate the chair of the UK Committee of IUCN. Therefore, when the government agencies' turn came round, my colleagues in SNH, including the Board and our sister bodies, were entirely supportive of me taking on that role. There was, therefore, strong support for Sandy and me to represent the three bodies at the World Conservation Congress in Montreal in 1996, as part of the UK Government delegation. Personally, that began my now long association with IUCN, which continues to this day, particularly as an active member of one its Commissions, the World Commission on Protected Areas (WCPA), and, most especially, its Geoheritage Specialist Group.

Another aspect developed from these connections came out of the blue. The Chair of IUCN's WCPA, Adrian Phillips, former Chief Executive of the Countryside Commission for England and Wales, along with the head of the Protected Areas Programme in the IUCN Secretariat, David Sheppard, wished to undertake a review of its operations in 1998. They asked me if I would take on this task. Magnus was keen for me to do so and gave me two weeks to undertake the task, involving spending a week in the IUCN HQ in Gland, Switzerland and a week finalising my report. He also allowed me to use my annual leave to present my findings to the Global Steering Committee of WCPA in Nassau, in the Bahamas, I should add, at no cost to SNH or the government. Writing about my report on the IUCN Protected Programme and the World Commission on Protected Areas, Adrian Phillips said:

> The WCPA Steering Committee were very pleased indeed with the quality of the report, which they regarded as comprehensive and penetrating. WCPA have taken the report as an extremely serious contribution to the development of our programme, structures and ways of working.

Scottish Office Agencies

A quite different informal group met periodically over dinner in Edinburgh: Crawford Beveridge of Scottish Enterprise (SE), Iain Robertson of Highlands and Islands Enterprise (HIE), Peter McKinlay of Scottish Homes (SH) and me. This was invaluable as it gave us different insights into our relationships with the sponsor divisions of the Scottish Government. It also helped to identify where there was potential conflict in our work because of our different remits and how we could overcome these through closer working and through joint initiatives. One such initiative involved rewarding local schools for good practice with their grounds through SE's responsibility for area improvement and SNH's responsibilities for environmental education. Inevitably, a media correspondent got to know of our meetings and *The Scotsman* headed Peter Clarke's article, 'Exposed: the after-dinner conspiracy' (*The Scotsman*, 27 April 1993), dubbed us 'The Conspirators Club'. Well, I suppose that is what sells newspapers. We were not challenged by our sponsor division in the government about this.

I have already noted in Chapter 6 the establishment of the CEOs group of Scottish Office funded NDPBs and the role we played in forcing coherency in the way they sponsored their NDPBs.

Relationships With Environmental Voluntary Bodies

It is notable that we did not sign any accords or concordats with the environmental NGOs individually or collectively through Scottish Environment LINK (SEL). There was not an appetite by either party for this, despite the fact that many SNH staff, including myself, were members of some of the constituent organisations, such as NTS, Ramblers, RSPB and SWT. It was more important to have good working relationships with the leading individuals in the main organisations, without compromising each other's positions. This was certainly my position. I have lots of good friends who are experts in nature and natural systems whom I have had the good fortune to work with, to learn from and spend insightful experiences in the field. Unfortunately, there remain those who cannot distinguish between what is reasonably well understood as a result of objective analysis and what they believe as nature organisation card carriers.

I had good links with successive chairs of SEL - Drennan Watson, Michael Scott and Kevin Dunion. Interestingly and helpfully to SNH, the latter two were appointed members of the SNH Board towards the end of my term. I had good working relations at a personal level with key individuals. These included the outstanding environmental campaigner Simon Pepper, who led WWF Scotland, as we were able to discuss privately so many issues, even when there were profound differences of opinion and approach. Indeed, Simon wrote to me later on:

> It has been a treat working with you and I'll miss you from the official scene, but I hope not from the unofficial one.

Michael Scott, the Scottish Officer of Plantlife, was also a great supporter, and he substantially increased my knowledge of mountain flowers. On the recreational side, my old hillwalking friend, Bob Aitken, was an excellent sounding board on recreation and access, wilderness and wildland, and on national parks internationally. And also Kevin Dunion, who wrote to me on my retirement:

> I just want to say how much I appreciated being able to meet with you over the years either through Scottish Environmental LINK and now through the SNH Board. Personally, I always felt you supported the perspective I sought to bring and encouraged a broadening of issues which in turn has prompted me to a much better engagement with SNH and its agenda. You have always been refreshingly frank.

We did provide significant funding to the Scottish Wildlife Trust for many years which rescued it financially. More importantly, this enabled it to deliver many conservation initiatives and volunteer work on its nature reserves which form an important component of protecting nature around Scotland. Also in my last two years, we provided funds for SEL, the collaborative group of environmental NGOs, to enable it to be more proactive.

We were also interested in having greater diversity in the ownership of conservation land. When the Rankin family decided it wanted to sell the Treshnish Isles, with its important seabird colony designated as an SSSI, the environmental NGOs decided that NTS should purchase it with funds from SNH. However, we were aware that the Hebridean Trust, which owned land on Tiree, were keen and had the funds. As a relative newcomer, but with a strong nature conservation progeny with Morton Boyd, a previous Director

Scotland of NCC, and his son, Ian, a Professor of Biology at St Andrews University, as Trustees, we thought that their aspiration should be supported. This arrangement survived for a number of decades until the Hebridean Trust agreed a transfer of ownership to NTS in 2023.

There was one relationship which was often difficult. It was with the RSPB. Bearing in mind my earlier recollections of its central role in the old NCC and the fact that Magnus had been a perhaps reluctant President, it's fair to say there was history. I had hoped for a more positive engagement, but this was not to be. It started badly when I was invited to lunch in The Scotty Bar in the Jock's Lodge area of Edinburgh in autumn 1991 by Frank Hamilton, the long-standing Scottish Director. Frank opened a small notebook. On the first page, it had a list of about five items which were commendations of SNH. Fine I thought and said so. He then turned over the page to reveal a list three times as long and began what I can only call a rant of instructions of what we were to do and how we were to operate. He never did get past the first item as I made it abundantly clear that RSPB was not the boss of SNH to dictate to us. Subsequent meetings with his successor and his staff were not always a meeting of minds. Yes, they were doing their job of defending the bird interests, but it was how they did it, which often failed to win friends and influence people. Later meetings with Barbara Young and Graeme Wynn, successive Chief Executives, sought to clear the air. In practice, we did joint projects, such as the Mull Sea Eagle Scheme and the various goose management schemes, and defining it as an Approved Body in owning and managing National Nature Reserves.

The Joint Nature Conservation Committee and Its Support Unit

I have indicated earlier the arguments which led to the establishment of this Committee. The appointment of its members rested with the Secretary of State for the Environment in consultation with Welsh and Scottish Environment Ministers. In addition, each of the three agencies nominated two members, in SNH's case always the Chair and one other with a more scientific background. The operation of the committee was never easy for the independent chair, in sequence Sir Fred Halliday, an eminent biologist and university leader, Sir Angus Stirling, the former Director General of the

National Trust, the Earl of Selbourne, a noted scientist himself and member of the House of Lords, and Professor Peter Bridgewater, an international expert on conservation. There was never really a meeting of minds as to who was in charge with the country agencies unwilling to cede control to the committee and its staff. Consequently, during my tenure it never really achieved its purpose of taking a UK overview of nature conservation matters and placing them in an international context. That was partly our fault in the country agencies, but also partly because the full time heads of the JNCC Support Unit were overly protective of their managerial role and sought, successfully, to build up the numbers of staff.

One matter was resolved - the funding. An official in the Department of the Environment came up with a funding formula, named the Hepworth Formula after him. This allocated the cost of running the JNCC and its Support Unit on a shared basis conjured up from some estimate of the relative scale of each organisation: 57.2 per cent England, 29.6 per cent Scotland and 13.2 per cent Wales. What was more difficult was that the staff were members of the country agencies, and this created management difficulties for the Chief Officer. It was resolved, in part, by the re-assignment of some staff back into the relevant country agency and partly by the establishment of the Support Unit as an employer in its own right.

Despite the fact that the JNCC was born out of a political comprise to placate opponents of the 'breakup' of NCC, it did and does have a role to play in putting the case for a UK wide approach to nature conservation, supported by nationwide data sets, advising on the use of common standards of monitoring, reporting on the state of health of nature and representing the UK at the European and international level.

I am sure that my former SNH colleagues who became members of the JNCC as independent members, Michael B. Usher and later on, Colin Galbraith, who became its Deputy Chair and then Chair, will have slightly different recollections. I hope that it moved on to play a more instrumental role in global conservation from a UK perspective

Partnership Working and Mandates

As partnership working was the mandate given to SNH by government, we had taken this on board in our logo and strapline. We made many arrangements to take this forward, through the establishment of Area Teams and the Regional Boards, for example. We made sure that the public knew what we were about and where we were located and how they could contact us through the publication and wide distribution of a simple brochure *Who we are, where we are and what we do.* The Area teams also produced brochures spelling out our work and the important issues for the natural heritage in their territory.

Nationally, we considered it essential to have formal arrangements with key bodies whom we were working with and, therefore, needed to interact with, even though at times our roles led us on collision courses. We used either the Memorandum of Understanding or the Concordant mechanism for no other reason than what felt more comfortable to both parties. Each included a statement of the respective roles of the two bodies and what we aimed to achieve through collaboration and through joint working. Some had specific targets and actions, others were more general. We signed these over the years. I will consider each one.

A Statement of Intent between Historic Scotland and Scottish Natural Heritage was signed in May 1995. It spelt out our mutual key aims on liaison, on policy matters, dealing with site management and casework related to it, such as Holyrood Park and buildings where there were bat roosts, and dealing with areas protected for natural or cultural heritage. It identified joint initiatives on interpretation, education, enjoyment of our heritage, and cooperation on research and on training.

One of the early accords was with the Ministry of Defence in the form of *Declaration of Intent for the natural heritage of Scotland*, signed in 1993 and revised in 1997. It was signed by the Parliamentary Under Secretary of State for Defence (a junior Minister). It covered all aspects of the relationship on military sites including biodiversity, access, site management and training. Interestingly, it notes MoD's commitment to avoidance of intensive land use on sites designated for their natural heritage interest. It heralded the establishment of a Joint SNH/MoD Liaison Committee.

A *Memorandum of Understanding Between SEPA and SNH* was signed in 1996 setting out a framework for liaison, working arrangements and training. It is interesting that it took until that date as the first Chair and Chief Executive of SEPA did not seem amenable to such an arrangement.

A *Memorandum of Agreement* was signed with Forest Enterprise, the government's forestry land management agency, this time between the Chief

Executives. It replaced an older Declaration of Intent between the Forestry Commission and NCC in 1986. Its wording was positive, aimed at developing mutual understanding with specific statements of what each would do.

An *Accord between SNH and the Scottish Museums Council* had the purpose of providing a framework for the two organisations to undertake appropriate joint initiatives to enhance public enjoyment and understanding of Scotland's natural and cultural heritages. The statement included specific actions.

A Statement of Common Interest and Cooperation between the Deer Commission for Scotland and Scottish Natural Heritage was signed by its Chair and our Chief Executive in August 1998. It covered our distinctive roles as well as setting out 6 partnership objectives and how each party would aim to achieve these. It took so long because of the continuing concern by the DCS Chair that we were trying to take it over, which was the last thing we wanted to do.

An interesting *Statement of Common Interest and Cooperation* was signed with the Game Conservancy Trust in 1997 by the respective chairs, The Earl Peel for the GCT. It stated the good working relationships enjoyed and the many common objectives for the countryside. It included seven key objectives and how these will be achieved. It is interesting that this statement came to fruition as there had been concerns that the GCT was more inclined towards the sporting interests, as reflected, for example, in its Chair being a major grouse moor owner in the northern Pennines.

A Concordat between the NTS and SNH was agreed in January 1999. This was significant given the large area of land owned by NTS that was of high conservation and scenic value. Also, NTS played a significant role in informal recreation and access to its properties. It recognised the financial contribution we made through management agreements and support for its Ranger Service.

There may have been others, but I have no record of them.

Were these statements useful and successful? Yes, to a degree, as they forced continuing liaison, formally and informally, between the parties at top representative levels, as well as, most importantly, at working levels. Without dialogues and acceptance of the different roles and responsibilities of the parties, and their sometimes diverse aspirations and action, standoffs would occur. Whether there was meeting of minds and the development of common objectives is another matter. It depended on the willingness or otherwise of the respective leaders and also, crucially, the power and influence of the interests pulling each organisation's strings behind the scenes.

Development of Forums

Pursuing the partnership objective given to us by the Scottish Office, we became the leader for the establishment of forums to bring often disparate interests together, to identify common ground, to develop codes of practice where there were disputes and to set out new ways of working.

The work on the inshore environment were cases in point, where fishing, recreational, tourism and conservation interests rarely came together. The establishment of estuary forums for the Moray Firth, the Forth Estuary, and the Clyde and Solway Firths was our initiative, working with partners, especially local authorities. Regional Board members were invited to chair them, and a broad membership of all of the interests was appointed.

Area partnerships were also important. I have already described the work of the Cairngorms and Loch Lomond and The Trossachs partnerships. In addition, following a call for a more cooperative approach across the Scottish Borders, the Southern Uplands Partnership was launched in 1998. We seconded Pip Tabor as the chief officer, and it proved an excellent arrangement for him with the partnership lasting until 2023.

Other forums were established to bring together interests in the hope of resolving disputed areas and to develop new approaches, such as the important and challenging work of both the Access Forum and the Moorland Forum, mentioned earlier. Suffice to say, through the willingness of the parties, guided by careful and astute chairing and excellent staff support, they achieved their purposes. Ultimately, they both led to fundamental legislative change, improving and clarifying the rights and responsibilities of all parties, particularly the owners and managers and the public. Without their establishment under our leadership, and the willingness of the disparate parties to develop co-operative working, the changes that were ultimately agreed by the Scottish Government Office and Parliament would not have been achieved.

Links Internationally

I was challenged by Magnus and Sandy Kerr, my International Manager in 1993, about what we were going to do about international connections. I responded that we should make professional links to share experience and learn from each other with equivalent agencies in the Nordic countries because of their similar biogeography, ie the Boreal region.

Magnus latched onto this immediately asking whether Iceland was included. I said that it definitely was, along with Denmark, Finland, Norway and Sweden. Magnus, therefore, organised for Michael B. Usher, himself and me to visit Iceland in May 1993 where we met senior staff from the Soil Conservation and Nature Conservation Services, and, of course, his close friend the President of Iceland, Vigdís Finnbogadóttir. As a result, we arranged staff exchanges, including with the two Ranger Services, and many lessons were learned for all of us involved. We continued this arrangement throughout my tenure. Personally, I have continued it ever since to my great intellectual benefit and a greater understanding of others' perspectives.

We made similar arrangements with the Danish, Finnish, Norwegian and Swedish equivalent government agencies. On all these visits, a Board member and two senior members of staff represented SNH. After every visit, I ensured that the lessons learned were reported back to colleagues through presentations and reports, and that the connections were kept alive through my International Manager, Sandy Kerr and latterly, Marion Hughes.

We also considered it important to further develop the links with international and European bodies that NCC and CCS had begun. In particular, we led on the UK government agency input into the IUCN World Conservation Congresses and specifically its World Commission on Protected Areas with me as lead, Ian Jardine in Eurosite, and John Thomson in the Europarc Federation. We were represented on the European Advisory Agencies Council by Michael Scott, where our contributions focussed on the marine environment.

Another initiative which the countryside agencies in Britain had fostered was a Countryside Exchange aimed at middle managerial level to gain experience. Colleagues chosen to attend always found the experience valuable personally and their feedback in SNH was very worthwhile.

There will always be those who criticise these links and their financial cost. Critics miss the point that we work in a global community and learning from the experience of others through face-to-face contact and ensuring that these lessons and contacts are shared with colleagues back home is vitally important. Insularity does not pay when the natural environment does not recognise human boundaries.

CHAPTER 9

Reflecting on a Decade

'I am sure that you can look back with great pride on the foundations you have laid and the structure you built in SNH. It is far more of an achievement than is given to most of us to aspire to in the public service and you have the happy talent of seizing opportunity when it was offered.'

Peter Mackay, CB, Former Head of the Industry Department for Scotland and SNH Board Member

'You can be deeply satisfied with all you have achieved – my impression is that SNH is in many ways the most effective of the national conservation agencies...Seeing Roger in such youthful vigour I am not sure he should retire at all. Roger has done an outstanding job at SNH.'

Sir Martin Holdgate, CB, former Director General UK Department of the Environment and former Director General IUCN

THIS HAS been a lengthy story covering a period of more than a dozen years. I now set out my reflections, focussing in this chapter on those I made at the time of my retiral, while Chapter 10 focusses on those I made writing this book.

First, let me restate what I said in our external newspaper on my retirement in 2002 in *Scotland's Natural Heritage*, the magazine of Scottish Natural Heritage (Issue 21).

> When SNH was first established, I pondered what I hoped the organisation would achieve by the end of my 10-year contractual term. For a public agency to be accepted as part of the institutional structure, which is respected for what it is seeking to achieve and the way it does it, and whose advice is sought by many interested parties was what I really hoped for. I am sure that readers will have

their own views and perspectives, but I would like to share my reflections with you.

SNH had an excellent starting point with strong government support, strong cross-party support and recognition that it was time to move on from the previous and separate arrangements for nature conservation and countryside, through NCC and CCS, respectively. The government's proposals were set in the context of the sustainable development agenda which seeks to remove traditional barriers between sectors and between institutions and encourage the interdependence between environmental stewardship, social wellbeing and economic prosperity. As a result, SNH's founding legislation gave us the first ever sustainable development duty for a public body in the UK. The artificial statutory divides between countryside and the rest of the land and between wildlife and landscape were removed. We were given many financial and other mechanisms to help us to be both innovative and continue the essential core work of the two predecessor bodies.

To me, coming from another part of the public sector to lead SNH, the most positive starting point was the quality of the new colleagues: the excellence of their expertise and their strong commitment to their work. This has continued throughout the decade and is one of the hallmarks of the organisation. In addition, and as a trailblazer which others have followed, SNH established four Regional Boards to help us engage with wider constituencies of interest. The value added by over 100 Board and Committee members over the period has been substantial and certainly well beyond the small amount of money paid to them.

On the other hand, there have been many things that have, in practice, not altogether helped us. This should not be surprising for a public agency whose role is to work with many, often conflicting, interests to safeguard, celebrate, improve and enjoy Scotland's priceless natural heritage assets. For most of the decade, and despite the outcome of the Rio Earth Summit a few months after our establishment, the environment had been low on the political and public agendas. Even 10 years on, the Rio agenda had not reached all of the parts it was meant to. Malcolm Rifkind's seminal speech on sustainable development in 1989 set the new framework and I am sure that Jack McConnell's equally seminal speech in February 2002 will have the same effect. Indeed, it is enormously encouraging for me that sustainable development is to be a key criterion in the decision making process for public spending in Scotland over the next three years.

There had been a healthy debate about the role of Quangos such as SNH. As a result, there is greater openness and transparency. For example, publishing the details of all of our grants and management agreements was a first and allowed anyone to scrutinise how we spend taxpayer's money. Also, our peripatetic open meetings were a first, begun in 1998 and expanded a year later. At the same time, we placed the minutes of Board meetings online, apart from confidential aspects. We held annual open meetings around the country to report on our work, spell out our future programme and to obtain feedback from attendees.

The resourcing of SNH and the natural heritage had been something of a rollercoaster, subject to a whole host of rules which get in the way of good management. Thankfully, there are now additional resources, and restrictions on staffing and pay in our early years have been removed.

One topic dominated our work throughout the decade: the designation and management of Scotland's special places. This has been driven by the government's obligations under EU Directives on Birds and on Habitats and Species and notification of Sites of Special Scientific Interest. This had not been anticipated by anyone at the outset. However, we should be proud that we now have in place Scotland's contribution to the new European wildlife network. That programme got SNH a bad name with some parties, perhaps inevitable given the timescales under which we had to work, the mechanisms which we had to use and the inadequate financial support for owners, tenants and managers of sites. In the vast majority of cases, through the professionalism of staff, the support of Board members and the positive engagement of key stakeholders, Scotland's internationally important wildlife assets and the way they are being managed are regarded as an exemplar in Europe.

So what have we achieved? I highlight some which I regard as particularly important. We have developed forward looking strategic policies and programmes across the whole of our very wide remit. For example, we have through our Natural Heritage Futures programme just published 21 local assessments, visions and actions reflecting the diversity of Scotland's natural heritage along with six national overviews on key sectors. This programme will guide our work and provide the basis for our input to major initiatives, such as community planning and biodiversity action. We have surveyed and assessed the terrestrial and marine habitats and species and the whole of Scotland's landscape and made all of the material available. We have reviewed the state of Scotland's natural heritage and published a seminal overview. We have supported local biodiversity data gathering and action. We have published many accessible booklets and posters on wildlife, geology and living landscapes. We have published full and summary versions of our commissioned research. We have taken forward the development of policy and action on National Parks and access to the countryside, and this has formed the basis of the Government's legislation and action. We sought and achieved solutions where conflict formerly occurred, for geese and agriculture on Islay, access and deer management in the hills, biodiversity and modern arable farming in some intensively farmed areas of the eastern lowlands. We have successfully reintroduced the Sea Eagle, although sadly the Red Kite has been subject to unjustifiable persecution. We have led the way in developing partnerships. For example, we have been involved in countless partnership activities on different scales and different topics around the country. Particular successes have been the Moorland Forum and the associated Statement of Intent, the Access Forum and the associated Access Code, the Focus on Firths initiatives and the various regional forums, such as the Spey and Tweed catchments and the Southern Uplands Partnership.

Also, very significant for me and my colleagues, we have

achieved many things on the ground which benefit people and the natural heritage: hundreds of projects in school grounds, thousands of people buying into the Plant for Wildlife Campaign through garden centres, and many kilometres of path creation and maintenance in and around cities, towns and villages, over long distances and up to mountain summits, thousands who benefit from our various schemes of positive land management and community grants, and we have reshaped the basis of supporting management for key wildlife sites through our Natural Care Programme and the evidence is there to see in Caithness and Sutherland and in Lewis.

All of this activity has created many jobs throughout Scotland, but especially in the remote and fragile rural areas of Scotland.

Also, we have consistently met our financial targets. We have achieved three-quarters of our operational targets each year, noting that 100% is never possible. We have instituted new ways of working which others have followed: our Regional and now Areas Boards, the dispersed staff and office structure, the approach to openness especially through national and local open meetings, the provision of detailed information on the way we spend taxpayers' money. Following the standard reviews of Quangos, our powers and functions have remained unchanged. We have modern internal and external communication systems, and we have proved that an organisation can work effectively through many offices based with our customers around the country.

I consider that SNH has been successful in delivering our responsibilities, but more to the point, improvements have been achieved for Scotland's natural heritage of landscape and wildlife, and greater ability for Scotland's people and visitors to enjoy it and understand it better.

In presenting my valedictory thoughts to the Management Forum on 21 March, *Reflections on a Decade: let's be proud of our successes*, I noted the things that have helped and those that have hindered. On the former, I praised the commitment and professionalism of staff, the continuity of leadership, changes being made at the appropriate time and the support of over 100 Board members. I noted the respect we had achieved, the initiatives we had stimulated, and the partnerships we had fostered. Yes, there were things we could have done better, such as less debate and more action, more fleet of foot on management, more delegation and trust, fewer old agendas, more customer focus, and better communication generally and of our successes to wider audiences. On the hindrances, I noted the lack of environmental leadership within government, continuing political opposition, and, from government, the perverse policies and funding mechanisms, micro management, a regressive running cost regime and stop/go financial support.

One area remained frustrating throughout. We were unable to achieve any fundamental changes in agriculture policy and the financial support schemes for farming. The apparent willingness of Ministers and officials, stated orally and in writing, never materialised into the quantum changes we were seeking with funding for goose management remaining our responsibility in all respects as a prime example. Yes, there were agri-environment schemes, but they were always at both the policy and financial margin of the support infrastructure for agriculture.

My final day as Chief Executive was 23 March 2002. It started with the formal launch of our *Natural Heritage Futures* programme. This was held in the Roxburghe Hotel in Charlotte Square in Edinburgh and was chaired by Michael Scott, our Deputy Chair and a kindred spirit on the environmental forward-looking agenda. The documentation had been prepared by colleagues throughout SNH who had consulted extensively around the country so its contents reflected a consensus of a different future founded in realism of what could be achieved and alongside visions and aspirations for a quarter of a century ahead. The fact that these documents have formed the basis of SNH strategy and action for well over a decade after I retired was testament to the combined work of all parts of the organisation and its agreement with partners for tangible actions. Michael Scott said:

> In combination, they represent an encyclopaedic assessment of the Scottish environment, and yet throughout they are written with a clarity and elegance of style that I find impressive. Their scope and their genuinely integrated vision is something that I believe will earn us huge credit with our partners and which even the arch

> sceptics will struggle hard to rubbish. Time and again they eloquently make clear the link between the natural heritage and the quality of life and the economic well-being of the communities that rely on it or simply coexist alongside it.

Peter Peacock, the Deputy Minister for Finance and Public Services and a former Board member, added:

> A rich and attractive and accessible natural heritage is a right for all citizens, not just the better off. I am pleased that these publications set out how the natural heritage can benefit people everywhere, thus making an important contribution to Community Plans.

Following this launch, I ensured, with Lindsay's help of course, that all of the women in the Secretariat were given a bouquet of flowers by me, always a trademark of mine to this day. On this occasion, they were bought from a florist in Newington rather than picked from our garden in Duddingston Village.

It was decided, by whom I'm not sure, that there should be gatherings at Battleby. Staff were given the option of whether to attend, and transport arrangements were made. I recall giving one of my typical presentations complete with slides of the decade reflecting, thanking and looking forward. By far the most interesting part of the events in Battleby, was about an hour with all of the senior and middle managers who formed our Management Forum for the previous five years. They asked and I answered was the format. Why did you do that? What were you thinking on that subject? What were the most difficult issues? What were the highlights? And many other questions of which I now have no recall. What struck me most was that colleagues wished to know the basis of thinking and acting across the whole range of our activity and I was happy to give open and honest answers. There were times when the position of Chief Executive is an isolated one with delicate choices to be judged and decisions made, whether about strategy, resource allocation, dealing with staff matters, or interacting with the Scottish Government and with partner organisations. That is why throughout my time at SNH my chief confidante was Lindsay, firstly as Personal Assistant to

Magnus and myself, and latterly as my wife.

The Board held a dinner for me at the Malt Whisky Society in Leith. This was a splendid occasion with many speeches from Board members with my reply based on three drams to reflect our successes, especially the role played by Board members and staff. And, finally, the family decided we would hold a thank you party. With the help of one of my lawyer friends, this was held at the Signet Library with well over a hundred SNH colleagues, and colleagues and friends from my wider working circle. We had the full panoply of a Ceilidh band and speeches by my children and by Roger Wheater. Curiously, I did not give a speech!

In my final email to all staff I said:

> It has been my great privilege and pleasure to be the founder Chief Executive of SNH. I would not have missed the last ten years for the world. I now know the difference between a Dotterel and a Hen Harrier, and some of you now know the difference between a protalus rampart and an esker. It has always been fascinating and interesting, learning so much from many colleagues. It has also been challenging and at times downright difficult. But not only have we survived as an organisation, we have made tremendous strides to create a new organisation which is widely known and respected in Scotland and beyond, which has succeeded on so many fronts on our natural heritage remit, and we have got our house in order internally.
>
> What distinguishes SNH from any other organisation I have worked in is the enormous commitment which you all have and the professionalism with which you do your job, irrespective of the role you play in SNH. That has made my job so much easier, and I know that my Management Team colleagues over the years would strongly agree with that. There seems to be one strong and common bond for all of us in SNH - our interest in and commitment to the natural heritage. This applies whether we are receptionists, administrators, technical specialists, Area Officers, scientists or other technical advisers. Compared with other parts of the public sector, where there is no such commitment to the organisation and the role it plays, SNH is in a league of its own.
>
> You should all be proud of the many successes that we have

had. I wish each and every one of you all success in your jobs in SNH and I wish SNH all success in the future. Please give Ian the support he rightly deserves as your new Chief Executive.

CHAPTER 10

Reflecting Twenty-Five Years On

'I might tactfully suggest that a few Government Ministers might also benefit from Roger's insights as they struggle to bring together dysfunctional departments! I hope it might also encourage current Scottish Ministers to reinvigorate their support for renamed NatureScot that now takes forward the work of SNH.'

Michael Scott

IN THIS chapter, I reflect on the developments in natural heritage over the past 25 years, with a specific focus on changes in legislation, policy and action within government and among Scottish partners. These comments are intended as personal reflections rather than a comprehensive review. My attention here is on the Scottish context, while a wider perspective will be discussed in a separate book, tentatively titled *Natural Common Sense.* Additionally, because one of my aims is to highlight my approach to public sector leadership, I also discuss key leadership lessons for others in this sector, which might also be relevant in other areas of leadership. I conclude with my final reflections.

Reflecting on Natural Heritage

One issue that is now at the top of the political and public agendas, the twin crises of climate change and biodiversity decline, was low in public profile and low in political understanding of their import and the need for action throughout my years leading SNH. This is without doubt a sea change. We had already begun work on many aspects of these issues to prepare for the future, but as we now know, the extent and direction of change is increasing and requires new thinking and new approaches to delivering solutions to combat these challenges.

The periodic reports on the *State of Nature,* developed jointly by environmental NGOs and NatureScot, make uncomfortable reading with continuing declines in many species and continuing loss of habitat, or at least little trend to improving their state of ecological health. Added to this are the predicted changes in climate. Many are already evident to some extent, such as increased storminess, more unpredictability in the precipitation regimes, especially the timing and scale of events, and in the wind regime, especially its direction and ferocity on land and at the coast, and the gradual rise in sea level in most parts of the country. We are seeing the effects of these changes on species migration polewards and the increase in pathogens, affecting both native and non-native species, and the growing extent of Invasive Non-Native Species. All of this means that a shift was needed and is being made from single species and small areas approaches to whole systems, backed by the outcomes from Earth System science and the adoption of whole landscape and whole seascape approaches, to address the changes already occurring and likely to occur on present trends.

The basis of policies, programmes, promised action and action has changed remarkably. There are so many examples. I highlight a few. We have seen the refreshment of the Golden Eagle population in the Borders, and the continuing growth of the reintroduced Red Kite and Sea Eagle population (albeit with some protest and demand for reductions on the latter). The European Beaver population has successfully grown in its formal introduction area and elsewhere with recognition given by the Scottish Government that it is a protected species, despite farmers' claims for compensation and licences issued for shooting. The need for concerted action to improve the ecological health of Scotland's rainforest is now well recognised.

Two Biosphere Reserves in Scotland, Galloway and Southern Ayrshire and Wester Ross, are up and running and the former has already passed the first ten-year assessment by UNESCO. This model of nature and community working together for the common good is an excellent one to follow. The two national parks have at long last refocussed their efforts on nature and landscape, rather than on the subsidiary purposes for which they were established. It is now time to reflect on what they have achieved and to refocus the legislation on their fundamental role in addressing the twin crises that have both environmental and people foci. This is better than the window-dressing changes to their subsidiary roles that have been inscribed in the Natural Environment (Scotland) Act 2026 as I write.

It is pleasing to know that UNESCO World Heritage Committee has now approved the inscription of the Flow Country on the World Heritage List. That is 30 years from the start of the process. It is testament to the hard work of colleagues in NatureScot, led by Graham Neville, and the willingness of key partner bodies, such as HIE and Highland Council, to be supportive. It just shows that persistence, along with hard work, in building alliances with partner bodies, backed by sound science, is necessary. And, on the ground in the Flow Country, the damage caused by the scientifically unsound and ecologically crazy ploughing of deep peats and planting of Invasive Non-Native Species of trees is gradually being overcome.

Pleasingly, nature has become an accepted word in the public vocabulary. There are around 100 Nature Champions of species and habitats among MSPs. Even SNH has been operationally renamed NatureScot. There has been the welcome addition of new programmes with new resources from the Scottish Government, such as the Nature Restoration Fund and the Peatland Acton Programme, both delivered by NatureScot.

The Scottish Government has developed new initiatives, including biodiversity targets and policies. It has also proposed, and the Parliament has passed, new legislation. Notable changes legislatively (listed in parentheses) have been: Nature Conservation (Scotland) Act 2004 (biodiversity planning and biodiversity duties); Flood Risk Management (Scotland) Act 2009 (moving towards a catchment management approach); the Climate Change (Scotland) Act 2009 (targets and a Land Use Strategy), along with the two Climate Change (Emissions Reduction Targets) (Scotland) Acts 2019 and 2024; Marine (Scotland) Act 2010 (marine spatial planning, protection of areas and wildlife); Wildlife and Natural Environment (Scotland) Act 2011 (vicarious liability for capture and killing of protected species, stronger biodiversity duty, regular biodiversity planning and reporting); Land Reform (Scotland) Act 2016 (Land Rights and Responsibilities Statements, landownership information, community input into land decisions); Wildlife and Muirburn (Scotland) Act 2024 (banning use of snares etc, licensing land where game shooting occurs, licensing muirburn) and the Natural Environment (Scotland) Act 2026 (biodiversity targets, national parks byelaws, deer management measures).

Of great significance is the establishment of Environmental Standards Scotland (ESS) through the UK Withdrawal from the European Union (Continuity) (Scotland) Act 2021. Its role of 'scrutinising and investigating public authorities' compliance with environmental law, the effectiveness of the law, and how it is implemented and applied in Scotland' is crucial, particularly as it is independent of the Scottish Government and reports directly to the Scottish Parliament. Its aim, 'to identify areas where environmental legislation is inadequate or could be improved', is essential if progress is to be made. I strongly support giving ESS further powers and responsibilities, and the resources needed to deliver their extended roles.

With all of this activity and legislative backing the way that climate change is being addressed and its effect on biodiversity means that trends should be improving. But are they really? It seems not. What is getting in the way?

Repositioning Other Government Programmes

I see real and continuing tensions between the agriculture and forestry agendas and perspectives on the one hand and those of the natural heritage on the other. There remains a fundamental failure that other government programmes are not being sufficiently reorientated to help reduce the consequences of traditional land uses through new ways of thinking and acting. The agricultural support budget of around £650 million is more than an order of magnitude greater than the NatureScot budget. There are clear examples in legislation, and action on the ground, to back up my observation. The Agriculture and Rural Communities (Scotland) Act 2024 is a classic reflection of retaining the *status quo*. A four tier system has been maintained with lack of real clarity on the inclusion and effectiveness of measures to combat climate change and to swing the biodiversity trends in a positive direction. There is urgency in developing and implementing the *Code of Practice on Sustainable and Regenerative Agriculture* specified in the 2024 Act. But will it recognise the climate change and nature recovery roles alongside the food production roles of agriculture and the soil, will it be linked to farm financial support and how will it be enforced? These are all fundamental questions that need to be addressed urgently by the Scottish Government. The need for changes in practice can be evidenced on the ground, particularly in the intensively farmed arable areas. For example, there is continuing loss of hedgerows and field margins to the detriment of wildlife on agricultural land; friable soils are still left open throughout the winter; and irrigation is needed to grow vegetable crops in the drought-prone eastern lowlands. Why has the Single

Farm Payment system remained as the basis for support to farming? What is needed is a two-pronged policy supporting production of healthy and nutritious food alongside improved stewardship of the land, especially the soil and water resources.

The position on forestry is becoming worse rather than better despite the administrative reforms establishing Scottish Forestry and Forest and Land Scotland under the Forestry and Land Management (Scotland) Act 2019. The ruling argument seems to be that more tree planting of Invasive Non-Native Species will be most beneficial in capturing and retaining carbon. However, the scientific evidence for this in the light of the planting, thinning and harvesting practices currently used is unproven. Yet the Royal Society of Edinburgh in its report, *Inquiry into Public Financial Support of Tree Planting and Forestry,* published in 2024, contested the scientific basis of this argument. Even more, the report challenged the use of public financial support through grant aid from the Scottish Government and through tax breaks agreed by the UK Treasury for commercial tree planting. Scandalously, nothing has changed.

I cannot help but conclude that the more powerful sources of influence on policy, legislation and practice are the industry lobbies, despite the oft-stated Scottish Government policies of the priority being given to addressing the twin crises of climate change and biodiversity loss. The situation compares unfavourably with, for example, the new policies in England, partly because of the government's insistence that it must keep its agricultural support policy in line with that of the European Union and partly because of the power of the traditionalists in the farming and forestry lobbies.

It is not in my character to end on a pessimistic note, being a hopeful optimist. It is obvious that despite the farming and forestry systems adhering rigidly to the past, there are many farmers and foresters of the younger generations and those newer entrants who are practising what many consider is the way forward. They are producing nutritious food with nature in mind and creating new environments by planting native tree species which benefit the soil and the landscape and are an aid to farming operations in providing moisture. We have to hope that they and their colleagues in the natural environment bodies will be able to move the position to one that is positive for both natural resources and food and fibre production, but I am not holding my breath on this!

Spatial Land Strategies

Where is the spatial strategy to deliver this? I indicated in Chapter 5 that the Scottish Government does not support spatial land use strategies in practice. The National Planning Framework 4 was a help in this direction but it does not deal effectively, nor can it, with land use outwith the town and country planning system. The earlier ideas of Indicative Forestry Strategies have long since wasted away in hidden government filing cabinets. However, there is clearly a great deal of conflict in land use and whether the nature and scale of land use change is being effectively considered in the context of the multiple objectives of producing food, fibre, biodiversity, landscape and community benefit. I fear not.

Let me repeat what I've said earlier because there remains a fundamental problem for the Scottish Government to resolve - land use conflict. Its refusal to develop locational guidance for wind turbines has resulted in a huge waste of public and private resources over so many years since then because of the arrogance and lack of strategic thinking within the Scottish Government. The same criticism of a lack of a strategic approach applies equally to afforestation and marine fish farms.

We have the means to address this through the Regional Land Use Strategies. These have been piloted and tested around Scotland, most recently in the south of Scotland, and locally, for example, in The Glenkens area of north Galloway. But there is a reluctance by the Scottish Government to support these approaches. Why the resistance? Is it again the dominant influence of the sector approaches and the industries backing them? I fear so. It is obvious from my observations in The Glenkens, for example, that the accumulation of commercial tree planting using Invasive Non-Native Species has reached the limit of local residents' wishes, radically changed the landscape and reduced its ecological diversity. Open moorland grazed with native cattle is no longer an economically viable business compared with selling the land for commercial forestry or wind turbine installation. This is a *crie de coeur* I hear from communities around the country. Yet the Community Empowerment (Scotland) Act 2015 and the recent Land Reform Acts mandate public participation in decision-making and lead to funding of community landownership. Why is the progress so slow on both these fronts? Again, it seems that traditional sector business-driven attitudes are more powerful in the corridors of power. This all makes the job of NatureScot even more difficult.

New Legislation

As I write, the Natural Environment (Scotland) Bill has just been passed by the Scottish Parliament. As a result of focused advocacy by the environmental NGOs and professional institutes, such as CIEEM and the Royal Society of Edinburgh the Biodiversity Targets are an advancement. The question remains whether there is the machinery to ensure full implementation, monitoring, and most of all compliance and enforcement of the targets to achieve the biodiversity gains needed. The attempt by the Scottish Government to give itself added powers to change the environmental Regulations inherited from the EU has been successfully resisted with strong opposition political party determination, as this would have resulted in weakening of well tried-and-tested powers.

Deer Management

I will not speculate on the reasons for merging the natural heritage and deer functions in 2010 under Section 1 of the Public Services (Reform) (Scotland) Act. However, it is abundantly clear that it is not working in practice to substantially reduce deer numbers at a time when the twin climate change and biodiversity crises suggest that reducing pressure on natural and managed habitats should be a priority. Hopefully, the sections in the Natural Environment (Scotland) Act, to implement the recommendations of the Working Group on the Management of Wild Deer completed in 2020, will be a step forward, despite opposition attempts to dilute the proposed provisions.

Raptor Protection and Grouse Moor Management

One of the major changes of benefit to Scotland's nature is the passing of the Wildlife Management and Muirburn (Scotland) Act in 2024. Persecution of protected bird species, long mandated under the Protection of Birds Act 1954, has remained at high levels, most particularly on moorlands devoted to grouse shooting, as the scientific evidence gathered by NatureScot has clearly demonstrated. Persecution has continued for many years until the Scottish Government set up a Review of Grouse Moor Management, chaired by the eminent geographical scientist, Emeritus Professor Alan Werritty. The outcome was groundbreaking by including powers to license grouse moors. Implementation is awaited. I hope that what constitutes a grouse moor will be the whole moor not, as the grouse protection lobby argue, just the area around the shooting butts and that implementation and enforcement will be rigorous.

Nature Protection

The major goal now is to achieve the international target of 30 per cent of the land and water area protected for nature by 2030 under the Convention on Biological Diversity Kunming-Montreal Global Biodiversity Framework 2022. This is a big ask. Progress is being made on the first step of designating the areas on land and at sea. This is not enough, as management of these areas to achieve favourable ecological status is essential. This needs time, financial commitment and management skills. It needs the buy-in of all who own and manage these areas and also the local communities whose livelihoods and health depend on these goals being achieved.

In the marine environment, substantial progress has been made on two fronts. The extension of the Natura 2000 programme has resulted in many new protected areas being designated. Additionally, Designation Orders for Nature Conservation Marine Protected Areas under the Marine (Scotland) Act 2020 for territorial waters and under the Marine and Coastal Access Act 2009 for offshore waters have been made. However, Marine Scotland's proposal to expand the government's policy of designating Highly Protected Marine Areas in 10 per cent of the nearshore area was contested to such an extent that Ministers withdrew the proposals. SNH's successor in another agency had not learnt how to pursue these measures as effectively as we had had to learn, nor learned from the international experience, as I pointed out in an article in *The Times* on 29 January 2024.

The static approach to protecting species and habitats is proving to be even more fallacious as a result of the impact of climate change on the migration of species and habitats in the northerly direction. Sadly, we do not have the tools to deal with the changes because SSSIs, SACs and SPAs, as the principal mechanisms for protection, are basically preserving a *status quo*, which is no longer the case. Some changes were made to nature conservation in the 2012 Act, but the system remains inadequate to deal with these issues which we identified decades ago. Some of the lessons learned were included in the Nature Conservation (Scotland) Act 2004, which, ironically, saw the demise of the statutory basis of NHAs with the repeal of Section 6 Natural Heritage Areas of the Natural Heritage (Scotland) Act 1991. I had not spotted this at the time, 'retirement' meant that I was probably doing something else, somewhere else at the time.

Scenic Protection

Improving the status of National Scenic Areas was not achieved until 2006 when NSAs were given a full statutory basis in Section 50 of the Planning etc (Scotland) Act. Significantly, the provisions were only as part of town and country planning legislation. Even this legislation did not materially improve the status of scenic protection, hence the arguments in the Landscape Alliances' report in 2021 for stronger statutory protection, but political support is still awaited. This is curious given that surveys have consistently pointed to the landscape and scenery of Scotland as a prime reason for visiting. Local communities have the same view of their local landscape.

Access

The position on public access to the countryside was changed radically by the Land Reform (Scotland) Act 2003 which, *inter alia*, provided for a statutory right of public access to private land taken with responsibility, and set out a clear legal basis for rights of way. This was a sea change. Work was well advanced under the aegis of the Access Forum on a Scottish Outdoor Access Code, setting out the codes of behaviour for users, as well as owners and managers of land and water. The establishment of Local Access Forums have helped also in developing local footpaths in and around settlements and in resolving disputes. We always knew that there would be cases of conflict which would have to be settled by the Courts, but these have been few and far between. This revolution in the legal position has been a great step forward. It is even more so given the growing evidence of the health and wellbeing benefits to people in undertaking informal recreation out of doors.

Without the leadership of SNH, and the work of the Access Forum, along with the political will as expressed in 1997, these beneficial changes could not have occurred.

Rights

One of the issues that has arisen recently is the question of human rights in relation to the environment. The United Nations General Assembly approved in 2022 a Resolution *The Human Right to a Clean, Healthy and Sustainable Environment* as part of the International Covenant on Economic, Social and Cultural Rights. The Scottish Government committed to bringing forward a Human Rights Bill during the current Parliament, following earlier consultation. This has now lapsed presumably due to lack of Parliamentary time. It proposed a provision on 'human rights to a healthy environment' flowing from the UN Resolution. I hope that this will be pursued in the new Parliament elected in spring 2026.

At the same time, a debate is beginning on the rights of nature. Globally, there are examples of nature's rights. Countries such as Colombia, Ecuador, India and New Zealand have it in various forms in their constitutions, national statutes and local laws. The anthropocentric approach of human rights is fine as far as it goes. However, it fails to recognise that society is continuing to cause the degradation of nature and to undermine its natural functionality, and therefore reducing the resources available to humankind. There is a reasonable argument, therefore, that we should not only recognise the pattern and speed of environmental degradation, but we should act beyond what is currently being done to help reverse the situation by developing a Scottish Charter for Nature.

Reflecting on Organisational Interactions
NatureScot

I do not intend to praise or criticise the progress of SNH/NatureScot since I retired; that is for others to do. The organisation will never be able to please all of the constituencies all of the time. Whether it feels that it can operate 'without fear or favour' in carrying out its statutory duties is a moot point. It partly depends on Ministers' views, as in earlier years, and partly on the attitude of the Chair and other members of the Board. Yes, it has been criticised for not taking, or seeming to take, a stance or for taking the wrong action. None of this is surprising given the very broad constituency it has to work with. In this context and given the approach developed by SNH in its earlier days, it is interesting to note that NatureScot stated in its Annual Report for 2023-24 that its purpose is to:

> Secure the conservation and enhancement of nature and landscapes
>
> Foster understanding and facilitate enjoyment of nature and landscapes
>
> Advise on the sustainable use and management of nature and landscapes
>
> Further the conservation, control and sustainable management of deer in Scotland
>
> We work in partnership with all relevant interests in Scotland, including public, private and voluntary organisations, and individuals
>
> We operate in a devolved manner, delegating decision-making to the local level, helping our organisation to be accessible, sensitive and responsive to local needs and circumstances
>
> We operate in an open and accountable way in all our activities.

So there is continuity in wording and focus in our ever-changing world. That is no bad thing, particularly as NatureScot recognises that 'we know that we still have a big challenge to reverse the trend of biodiversity loss by 2030 and regenerate nature by 2045'.

It is not clear whether NatureScot is allowed to inform the public why it is doing certain things in a certain way when acting as statutory adviser to the government. However, recently publishing its advice and recommendations on the Galloway National Parks proposals both as statutory Reporter and as a state agency, was a welcome step.

Government Control

More broadly, what is the working environment for Scottish NDPBs? I do not wish to comment on this in detail. I would observe that there is greater control in a 'top down' manner over the last twenty years. But has the real scrutiny of performance improved? Yes, performance targets and indicators of performance have been imposed and have to be formally reported on annually as is right and proper for the public money expended.

I have not detected greater scrutiny by the Scottish Parliament of government bodies, but maybe it does exist. What is needed is a more strategic approach to NDPBs by the Scottish Government with an agreed five-year strategy and agreed funding, with government scrutiny of performance annually and periodic review by Parliament. What about officials? Are they really briefed to apply an overseeing role rather than an interfering pernickety one? Hopefully, Ministers might see it in their interest to do so.

Given what I have written earlier in this chapter about government policies operating in silos, one has to question whether the bigrading of portfolios at Cabinet Secretary and junior Minister levels, and by implication at official level, really works. It comes back to my earlier point about who do Ministers really listen to and why do they accept their viewpoints.

Reflecting on Leadership and Management

I do not want this final section to read like a mini leadership and management textbook, but I have messages for others which I have learnt from experience which might be useful.

Two lessons are by far the most important - knowing oneself and knowing one's colleagues. Let me elaborate. It is essential to know your own strengths, and especially your weaknesses and foibles, as well as your likes and dislikes. Only then can you ensure that you know how to work within your organisation and with partners outside. It means being, at times, introspective rather than being a so-called 'flash in the pan'. It also means that you are true to yourself and especially to your own set of values and ethics. In effect, you have been appointed to a specific leadership role and have the opportunity to set the ethos of the organisation. Just do not do it without understanding your colleagues. I always felt that I was so fortunate in playing a leading role in the Scottish Office on its proposals for the natural heritage and then being appointed to lead it ultimately for a decade. I often describe one of my characteristics as 'tilting at windmills and kicking sacred cows'. I hope that I have learnt to do this judiciously as I became more experienced at least during my working life, even if not in retirement from paid employment! Flying a kite of an idea is a good approach when one is not sure about whether it will really fly or whether it is just an idle notion. Equally, it is important to question established thinking to test whether there is a more appropriate approach for now and for the future. What is essential is to listen to colleagues' reactions, to weigh them up in the circumstances of the moment, bearing the future in mind, and, importantly, being prepared to change one's mind. Another characteristic that needs to be honed is the ability to make friends and work with others outside the organisation.

Alongside this it is, therefore, absolutely essential to have the time and patience to get to know your colleagues. Most important is to know and understand what their personal interests and aspirations are, what their knowledge and expertise is, what their commitment is, what makes them tick, and what their limitations are. Finding out why colleagues want to work for the organisation is a necessary part of this process, remembering that commitment and motivation are as important for those providing infrastructure services such as administration, finance, human resources and information systems, as it is for those who have expertise in the subject matter as specialists. If you've never asked staff in personnel or in finance this question, I am sure you would be positively surprised by their answers, as I always was. All of this is a slow process and cannot be achieved through a remote questionnaire type approach, although that can be helpful as a first introduction as I did at the beginning of SNH. Face-to-face in their workspace is by far the best, either in the office or in the field, preferably a mixture of the two; never make the excuse that you are too busy to meet colleagues in their space. Knowing and remembering colleagues' names helps a great deal. I had that facility and what a difference it made as colleagues told me. Sadly, it is fast disappearing now! It follows from this that when new opportunities arise or obstacles appear you know who to turn to. It also means that colleagues feel able to volunteer to participate in something that is beyond their day job. Learning how to encourage that is necessary. Allowing colleagues to articulate their need for a change in job, maybe as part of a career change or to undertake some training to advance themselves, is equally important. Overall, a Chief Executive should be playing to colleagues' strengths as long as they benefit the organisation. Making sure that colleagues know what is expected of them is a key element in leadership – a job description and sensible performance targets for assessing their progress are well tried-and-tested tools, as are periodic reviews and annual conversations and a written report of performance, including the ability to feed back to the line manager in a 360° circle. One final point here is to be able to give sympathy and support to help deal with health and domestic issues where this would be genuinely helpful. I often operated a 'family comes first' approach when a colleague had issues needing to be dealt with.

Executive staff often feel that the non-executives, paid in our case, could at times be an irritant or at times a buffer and help for us. The trick is to know your non-executive colleagues and in particular their strengths and weaknesses, and their motivations. Some, after all, will be entirely working for the organisation, whereas others may well have their own agendas or carrying the agendas of others, and some may think they could do a better job than paid staff. They certainly can be used effectively as a buffer or go-between with external bodies, certainly in our case local people who were unhappy with our decisions or our approach, or Ministers and their officials who felt we were not heeding their instructions. The most essential relationship is between the Chair and the Chief Executive. As I noted earlier, open disputes about direction of the organisation or ways of doing things are very internally disturbing for colleagues and externally are very damaging to the organisation as it affects others' perception of its effectiveness. In the end, as we discovered in SNH, creative working between staff and Board members can bring so many benefits: a slightly more detached perspective, and bringing different skills and experience. Ensuring that the tasks allotted are clearly articulated, including the reasons, the desired outcomes, the timeframes and the ways of operating, are the essential components to get the best for the organisation out of these situations.

One simple message is, therefore, to make sure that everyone knows their role and their degree of responsibility. This means setting out clearly the purpose and roles of each level in the organisation at board and committee level and as individuals. This may sound typical of a civil and public servant like me, but all too often failure to provide these delineations causes confusion, overlap and duplication to the detriment of the work of individuals and the organisation as a whole. One important aspect is to have a system of delegation, so that not everything has to be decided by the Chief Executive or Directors. In deciding what types and levels of delegation should be put in place, it is important to see these as motivating factors for staff given the responsibilities, and at the same time to be sure that they are able to take on the responsibility and given the necessary training and support. How far the Chief Executive is prepared to take the risk of delegation depends on the maturity of the organisation and the ability and commitment of line managers and those delegated to take on the roles. This cannot be done too early in a new organisation, equally it cannot be left undone as it will demotivate staff and clog up decision-making at the upper levels.

Organisations have to deal with change all of the time. When colleagues say 'can we have a period of no change' one has to persuade them that this is not usually possible if the organisation is going to keep abreast of developments and be in as much control as possible when external changes are being imposed. Often the trick is to see how many colleagues are willing to volunteer to work on the changes needed and help to champion them around the organisation. I have found that resort to external consultants can be really demotivating for colleagues, as it ignores what they know and how they can help, and places a burden on them on how to bring these external folk up to speed. Sometimes an external view is helpful, as long as it can be positively managed to benefit the organisation and the colleagues affected.

Changing the organisational structure is rather like moving jobs and functions around just for the sake of being seen to be doing something, when there are real issues to resolve. My experience is that structural change has to be a way of implementing change, ie a means and not a purpose in itself.

Leading on from dealing with changes is my metier of *strategic opportunism* - plan for the future to be ready when the opportunity arises. As I explained earlier, this means having a clear view of what the organisation wishes to achieve and preparing the ground so you, as Chief Executive, and colleagues are ready when the opportunity arises. It may not be precisely how you had imagined or expected it to be, but at least you will be prepared better than starting from scratch. It means thinking long and creatively about the goals the organisation wishes to achieve, considering what steps need to be made to achieve these and doing some preliminary planning with colleagues to prepare the way when the opportunity arises. One has to be ready to implement one's opportunity when the time is right, meaning your and colleagues' judgement is essential. Push too soon and there may well be irresolvable resistance, or fail to notice when an opportunity is likely to arise means that it is missed and your preparation time is wasted. An essential element of this approach is to be aware of what is happening in the wider world. Having the ability to undertake what is generally called 'horizon scanning', and even to consider the unthinkable and what it might mean for the organisation's work and direction is important. In SNH's case this meant having the political nous to understand the government's evolving thinking and direction, both in Scotland and at UK Level. On our natural heritage agenda, it is knowing the new thinking and practice internationally. By having colleagues and Board members tasked with this as one of their roles is important. Equally, being part of international circles, in our case IUCN, gave us a window on the world that was so valuable in developing our forward strategies and revising our actions.

This also means that a shift from the traditional way of doing things is sometimes necessary. If you are not entirely in control, as in a government agency for example, you will have to argue why this is valuable and identify the benefits to the system remembering that there are always forces of resistance to making changes.

One necessary component of this approach is to gather information to inform and guide decisions. This means gathering long time series of data when dealing with the natural world that are resonant with the time frames of changes in the natural world. But that is only the start of this process. An organisation needs the ability to be able to understand the causes of the trends either through experience and research or by commissioning others to help. Without understanding the causes of changes and the trends, the data itself is, to my mind, worthless. The rapidly changing availability of analytical tools to review data in space and time means that colleagues need the tools and have the technological systems and expert helpers to be able to use them effectively.

One characteristic of a successful leader is to know when to resist and when to go with the flow. There is, of course, no right answer. Using considered judgement is essential, not only oneself but collectively with the help of colleagues. Taking a stance against tradition or against change has to be done with the best interests of the organisation and the functions it performs in mind. For example, this may mean that if continuing a long-term data set is questioned for resource reasons or its utility, you need to stand your ground if you and your colleagues consider that discontinuing could mean that past costs are nullified or that changing external factors impacting on the data would be lost. This is what we did with the longer-term surveys of bird monitoring; in hindsight this has proved to be an even more sensible decision than we first thought given the impact of climate change on species distribution and behaviour. Similarly, the argument for discontinuing a series already underway but not yet complete, did not make sense for Geological Conservation Review, so we obtained agreement to continue with the series until it was completed and made publicly available.

A Final Reflection

Moving to the present, what are my reflections? First and foremost, I was very fortunate to have been in the right place at the right time. I was there playing a key role from the decisions about a new agency, developing thinking about its role and purpose in Scottish society, leading the Bill team and then being Chief Executive for a decade. I admit that it was hard at times and that the hours were long. I may have done things differently on reflection, but honestly, it is a waste of time even considering that point. But I have no doubt that it was a job I never thought I would have the opportunity to do, and especially one I have never regretted doing. How fortunate to have been at the initiation of this whole new approach from thinker and influencer, to developer, to leader and manager. What a great privilege.

I could not have done it without the immense contribution of the staff throughout as they were all so professional, durable and committed to our work and the way we did it in whatever role they played. The guidance and support of the Board was generally helpful, and especially the inspiring leadership of Magnus Magnusson, with Chris Smout, Michael Scott, Roger Wheater and John Markland as key people playing to their strengths and using their networks; and so many other Board members playing formative roles. Joint working of staff and Board members proved to be a great bonus in reviewing policies, developing initiatives, leading on partnerships, using their networks and helping to defuse contentious matters around the country.

What is most amazing is that we survived the political criticism from the Conservative administration which set us up and the continual griping of some of the government officials. The media criticism continued, much of it ill-informed but very damaging to our work and to my colleagues, especially those who lived locally who had to face this outside the office. We covered our vast remit with many initiatives that were not decreed by the government. We gained many supporters through our work and the way we carried it out, internationally, nationally and locally as the feedback from the *Natural Heritage Futures* exercise made clear. Partnership working was carried out with a purpose and the outcomes in terms of agreements of all types, for example on access, moorlands, the Firths and more, were beyond even my wildest expectations at the outset. They were a testament to the willingness of all the parties to come round the table, to state their positions and gradually for common ground to be identified and worked into deliverable solutions of whatever kind were appropriate.

An obvious question is what am I most proud of? Goodness, that is difficult. Three aspects bear mention. I can honestly say that the two programmes in my middle years were high points. I devised and led the implementation of the *Natural Heritage Futures* and the *Organisational Development Programmes*. Collectively, we grasped the ball ourselves with leadership and implementation of change. Making a difference in so many ways on the ground is a second highlight. Through our projects new approaches were established, barriers were removed, and, significantly, we changed our attitudes and behaviours and helped others to do likewise. At a personal level, visiting staff around the country on a rolling programme and hopefully remembering their names, what they did and what made them tick was a privilege and a pleasure - all part of a proper Chief Executive's job. It meant that I also learned even more about my adopted country and the diversity of Scotland in all respects. It should be no surprise that when I was asked if I would retire back to England, I responded that it never entered my head. I had already celebrated over half of my life living and working in Scotland and intended to stay.

ACKNOWLEDGEMENTS

There are far too many people with whom I have worked to thank individually. Colleagues in the Scottish Office and the Scottish Government, in Scottish Natural Heritage, in other UK and international government agencies, and in the environmental movement in Scotland and further afield are included. I was fortunate to be given wise advice, briefed on what was really happening and why, taken around Scotland to meet others, and be able to engage with my opposite numbers in England and Wales, and in agencies in the Nordic countries. My thanks to them all for opening my eyes to new situations, ideas and ways of doing things, for listening and commenting on my ideas and the issues we faced in Scotland, and for helping me make decisions.

I learnt a lot working with my SNH Management Team colleagues and welcomed their different personalities, knowledge and approaches to complement my own: the late Duncan Campbell, Jane Dalgleish, Ian Edgeler, Chris Fox, Ian Jardine, Lindsay Montgomery, John Thomson, the late Peter Tilbrook, Michael B Usher and the late Jeff Watson.

I must personally thank Gavin McCrone and Hamish Laing, who set me on this course in the Scottish Office by believing I was the right person and encouraged me to think and act creatively.

My years working with the late Magnus Magnusson were a privilege and a pleasure. He taught me so much in so many ways - in speaking and writing, in dealing with difficult situations and encouraging me to take a positive stand even when there were difficulties. Significantly, he introduced me to Iceland, which started my enduring links with that country and its people.

Chris Smout always gave wise counsel and was a steadying influence, as well as introducing me to so many species in the field. Roger Wheater was always encouraging, and his network of contacts here and overseas was most valuable. Michael Scott was a great conduit to the environmental movement and an enthusiast for what SNH was doing. John Markland, a fellow geographer, with much chief executive experience, gave me my head and especially made good links with the government. Other board members provided support and guidance. It is significant of their influence and friendship that I am still in touch with some of them.

Being out on the hill with Bob Aitken had always been a pleasure; his perceptive views and well-honed thoughts have always been invaluable. Calls and private meetings with the late Simon Pepper helped break down many barriers as we had a common purpose, albeit operating in different milieus. His premature death was a grievous loss to the environmental movement in Scotland.

My personal assistants all gave me invaluable support in sharing the load, keeping the paperwork flowing, being good organisers and especially, being the eyes and ears of what was happening around SNH. There was one of those, of course, Lindsay Manson, without whom I could never have done my job. I treasured her calm approach and wise judgement as my assistant and later as my dear wife. I valued beyond measure the care and love she gave me. As I write these words, I remember her so well, giving me strength when needed and enriching my life beyond all imagining. My sadness is that she died after a long and brave fight against breast cancer and was not able to give me her wise counsel in writing this account.

Thanks to Colin Galbraith (now the Chair of NatureScot) and Des Thompson, who have persuaded me to set down my story and have given me good advice on the issues from their own perspectives. Thanks to Jenny Brown, a friend and literary agent, for her perceptive comments on an earlier draft and for her continuing encouragement. Special thanks to Michael Scott, my longstanding colleague and friend, for his very perceptive comments, which have resulted in improvements to the text and for writing the Foreword. Thanks to Sally Magnusson for helping me access her father's archive. Thanks to Erica Caldwell, Hew Dalrymple and Des Thompson for reviewing the draft and offering many helpful comments. It has been a pleasure working with Dr Paul S Philippou and his colleagues at Tippermuir Books, who have helped me to improve the text and provided excellent designs.

ABOUT THE AUTHOR

Roger Crofts had the unique position of working within government to develop proposals and legislation for Scottish Natural Heritage and then to establish the new body and lead it as its Chief Executive for its first decade. He is an unashamed geographer, specialising in assessing nature and how it is better managed from his early research and in later life on geoheritage conservation. More than that, he has inside knowledge of how government works as a civil servant, including responsibility for government bodies dealing with development and the natural environment. Since then, he has written and lectured widely on caring for the environment without fear or favour. Roger has been a trustee and non-executive director of many organisations, contributing especially on strategy, policy and resource management. His work has been recognised by the award of many honours in the academic and environmental worlds in Scotland, the UK, Iceland and globally. www.rogercrofts.net.

TIPPERMUIR BOOKS

Tippermuir Books Ltd is an independent publishing company based in Perth, Scotland

PUBLISHING HISTORY

Spanish Thermopylae (2009)

Battleground Perthshire (2009)

Perth: Street by Street (2012)

Born in Perthshire (2012)

In Spain with Orwell (2013)

Trust (2014)

Perth: As Others Saw Us (2014)

Love All (2015)

A Chocolate Soldier (2016)

The Early Photographers of Perthshire (2016)

Taking Detective Novels Seriously: The Collected Crime Reviews of Dorothy L Sayers (2017)

Walking with Ghosts (2017)

No Fair City: Dark Tales from Perth's Past (2017)

The Tale o the Wee Mowdie that wantit tae ken wha keeched on his heid (2017)

Hunters: Wee Stories from the Crescent: A Reminiscence of Perth's Hunter Crescent (2017)

A Little Book of Carol's (2018)

Flipstones (2018)

Perth: Scott's Fair City: The Fair Maid of Perth & Sir Walter Scott – A Celebration & Guided Tour (2018)

God, Hitler, and Lord Peter Wimsey: Selected Essays, Speeches and Articles by Dorothy L Sayers (2019)

Perth & Kinross: A Pocket Miscellany: A Companion for Visitors and Residents (2019)

The Piper of Tobruk: Pipe Major Robert Roy, MBE, DCM (2019)

The 'Gig Docter o Athole': Dr William Irvine & The Irvine Memorial Hospital (2019)

Afore the Highlands: The Jacobites in Perth, 1715–16 (2019)

'Where Sky and Summit Meet': Flight Over Perthshire – A History: Tales of Pilots, Airfields, Aeronautical Feats, & War (2019)

Diverted Traffic (2020)

Authentic Democracy: An Ethical Justification of Anarchism (2020)

'If Rivers Could Sing': A Scottish River Wildlife Journey. A Year in the Life of the River Devon as it flows through the Counties of Perthshire, Kinross-shire & Clackmannanshire (2020)

A Squatter o Bairnrhymes (2020)

In a Sma Room Songbook: From the Poems by William Soutar (2020)

The Nicht Afore Christmas: the much-loved yuletide tale in Scots (2020)

Ice Cold Blood (2021)

The Perth Riverside Nursery & Beyond: A Spirit of Enterprise and Improvement (2021)

Fatal Duty: Police Killers and Killer Cops: the Scottish Police Force 1812–1952 (2021)

The Shanter Legacy: The Search for the Grey Mare's Tail (2021)

'Dying to Live': The Story of Grant McIntyre, Covid's Sickest Patient (2021)

The Black Watch and the Great War (2021)

Beyond the Swelkie: A Collection of Poems & Writings to Mark the Centenary of George Mackay Brown (2021)

Sweet F.A. (2022)

A War of Two Halves (2022)

A Scottish Wildlife Odyssey (2022)

In the Shadow of Piper Alpha (2022)

Mind the Links: Golf Memories (2022)

Perthshire 101: A Poetic Gazetteer of the Big County (2022)

The Banes o the Turas: An Owersettin in Scots o the Poems bi Pino Mereu scrievit in Tribute tae Hamish Henderson (2022)

Walking the Antonine Wall: A Journey from East to West Scotland (2022)

The Japan Lights: On the Trail of the Scot Who Lit Up Japan's Coast (2022)

Fat Girl Best Friend: 'Claiming Our Space' – Plus Size Women in Film & Television (2023)

Wild Quest Britain: A Nature Journey of Discovery through England, Scotland & Wales – from Lizard Point to Dunnet Head (2023)

Guid Mornin! Guid Nicht! (2023)

Madainn Mhath! Oidhche Mhath! (2023)

Who's Aldo? (2023)

A History of Irish Republicanism in Dundee (c1840 to 1985) (2024)

The Stone of Destiny & The Scots (2024)

The Mysterious Case of the Stone of Destiny: A Scottish Historical Detective Whodunnit! (2024)

Salvage (2024)

A Most Unsuitable Game: Celebrating Scottish Women's Football Fifty Years After the Ban (2024)

The Scottish Murder Book: Sensational Scottish Murder Trials. Book 1: Perth, Angus and Fife (2024)

Perthshire's Pound of Flesh: True Stories of Revenge & Retribution From Perthshire's Dark Past (2024)

Blood Beneath Ben Nevis: Tales of Murder, Myth & Mystery From Lochaber's Dark Past.

William Soutar: Collected Works, Volume 1 Published Poetry (1923–1946) (2024)

William Soutar: Collected Works, Volume 2 Published Poetry (1948–2000) (2024)

The Road to Mons Graupius (2025)

'The Wheesht': The Best o Scots Hoose Yaldi (2025)

'The Perth Steamies': the Story of the Fair City's Public Washhouses, 1846–1976 (2025)

The Lass and The Quine (2025)

Balkan Rhapsody (2025)

The Royal Edinburgh Military Tattoo: 'The Show Must Go On' – Travels of the Tattoo Producer (2025)

Wild Edinburgh: A Wildlife Guide to Edinburgh (2025)

'The Old Divide': A History of Sectarianism in Scotland (2025)

A Gentleman of Great Enterprise: William Sandeman (1722–1790) Perthshire Entrepreneur and Cotton Pioneer (2025)

A History of Perth Academy (2025)

'An Odious Campaign': The 1936 Ross & Cromarty By-election of 1936 (2025)

Shout: Collected Poems From The Corbenic Poets (2025)

Barvick Falls (2025)

Scottish Natural Heritage: An Insider's View (2026)

Tuula: A True Crime Tragedy. The Story of Jersey's Only Unsolved Murder and the Dark Decades That Changed the Island Forever (2026)

Curious Histories & Mysterious Tales: Galloway Adventures (2026)

Mothsoul (Jon Plunkett, 2026)

Family Man (Colin Burnett, 2026)

FORTHCOMING

Disasters, Accidents & Enquirers in Scotland (Gillian Mawdsley, 2026)

City Lives! A Dundee GP's Memoir of the NHS at its Height (John Hulbert, 2026)

The Black Watch From the Crimean, Coomasie & Beyond (Derek Patrick and Fraser Brown (eds), 2026)

William Soutar: Collected Works, Volume 3 (Miscellaneous & Unpublished Poetry) (Paul S Philippou (Editor-in-Chief) & Kirsteen McCue and Philippa Osmond-Williams (eds), 2027+)

William Soutar: Collected Works, Volumes 4–6 (Prose Selections) (Paul S Philippou (Editor-in-Chief) & Kirsteen McCue and Philippa Osmond (eds), 2028+)

Ayont the Thistle (Jim Mackintosh, James Robertson and Alan Riach (eds), 2026)

R F Scott & E H Shackleton in Scotland, 1903-1906 (Liam Maloney, 2026)

Seal Song (Ian Spring, 2026)

Scottish Gothic (Ian Spring and Tom Hubbard, 2026)

TIPPERMUIR
BOOKS LIMITED

Tippermuir Books titles are available from bookshops and online booksellers.
They can also be purchased directly (with free postage & packing (UK only) – minimum charges for overseas delivery)
from www.tippermuirbooks.co.uk.
Tippermuir Books Ltd can be contacted at
mail@tippermuirbooks.co.uk.